The Organization and Administration of the Union Army

Volume I

ZOUAVES OF 1861

The Organization and Administration of the Union Army 1861-1865

by

FRED ALBERT SHANNON, Ph.D.

Associate professor of History, Kansas State Agricultural College

Volume I

GLOUCESTER, MASS.

PETER SMITH

1965

RCh

8/70

Contents of Volume I

Illustrations, Volume I

Preface

Histories dealing with the Civil War have, in the past, almost without exception passed over the whole subject of the creation of the armies. Emory Upton in his book, *The Military Policy of the United States* (Washington, 1912), is concerned primarily with the period before the Civil War, and he closes with the year 1862. His chief interest is in military legislation. Frederic Louis Huidekoper, in *The Military Unpreparedness of the United States, A History of American Land Forces from Colonial Times until June 1, 1915* (New York, 1915), summarizes and continues the work of Upton but he devotes only thirty pages to the Civil War exclusive of campaigns, and his work is chiefly propaganda. Some of the problems connected with recruiting and the draft have been considered by William B. Weeden, in *War Government Federal and State in Massachusetts, New York, Pennsylvania, and Indiana* (Boston and New York, 1906). The party and sectional prejudices of Weeden and occasional gross misstatements of facts, as well as a too optimistic view of the activities of the war governors and an uncritical approach, detract much from the value of the book. The present work was completed before the appearance of Edward Channing's sixth volume of his *History of the United States*.

In this work an attempt has been made to show how the Union changed from a peace to a war basis, to describe the evolution of the military policy and of the army, and to outline the inter-relations of state and national governments in the solution of various problems of recruiting, equipping, supplying, and training the soldiers. Limitations of time and space have made necessary the omission of some topics which might otherwise have been included. Among these are the work of the Surgeon-general's office, the military control of railroads, and the problems of the Signal-officer's bureau.

I am indebted to Professor James A. Woodburn, formerly of Indiana University, for first directing my attention to this field of work, and for help in the early stages of its preparation. Thanks are due to the librarians of Indiana University, the State University of Iowa, the State Historical Society of Iowa, the Iowa State Teachers College, and the State Historical Society of Wisconsin for valuable assistance in the gathering of materials; also to the editors of the *Mississippi Valley Historical Review* and the *Journal of Negro History* for permission to use materials from articles first printed in those journals. I am especially obligated to Professor Arthur M. Schlesinger of Harvard University for valuable suggestions and criticisms at every stage in the work and for reading and helping correct the manuscript, and to my wife, Edna Jones, for countless hours of assistance in elimination of errors, proof reading, and preparation of the index.

FRED A. SHANNON

MANHATTAN, KANSAS: September, 1927

The State-Rights Principle applied to the Army

The State-Rights Principle applied to the Army

THE problem of recruiting, equipping, and training the Union army in the Civil War cannot be adequately considered without taking into consideration the influence of the state-rights theory in the North The powerful impulse of that doctrine was felt no less in the free than in the slave states. Indeed it may well be maintained that, as soon as secession was an accomplished fact, the Confederacy was much the more expeditious of the two sections in abandoning the no longer profitable theory. The state-rights philosophy was not indigenous to or permanently held by any section of the country or of the people. It was merely a tool to be wielded by any group or section that found it the most ready means to an end. Prior to 1860 the North had sought refuge behind the doctrine at least as often as the South and, at the outbreak of the war, except from the extremity of secession, she was as ardently attached to it as at any earlier period of the national existence.

For developing a centralized control of her army the North, at the beginning of the war, was at a positive disadvantage as compared with the South. The latter section was composed wholly of cotton states or states of closely allied interests and traditions. The common dread of northern intervention was enough to dissipate the memory of such inter-state jealousies as existed, and the early invasion by northern troops helped to weld the southern republic into something very closely resembling a nation. Early national supremacy in the Confederate army was the result. In the North, on the contrary, no such unity existed. Instead of one section there were several, each with a different set of interests and traditions. New England, the trans-Allegheny West, and the border slave states were so widely different in their interests that close coöperation between them was rendered almost impossible. National good was likely to be sacrificed for local prejudices. State-rights sympathies predominated in the federal councils, and as a consequence, the same principle was applied to army organization.

Of the various sections of the North, New England had ever been ready to place her interests above those of the nation. The very doctrine of secession bore the stamp "Made in New England." That product of the Hartford Convention was hastily repudiated by the constituency, once the War of 1812 was ended, but the memory of it lingered on. In later years, when New England became the manufacturing center of the country, her interests became more national. In order to control the markets of the country, she began to advocate a national mercantile system and to favor federal supremacy, so long as it was conducive to that system. Accordingly she denounced nullification, and opposed the annexation of Texas and the Mexican War. She heaped condemnations upon the head of Webster in 1850 and Douglas in 1854, because of their obeisance to popular sovereignty. But thereafter her attitude underwent a change. Popular sovereignty was working out to her interest. Therefore she welcomed the antislavery constitution of California and, by means of Emigrant Aid Societies, helped to achieve a like result in Kansas. So well was popular sovereignty serving her purposes that, when it was blasted by the strongly national pronouncements of the Dred Scott decision, none denounced that document with greater vehemence than did she. Finally in 1860 New England had just about completed the political cycle begun during the second war with Great Britain. There were those in the section who were even ready to advocate secession if John C. Breckinridge won the election. There was nothing in the past of New England that bound her to any strongly national program during the war.

The West represented another sectional group of interests. Relatively poor, decidedly democratic, and definitely dependent upon the East and South for the marketing of her produce, she ever looked longingly westward for opportunities of expansion. Like the cotton states and New England, her attitude toward state rights and centralization was dependent on her own advantage. With this object in mind she had, in the past, been willing to barter her political influence either to the East or the South according to the support for her projects likely to be derived. In order to secure Oregon she joined with the South in a demand for both Oregon and Texas. She was inclined to be benevolent in her attitude toward the Mexican War and cession, since it gave her more excuse for organizing the territory between the Missouri River and Oregon.

As to state rights, the theory found a welcome home in the West. The doctrine of popular sovereignty was from first to last a product of that section. As the doctrine applied to Kansas, the West was passively willing to surrender that state as a small price to pay for the opportunity of developing the far West. This complacency was rudely interrupted by the Dred Scott decision. There arose an ungrounded fear that legal slave territory would result in slave settlement and that the legitimate field of expansion for the West would be preëmpted by the South. This fear drove the West into the arms of the republican party in spite of the Freeport Doctrine of Douglas. With the outbreak of war the West was ready to take up arms, but for a different reason than that of the East. She would fight, not for the preservation of a mercantile system, but to keep the western territories open for her exploitation and free from negroes. It was in the frontier states of this group that the most enthusiasm was shown.

The motive was less active in the older and more settled states of the section than in the frontier group. In Illinois, Indiana, and Ohio less interest was shown in westward expansion and less interest was felt in the war. Neither abolition, mercantilism, nor freedom of the far West had any strong appeal for them. Regard for the traditions of union was about the only motive left. It was in this section that the Knights of the Golden Circle did their most effective work, not because the people were intrinsically less loyal than elsewhere but because fewer of them had what they felt to be a direct interest in the war. State control of the recruiting and organization of the army was there held to be essential even by ardent advocates of the war.

In the loyal border states the predominant sectional interest was that of slavery. This was especially true in Maryland, Kentucky, and Missouri. These were not essentially cotton states. There was not even in them the

same traditional connection with the South that tended
to bind Virginia to the Confederacy. Economically
their interests were more bound up with the North. It
was only in their institution of slavery that they were
connected with the South. Their problem was a complex one. If they seceded and the Confederacy endured
they would be cut off from their natural economic
affinities. They would be aliens in a cotton confederacy;
in a hopeless minority; helpless to control their own
fate. If they remained in the Union they would be a
small slave-holding group in a free republic; an easy
prey to the abolitionists. Even if unmolested by them,
slavery would become a burden rather than an asset,
because of the loss of the southern slave market. The
only hope for them was the preservation of the Union
and of slavery at the same time. If the Union could not
be saved they had to take their choice between their
major economic connections and their slaves. Because
of the peculiar position in which they were placed,
these border states were the only parties in the conflict,
in which the slavery issue, as such, was from the beginning predominant. They were almost ruinously divided
from the start on the question of secession. Nothing
could be expected from them in the way of national
control of army organization.

The middle Atlantic states had no distinctive sectional prejudices. It is only for purposes of classification that they can be considered as a section at all. Yet
a combination of prejudices, shared with the neighboring sections, reacted as definitely in favor of state supremacy as was the case in any other part of the country.
In general the more populous regions around the ports
and along the seaboard were dominated by commercial

and industrial pursuits. The back country of New York and Pennsylvania had as much in common with the old Northwest as with the Atlantic seaboard.

The large foreign population in the industrial centers presented the distinctive problem of this section. From the time of the earliest settlement, the Dutch and Quaker colonies had been composed of diverse ethnical elements. This condition had become even more pronounced with the advent of the industrial revolution. The various unassimilated groups were rapidly increasing, especially in New York City and the mining districts of Pennsylvania. The unprecedented Irish immigration into New York before 1860 seemed to be transforming that city into a New Hibernia, leaving a later generation to perform the metamorphosis into the present New Jerusalem. These "Milesians" asked nothing better than a fair chance to make a living, mix in ward politics, and hate Great Britain. They had little interest in the quarrel between North and South so long as it did not interfere with their livelihood. They opposed emancipation of negroes because they feared competition with them in the labor market. Yet, if they could have been led to believe that Great Britain was whole-heartedly friendly with the South they would have been united in their loyalty to the Union.

The problem in the Pennsylvania mining region was largely one of industrial strife. The miners, largely foreign born, were seeking economic independence from their employers but were meeting with little success. The results were perpetual hatred, strikes, and riots. The miners could not consider enemies of their masters in any other light than as friends to themselves. Hence they later assumed the attitude that was branded as treason.

Such were the tendencies operating against centralization of government at the outbreak of the Civil War.
Should the war be a "National Crusade" or a coalition
of state and class interests, each fighting for union but
each for a different reason? Crusades have always been
of the latter variety. Unity of interest has ever been
the part of the party of the defense, whether it be the
Paynim of the East, the Albigeois, the Moors of Spain,
or the cotton-state aristocracy of America. Hence comes
the powerful tenacity of resistance which they have
always shown.

In contrast with the relative unity of interest of the
belligerent South, the North presented a motley array
of widely differing and sometimes conflicting elements.
The abolitionist would fight to free the slaves, the Ken-
tuckian to save the Union so that slavery might be preserved. The capitalist would fight, by proxy, to preserve
the southern market and to exclude therefrom the competition of foreign states. The frontier states would
fight to keep the far West negroless and open for their
settlement. The older settlements west of the Alle-
ghenies and north of the Ohio would fight, when at all,
for sentiment or for various of the other mentioned
motives. The wage victims of the industrial revolution
would fight, if at all, by compulsion or for pay.

Since these various sectional differences could not be
represented in the government by sections they were
represented by states. One bloc of states represented
one interest, another represented another. Each was
careful to see that its rights were not impaired either
by neighbors or by national encroachment.

How, then, should the armies be recruited, trained
and mobilized, and the war conducted? If by the nation, then one section might predominate over another

and subvert the other's men and money to its own interests. State interest, therefore, dictated that the troops should be raised and managed, and that the war policies should be controlled, as far as possible, by the individual states. The representatives and senators in congress were obsessed by the same ideas. But a successful war could not be conducted on such principles. The South, wherein state differences were less pronounced, learned this lesson first and best. Accordingly, for three years she held at bay an army nearly twice the size of her own. The North, by the end of the war, was, as a result of lessons learned from her blunders, being led toward the same solution.

The federal government in the spring of 1861 was in a relatively feeble condition as compared with the more robust state governments. Therefore the states were able to assume that initiative in recruiting which their self interest dictated. Secession had left the federal government tottering at a time when the states, with the exception of the border group, were, as yet, unrent by internal dissension.

The state governments were stable and financially sound. Each had a complete military organization, usually more elaborate than efficient. Several still had fragments of those ebullient militia organizations, so popular for a few years following the Mexican War, but, in recent years, degenerated to gaudy vanguards for parades. Legislatures, however, were ready and prompt to pass military legislation and make grants of money. Banks were eager to make loans on the ample security of the state. Private organizations and individuals were profuse in their donations for purposes of arming and equipping volunteers. The states were fairly bubbling over with vitality.

The vigor of the state governments was shown in the zeal with which they responded to the Union's cause. Some states did not wait for a call for troops but made their preparations for warfare in advance. By April 13, a day before the surrender of Fort Sumter, a war act passed the legislature of Wisconsin and received the signature of the governor. It was designed to anticipate the President's proclamation. It decreed that: "In case a call shall be made by the President of the United States upon this state, to aid in maintaining the union and the supremacy of the laws, or to suppress rebellion or insurrection, or to repel invasion within the United States, the governor is hereby authorized, and it shall be his duty, to take such measures as in his judgment shall provide in the speediest and most efficient manner for responding to such call. . . ." This declaration was rendered effective by a grant of $100,000 for raising troops.[1]

New York was just two days behind Wisconsin in the passage of similar legislation. On April 15 her legislature made a grant of $3,000,000, secured by a two-mill tax, to cover the cost of recruiting and equipping the militia. Thirty thousand two-year troops were provided for and, to provide for their needs, $500,000 of the grant was made immediately available.[2]

Other states, whose legislatures were in session, were quick to follow. Rhode Island, by April 17, appropriated half a million dollars.[3] Massachusetts was somewhat slower in her appropriations but was none the less thorough. By two acts passed on May 21, 1861,

---

[1] *General Laws passed by Legislature of Wisconsin in Year 1861* (Madison, 1861), pp. 266-267.

[2] *Laws of New York, passed at eighty-fourth session of Legislature,* 1861 (Albany, 1861), pp. 634-636.

[3] *New York Daily Tribune,* April 18, 1861.

she provided for a maximum fund of $10,000,000, to be raised by the sale of bonds, for war purposes.[4]

The governors of other states, whose legislatures were not in session, took prompt measures to call the lawmakers together. Governor Andrew Curtin of Pennsylvania issued such a call on April 20.[5] But none exceeded the speed of New Jersey. Her legislature had adjourned from regular session in March but was in session again by April 30 and within a week was passing military legislation.[6]

Individuals and corporations were equally active in making advances to the states. The banks of Chicago offered Governor Richard Yates $500,000 for extraordinary expenses. There was very strong competition among moneyed men in Wisconsin to subscribe a $200,-000 loan for that state, the Juneau Bank offering to take it all at par. Two Trenton, New Jersey, banks offered a $25,000 loan each to raise four regiments for the war.[7] Hartford, Connecticut, banks offered $500,-000 and Rhode Island banks offered $235,000. The Cincinnati city council offered the governor of Ohio $255,-000 in cash from the sinking fund.[8] All these were manifestations of the first week of the war. For weeks afterward offers continued to pour in, from individuals, corporations, and local governmental organizations, of gifts or loans of money to be used in the raising of troops or the relief of the soldiers' families.[9]

But while the states were showing all these symptoms

---

[4] *Supplement to General Statutes of Massachusetts* (Boston, 1873), vol. 1 (1860-1872), pp. 81-83.

[5] *New York Tribune*, April 22, 1861.

[6] *Acts of eighty-fifth Legislature of New Jersey* (Freehold, 1861), cf. especially pp. 545-553.

[7] *New York Tribune*, April 19, 1861.

[8] *Ibid.*, April 18, 1861.

[9] *Ibid.*, April, May, 1861, *passim*.

of vigorous vitality, the federal government was still at its lowest ebb of authority. President James Buchanan merely adopted a policy of watchful waiting, hoping against an attack but unwilling to adopt coercion. Meanwhile his cabinet was going to pieces on sectional lines. Howell Cobb of Georgia, Secretary of the Treasury; John B. Floyd of Virginia, Secretary of War; and Jacob Thompson of Mississippi, Secretary of the Interior, all went over to the secessionists after doing what little they could to strengthen the Confederacy at the expense of the Union.

The incoming administration not only inherited the perplexities of the old but rapidly acquired a full share of its own. Seven states were in open rebellion and eight more were on the verge. For over a month President Abraham Lincoln merely continued the policy of watchful waiting adopted by Buchanan. He made no more preparation than his predecessor to strengthen the military position of the United States, though he was more ready to adopt coercion in case of attack. Submerged by the pleas of hungry office seekers of a party for the first time in power, the ordinary routine of business was more than enough for his attention. The secession of four more states, following the firing on Fort Sumter and the call for the militia, seemed to herald a still further dissolution of the Union. The riotous attack on the Massachusetts Sixth at Baltimore, on April 19, following as it did on the secession ordinance of Virginia and followed in turn by the cutting off of all communications from Washington, seemed to announce to the world that the federal capital itself was as good as captured.[10]

---

[10] The despondency at Washington is described in W. R. Thayer, *Life and Letters of John Hay* (Boston, 1916), vol. 1, pp. 105-107. An account of

Not only did the federal government have the appearance of weakness, in various respects it was weak. A special evidence of this was the total lack of any military policy. For the maintenance of self respect Maryland, with the enclosed District of Columbia, had to be saved for the Union. A quick military coup was the logical way to attain this end, yet not even decent precautions were taken to provide for the contingency of resistance in Baltimore. For lack of this much foresight the whole administration was for several days hurled into more utter confusion than before, through threatened loss of the capital. Worse than this there was not even at hand any means of really increasing the military force of the country. War had been imminent ever since the inauguration of the new government yet congress was not in session nor even called in session. If a special session had been convened with the rapidity that the crisis demanded the authorization for 500,-000 volunteers could have been passed in April instead of July. An army instead of an "armed mob" could have appeared at Bull Run.

The weakest cog in the federal machine was the one that should have been the strongest. Simon Cameron was Secretary of War. He was purely a political appointee, enjoying the confidence neither of the President nor, apparently, of himself. From the beginning he was at a loss how to conduct the office. His sole virtue was that he did not resent assistance from outside his department. Hence for several months Salmon Portland Chase maintained whatever semblance of order was to be found in the Department of War, besides managing his own portfolio of the Treasury and offer-

---

riots, written by the mayor of the city – G. W. Brown, *Baltimore and Nineteenth of April, 1861* (Baltimore, 1887), *passim.*

ing his advice, whether sought for or not, elsewhere in the government. This interference was not solely officiousness on his own part, but was partly due to the wish of the President, and was at least tolerated by Cameron, whose friendship Chase retained even after Cameron's dismissal the following year. Chase drafted the orders for the enlargement of the regular army and the creation of the volunteer army, May 3, 1861. He advised forcible means of quelling the secession movement in Maryland, he directed the organization of the western troops, and had much to do with the early elevation of George B. McClellan.[11] But, in spite of all his marvelous energy, Chase, with his divided responsibilities, could not take the place of an expert devoting his whole attention to the problems of mobilization.

The troops available for service at this crisis consisted of a regular army, well trained, and at least adequate in size for the policing of New York City. On January 1, 1861, the total number of enlisted men and officers barely exceeded 16,000 [12] and even this small army was further decimated by the defection of the last four seceding states. Robert E. Lee, slated for the active command of the armies in the field, deserted at the last moment and took with him many able officers of cotton-state sympathies. The remnant of an army still remaining was just sufficient for officering the first half million of a national army, if such a mythical thing had been in existence.

In addition to this potentially invaluable contingent,

---

[11] A. B. Hart, *Salmon Portland Chase* (Boston, 1899), pp. 211-213; Emory Upton, *Military Policy of United States* (Washington, 1912), pp. 233-235.

[12] "Report of Provost-marshal-general [J. B. Fry]," in *House Exec. Doc.*, 39 Cong., 1 sess., appendix to "Report of Secretary of War, 1865," part i, p. 102. This is referred to hereafter as "Fry's *Report*." The "*Report*," with

the decadent militia regiments were the sole remaining organized resources. A few of these still retained a fair share of their original numbers and vigor. Of these the most famous, because the first in action, was the Sixth Massachusetts. Four days after the call for 75,000 militia, this regiment achieved distinction through conflict with a secessionist mob at Baltimore. Four of their number were killed and thirty-six were wounded in the engagement.[18] Several Iowa militia companies had offered their services even before April 12th, the Washington, Iowa, Light Guards having been accepted by the governor on January 17, 1861.[14] But most of the regiments and companies were so short of men and equipment as to be unready for immediate service. The *New York Tribune* complained, on April 19, that Massachusetts and Pennsylvania had already sent regiments to the defense of Washington, whereas New York had not yet sent its first company. The Fifty-fifth New York, a regiment of Frenchmen, beautifully equipped with red pantaloons and caps, had only three hundred fifty enrolled – just enough for its peace-time requirement for parades, marches, and funerals.[15]

With all their potential vigor, the states had, in recent years, borne lightly the duty of local self protection. Even in the frontier state of Iowa, on the eve of the Spirit Lake Massacre of 1857, the Committee on

---

some excisions, is also found in *Official Records*, series iii, vol. 5, *cf. post,* note 21.

[13] See account in J. F. Rhodes, *History of Civil War 1861-1865* (New York, 1917), pp. 17-19.

[14] J. E. Briggs, "Enlistment of Iowa troops during Civil War," in *Iowa Journal of History and Politics*, vol. 15, pp. 333-337; S. H. M. Byers, *Iowa in War Times* (Des Moines, 1888), pp. 39-40.

[15] Regis de Trobriand, *Four Years with Army of Potomac* (Boston, 1889), p. 70.

Military Affairs in the House of Representatives presented a report on the military condition of the state,
which was intended merely as a burlesque for the enter-
tainment of the House.[16] It was replete with puns, more
or less brilliant, on the infantry, dragoons, and artillery,
but was, evidently, no more of a joke than was the
military status it affected to describe. A typical western
military company was the Waupun, Wisconsin, Light
Guard, which had arms for about forty – and these
were borrowed from the state with no security of continued possession – and uniforms for twenty.[17] Governor
Samuel J. Kirkwood of Iowa estimated that there
were in the possession of the entire state, at the outbreak
of war, only about 1,500 old muskets, two hundred
rifles, and four six-pound guns. These antiquated relics
were loaned to militia organizations, on sufficient bond,
for special occasions and at other times they worried
along without arms.[18] Though the states were capable
of displaying great vigor in recruiting they had to start
from practically nothing in so doing.

The legal means by which the federal government
might increase these miniature forces were almost as
inadequate as the forces themselves: two militia acts
of ancient vintage – nothing more. The first of these
had been adopted February 28, 1795, and empowered
the President to call forth the militia of any state or
states, whenever the laws of the United States should
"be opposed or the operation thereof obstructed in any
State, by combinations too powerful to be suppressed

[16] Briggs, *loc. cit.*, pp. 325-328.

[17] J. W. Hinkley, *Narrative of service with Third Wisconsin Infantry*
(Madison, 1912), p. 3.

[18] C. B. Upham, "Arms and equipment for Iowa troops in Civil War," in
Iowa Journal of History and Politics, vol. 16, pp. 5-6.

by the ordinary course of judicial proceedings or by the powers vested in the Marshals by this Act." The militia could continue to be employed "until the expiration of thirty days after the commencement of the then next session of Congress," provided that no militiaman should "be compelled to serve longer than three months, after his arrival at the place of rendezvous, in any one year." [19] The other law, approved March 3, 1803, provided merely for the calling out of the militia for the preservation of law and order in the District of Columbia.[20] Since congress was not in session, though there was no valid reason why it could not or should not have been, recourse had to be taken to whatever other means, however feeble, were immediately available. The first care, after determining to provision the garrison at Fort Sumter, was to provide for the safety of the capital in case hostilities ensued. Under authority of the act of 1803 the President issued calls, through the War Department, for ten companies of militia on April 9, five more companies April 13, one company April 15, and eight companies April 16, to be furnished by the District of Columbia.[21] These three abbreviated regiments represent the first step toward mobilization: a step of such meager dimensions as to cause not even a ripple of comment outside of the Dis-

---

[19] *U. S. Public Statutes at Large* (Boston, 1845-1846), vol. 1, pp. 424-425. This work, begun in 1845, was continued under various titles and under different editors until it assumed the form in which the volumes since 1873 have appeared. Hereafter in this work it will be referred to as *U. S. Statutes at Large*, those being the key words of the majority of the volumes. For complete title and editor of any volume later cited see the formal bibliography.

[20] *Idem*, vol. 2, pp. 215-225.

[21] *War of the Rebellion: compilation of official records of Union and Confederate Armies* (Washington, 1880-1901), series i, vol. 51, part i, pp. 321-325; *idem*, series iii, vol. 1, p. 75. This compilation will be referred to hereafter as *Official Records*.

trict. Here too was exhibited the first opposition to federal control. Many of the men of the first ten companies refused to take the oath at muster for fear that, by so doing, they would be made regular soldiers of the United States. Nor were their fears overcome until they were assured that they were merely "the militia of the District, taken into the United States Service for the protection of the District, and would not be ordered off." [22]

In the meantime a state of war had been recognized. Now, if ever, the authority and strength of the residual Union must be shown. The display that ensued was couched in the form of a call, under authority of the act of 1795, for 75,000 three-months militia. Seventy-five thousand raw, green militiamen, who could not be trained for the field by the time their three months' term of service had expired, for the suppression of a rebellion thoroughly organized in seven of the strongest states of the Union and more than incipient in eight more.[23]

Because of the unpardonable neglect to call for an immediate session of congress, militia were the only troops available but, even so, seventy-five thousand was an absurdly small request at a time when New York alone was contemplating raising as many as thirty thousand for two years. Governor Oliver P. Morton of Indiana was expecting as many more,[24] and Massa-

[22] *Idem*, series i, vol. 51, part i, pp. 322-323.

[23] In "Fry's Report," part i, p. 7, the provost-marshal-general states that this call was made "under the 24th section of the act approved March 3, 1803." However text of proclamation is thoroughly in accord with act of February 28, 1795, and nowhere makes any provisions which would fall under act of 1803. Furthermore, the Secretary of War, in his call to states in pursuance of proclamation, *Official Records*, series iii, vol. 1, pp. 68-69, expressly states that he is making call under authority of act of February 28, 1795.

[24] *New York Tribune*, April 16, 1861.

chusetts was offering twenty thousand. Three states
were willing to furnish more than the total number
requested. The *New York Tribune* estimated that
Pennsylvania alone would offer more than the number
required and that almost the whole number could be
supplied from New York City.[25]

Nor were these estimates greatly exaggerated, as the
immediate and subsequent fervor of enlistment was to
show. Seventy-five thousand was but a fraction of what
the nation was willing to furnish but it was more than
enough of the kind of troops called for. A belated call
for an extraordinary session of congress accompanied
the call for militia, but the date of convening was postponed till July 4 [26] and it was not until August that the
United States was ready to make a serious effort to
raise an army.

In the meantime the first flush of recruiting fervor
was almost wholly wasted. Bull Run may have been
necessary to awaken the administration and congress
but the people were ready to act in April. Undoubtedly
the people underestimated the size of the task ahead of
them but, if the vigor of the government had equalled
the enthusiasm of the people, the task itself would
indubitably have been smaller. It was the half-hearted
military policies of the Union that gave the Confederacy its tremendous advantage during the first year of
the war.

Outside of the slave states the replies to the President's call were more than gratifying. Responses poured
in from the governors of free states promising troops

[25] *Ibid.*, April 15, 1861.

[26] J. D. Richardson, ed., *Compilation of Messages and Papers of Presi-
dents 1789-1897* (Washington, 1897), vol. 6, pp. 13-14. See note at end of
chapter for dissenting opinion on this subject.

and offering many more than were called for.[27] But from none of the slave states was the answer cordial and from most it was hostile. Governor Thomas P. Hicks of Maryland secured a promise that the troops of that state would not be taken across the borders of the state or of the District of Columbia. Governor William Burton of Delaware, in a belated reply, pleaded the constitution of his state in refusal to turn the militia over to the President. Governor Beriah Magoffin of Kentucky stated emphatically, "Kentucky will furnish no troops for the wicked purpose of subduing her sister Southern States." Governors John Ellis and John Letcher of North Carolina and Virginia respectively, professed to doubt the genuineness of the document sent to them, denounced the policy and threatened retaliation. Governor Isham G. Harris of Tennessee was willing to furnish 50,000 men for the Confederacy but not one man for the purpose of coercion. Governor Claiborne F. Jackson declared the demand "illegal, unconstitutional and revolutionary" and the object "inhuman and diabolical." Not one man would Missouri furnish "to carry on any such unholy crusade." Governor Henry M. Rector of Arkansas declared that the call merely added insult to injury. His constituents were "freemen, not slaves" and they would defend themselves to the last extremity "against Northern mendacity and usurpation."[28]

This opposition was only to be expected. Four of the states seceded shortly afterward and furnished no troops officially throughout the war. In the other four

[27] *Official Records*, series iii, vol. 1, pp. 70 *et seq.*
[28] *Ibid.*, reply of Kentucky, p. 70; North Carolina, p. 72; Virginia, p. 76; Maryland, pp. 79-80; Tennessee, pp. 81, 91-92; Missouri, pp. 82-83; Arkansas, p. 99; Delaware, p. 114.

the loyal governments ultimately prevailed and maintained their quotas throughout the war, although in
Missouri and Kentucky a duplicate drain placed an
almost equal number of men, at least of volunteers, in
the Confederate army. The militia call forced these
states to take a stand and thereafter the government
knew just about how much support was to be had from
them.

In the free states the performance in recruiting was
at least equal to the promise. The call, apportioned
approximately according to population, was not heavy
on any state. Seventeen regiments of 780 men each from
New York, fourteen from Pennsylvania, and thirteen
from Ohio were the largest contingents, the other states
being assessed from one to six regiments each. All
officers even to brigadier and major-generals were to
be furnished by the states.[29] There was plenty of chance
for individual initiative, and within a week various
quotas were filled, and governors were being embar-
rassed by offers of more men than they knew what to
do with. General Benjamin F. Butler tendered his
services with his entire brigade.

Acceptance by the governors of a surplus would only
entail an extra expense to the states for the maintenance
of those not accepted by the War Department. Accordingly zealous organizations were put off with indefinite
promises or tentative acceptances.[30] In less than two
weeks 35,000 were in Washington or en route thither
and nearly 20,000 more were ready for transportation.[31]

At the same time governors were clamoring for the
War Department to accept more troops. Governor

[29] *Ibid.*, p. 69.
[30] Byers, *op. cit.*, p. 46; *New York Tribune*, April 16, 27, 1861.
[31] *New York Tribune*, April 28, 1861.

Alexander W. Randall of Wisconsin was, from the first, offended because his state was called upon for only one regiment, while Illinois was allowed to furnish six. As early as April 19 he suggested that 100,000 more men be called. Again on May 6, he acted as spokesman for a recently held conference of western governors. This time he insisted, in a personal letter to the President, that, even though it were positively certain that the rebellion could be suppressed in three weeks, yet, in order to show its authority and properly impress the world, 300,000 more men should be called into the field at once.[32] The governors of Indiana, Maine, New Jersey, Connecticut, Michigan, New Hampshire, and Ohio were especially persistent in their requests that many more regiments should be accepted from their states. The attorney-general of New York urged on May 1, that the government accept thirty-eight regiments of two-year militia in place of the seventeen called for. The state had appropriated $3,500,000 for this purpose and was willing to arm and equip them completely if the government would only accept them and pay and provide for them after reaching the depots.[33]

So far, instead of the federal government assuming the initiative in recruiting, the states seemed to be pursuing a hopeless policy in trying to stimulate the federal administration to energetic activity. On the third of May their urgings began to bear fruit. The President, trusting to the approaching congress to legalize his actions, issued a proclamation calling for 42,034 volunteers (the maximum number for forty regiments) and ten regiments of regulars, totaling 22,714. These and

---

[32] *Official Records*, series iii, vol. 1, pp. 91, 169.
[33] *Ibid.*, pp. 93 *et seq.*, especially pp. 93, 94, 97, 100-102, 143-144.

18,000 additional seamen were to serve for three years unless sooner discharged.[34] Thus, for the first time, the President gave dynamic expression of response to the insistent demands for an army.

The total number of volunteers called for was only a third greater than the number New York alone was urging the acceptance of. This is to be explained very largely by the fact that the purpose of the new call was not so much to increase the size of the federal defense, as to make the force already raised more permanent. The term of the militia would have expired before the belated congress could provide for their successors. In this case the North would be wholly at the mercy of the South even if another contingent of militia were called into the field to succeed the first. The thing to do was to continue the terms of those already in the service, and at least partially trained. To secure this continuity the Secretary of War called upon the governors of seventeen states which still had militia regiments mustered into the service of the government but not yet sent forward, to muster them into the service for three years or during the war. If any individuals should refuse to be so mustered the governors were asked to fill their places by others.[35]

No difficulties were encountered in filling up the quotas under the new calls. Governors were again overwhelmed with applications from volunteer organizations, and they, in turn, besieged the War Department to accept additional regiments and to hasten to assign quotas.[36] After nearly two weeks' delay some relief

---

[34] *Ibid.*, pp. 145-146.

[35] May 6, 1861. Pacific states and slave states except Delaware were omitted, *ibid.*, p. 161.

[36] *Ibid.*, pp. 162, 166, 170-173, 179, 181, 185-189, 198-200.

was doled out to the anxious governors. A maximum number of three-years regiments was assigned to each in addition to the three-months regiments, but the sanction was accompanied with the admonition that "It is important to reduce rather than enlarge this number, and in no event to exceed it." [37] In other words, the decision was still adhered to to draw as many as possible of the new troops from the earlier militia regiments. As much advantage as possible was taken of the latitude allowed, and few instances were recorded of the anticipated refusal to take the oath on muster. Where such cases occurred the soldiers usually took the matter in hand themselves. Instances are recorded of such non-jurors being stripped of all clothing except underwear and "kicked by all from the Colonel down," [38] and of others being "stripped of their arms, a white feather stuck over each ear and . . . marched out of the Armory grounds [at Albany] with the drums playing the Rogue's March. Crowds of people assembled to see them undergo the degrading penance." [39]

Just how many volunteers for three years or the war could have been raised in these first months, if the government had been in a position to receive them, cannot be ascertained. The prevailing opinion was that the war would be a short one. A person who enlisted for three years or the war understood that, in reality, he was enlisting for only a short period. Multitudes wished to be in the fight to see the finish: hence the keen competition to secure places in the thin regiments of the early months. As early as May 10 it was estimated

---

[37] *Ibid.*, pp. 203-204. By orders of May 15, 16, 1861.
[38] *New York Tribune*, June 2, 1861.
[39] *Harper's Weekly*, vol. 5 (June 1, 1861), p. 384.

that at least 300,000 had offered their services.[40] On the same date the *New York Tribune* declared that "Had the President called – as we fervently wish he had – for Five Hundred Thousand men . . . they would all have been promptly furnished by the Free States alone and every man a glad volunteer. And they would have been armed and equipped too. . . ."[41] Regardless of the exact degree of exaggeration in these estimates, the fact is glaringly apparent that the spring, rather than the late summer and fall, of 1861, was the time for the federal government to take the initiative in recruiting. The later soldiers had a clearer notion of the task ahead of them, but it is not at all apparent that this made them any abler as soldiers than if they had been mustered earlier and learned the magnitude of the enterprise as it developed.

A very considerable difficulty in ascertaining the exact degree of recruiting fervor in the first months, is due to the fact that many of the regiments offered to the federal government, and upon which the estimates are based, were either incomplete or only in prospect, at the time of the offer. The expedients adopted to complete these regiments were many and varied. Daily advertisements appeared in the newspapers calling for men to complete regiments or companies in process of organization.[42] Blazing posters "plastered along the city streets and spread broadcast over the countryside, dwelt not only on the generous pay offered by the United States, and its land bounties and pensions, but very frequently on the care that would be taken of those

---

[40] *New York Tribune*, May 11, 1861.
[41] *Ibid.*, May 10, 1861.
[42] For example see *ibid.*, April, May, 1861, *passim.*

at home." [43] Almost unlimited capital was made of the
mob and subsequent minor disturbances at Baltimore,
and hyperbolic boasts were made of how the brave
soldiers would handle the Plug Uglies if they were
only given the opportunity. For lack of anything more
exciting, the newspapers played up the riot and the
murder on May 24 of Colonel Ephraim E. Ellsworth,
until the news of Bull Run was almost a welcome relief
to the readers. Repeated accounts of the departure of
"gallant troops" and of the exuberant celebrations that
attended such events tended to inspire the emulation of
others. [44]

Individual motives for enlistment were varied. Many
were inspired by the influences above mentioned. Perhaps a great number were influenced by the same motive as a Wisconsin private who confessed that he was
not "very strongly animated by a love for the Union
in the abstract" nor did he consider the abolition of
slavery worth fighting for but he "felt that the dismem-
berment of the Union by armed force, submitted to
without a struggle, would be a disgrace to the whole
north." [45] Many enlisted for lack of other employment.
The temporary derangement of business, due to seces-

---

[43] C. R. Fish, "Social Relief in Northwest during the Civil War," in *American Historical Review*, vol. 22, pp. 312-313; Louis Philippe Albert d'Or-
leans, Comte de Paris, *History of Civil War in America* (Philadelphia, 1875-
1888), vol. 1, p. 177.

[44] See files of *New York Tribune* and *Harper's Weekly*, vol. 5 (April,
May, and June, 1861), *passim*. For murder of Ellsworth see Nicolay and
Hay, *Abraham Lincoln, a History* (New York, 1890), vol. 4, pp. 312-314;
"Ellsworth, Ephraim Elmer," in *American Annual Cyclopaedia*, vol. 1 (1861),
pp. 284-285. See also C. A. Ingraham, *Elmer E. Ellsworth and the Zouaves
of '61* (Chicago, 1926).

[45] Hinkley, *op. cit.*, pp. 2-3. His account was written many years after
the war, thus accounting for reference to antislavery motive which, in 1861,
was confined to seasoned abolitionists.

sion, had created a rather large group of this class. Irishmen enlisted hoping in some way to strike a blow at England, and carried the green flag along with the American colors in their regiments.[46] But whatever the motive or inducement volunteering went on steadily with little hindrance except from the federal government.

The favorite method of raising a company was by mass meetings and many of these have been described by regimental historians. A typical meeting of this kind was presided over at Galena, Illinois, on April 16 by ex-Captain Ulysses S. Grant and was addressed by his future Chief of Staff and Secretary of War, John A. Rawlins. The meeting was not much of a success and the promoters had to hold subsidiary meetings in neighboring villages to complete one company, whereas two companies had been the goal. At one of these meetings Grant himself made one of the first speeches of his reticent career. Twelve recruits were the result, but the records are silent as to whether Grant's address had anything to do with the paucity of the returns.[47]

A similar but more successful meeting, held in Milwaukee while raising the first three-year men, was attended by the newly appointed captain of the prospective company, who was very anxious to cut a dashing figure and impress the people with his bravery. While the meeting was in progress he "stood apart, the hero of the moment, and with a bright new sword, made cuts at space which offered no resistance." [48]

But the height of the histrionic, in these perform-

[46] Count of Paris, *op. cit.*, vol. 1, pp. 177-178.
[47] A. L. Chetlain, *Recollections of Seventy Years* (Galena, Illinois, 1899), pp. 69-70.
[48] E. R. Jones, *Four Years in Army of Potomac* (London, n. d.), pp. 40-41.

ances, was shown in the organization of the Wilson Fighting Zouaves in New York City. They were sworn in midst cries of "Death to the Plug Uglies." Then the colonel, William Wilson, "illustrated with his sword how they should hew their way, and said though he should be the first man slain, he had but one thing to ask, that was that each of his followers should secure his man and avenge his blood. That they would do this, he again called upon them to swear, and marching around the hall, holding up the flag and the sword and accompanied by two officers, the one on his right bearing a banner inscribed 'The Union Battalion of Zouaves. Death to Secessionists,' the other officer on his left holding up in both hands a bowie-knife and revolver, Wilson shouted to them to swear, and they responded with shouts of 'Blood! Blood! Blood! We swear'." [49] Fantastic as this may sound these men, at least, were equal to their sanguinary professions. They included hardened veterans of many wars in many parts of the world and, if current comment is to be believed, they also included the dregs of the city. "It was observed that the average of crime in the great city of New York decreased by one-half after the departure of the Wilson Zouaves." [50]

When once organized these companies and regiments made up in enthusiasm for what they lacked in skill. An Iowa company contemplated mobbing and egging the governor when he proposed to place them in a later regiment than the one then forming. [51] Other companies were beset with fear that the trouble between

---

[49] *Harper's Weekly*, vol. 5 (May 18, 1861), p. 311.

[50] Count of Paris, *op. cit.*, vol. 1, p. 178; *New York Tribune*, April 22, 1861.

[51] Byers, *With Fire and Sword* (New York, 1911), p. 1.

the North and the South would be settled before they should engage in any fight, and they were downcast at the prospect.[52] When a New York regiment was slow in starting for the front, the colonel was blamed for using his influence to keep them at home and many volunteers deserted the regiment to enlist in others.[53] It was long before such desertions were considered or treated as anything else than permissable. Yet, anxious as these volunteers thought themselves to be to smell burnt powder, their holiday attitude toward the war was attested by the fact that many, who were entirely willing to enlist for the war, objected to a three-year term. Yet some of these very persons served out such terms and enlisted again as veteran volunteers before the war was over.[54]

Another form of enthusiasm was exhibited in the desire to form regiments and companies along racial, occupational, sentimental, or even freakish lines. The Irish regiments of the East have already been mentioned. Many western organizations were German and, in the East, there were to be found regiments of French likewise. The presence of the exiled Count of Paris and his uncle the Prince de Joinville on the staff of Mc-Clellan was a special incentive to the formation of the latter type of organization. The Fifty-fifth New York Volunteers was one of this kind, made up very largely of relatively wealthy Frenchmen, but including also veterans of the Algerian, Crimean, and Italian wars.[55] The voluntary fire companies checked their "prover-

---

[52] F. B. Wilkie, *The Iowa First; letters from the War* (Dubuque, 1861), p. 11.

[53] Trobriand, *op. cit.*, pp. 70-71.

[54] Hinkley, *op. cit.*, p. 6.

[55] Trobriand, *op. cit.*, pp. 70, 73.

bial turbulence" long enough to form a regiment of
Fire Zouaves. A temperance regiment was organized in Iowa. But of caste or occupational organizations one of the strangest was a company of black-
smiths from Phoenixville, Pennsylvania. With no reference to the organization just mentioned, a New York
bank clerk named Smith proposed to raise a regiment
of Smiths: nobody whose surname was not Smith
should apply for membership. Surely this was not an
impossible task, nor was that of another New Yorker
who advertised for recruits for a regiment of Gren-
nadier Household Guards. None but able bodied men,
six feet or more in height would be accepted. As a further incentive to such enlistment, the promise was made
that these delicate youngsters would be used solely to
guard the city and its suburbs, though their stature
would indicate that they were better fitted for active
field service.[56]

But the most frequent type of organization was the
Zouave. The picturesqueness as well as the valor of
the French Zouaves in Algeria and elsewhere had
struck a responsive chord in America. Literally scores
of companies and many regiments bore this name. Differences of opinion existed as to the exact regulation
Zouave uniform, but all were agreed upon some kind
of loose, baggy, Turkish trousers, a fez, and an exuberance of color, red predominating.[57] The making
of Zouave fez caps became a specialized industry in
itself. Alongside of advertisements of Gifford's Home-

---

[56] Count of Paris, *op. cit.*, vol. 1, pp. 178-179; Upham, *loc. cit.*, p. 24; *New York Tribune*, April 22, 27, 1861.

[57] The newspapers of April-June, 1861, and the regimental histories are replete with descriptions of Zouave organizations. *E. g. New York Tribune*, April 18, 1861; Jones, *op. cit.*, pp. 42-43.

opathic Pills appear advertisements of Warnock's Zouave Fez Caps,[58] both of inestimable value to the army. A year after the outbreak of the war these Zouave organizations were still in evidence, still retaining their ridiculous but rather faded costumes.[59]

The zeal of the volunteers was but a part of the general enthusiasm of the day. Union pins and highly decorated Union envelopes were as widely advertised as patent medicine and Phineas T. Barnum's whales. Frank Moore, the publisher, started the publication of the *Rebellion Record* filled with poems, anecdotes, and official records of the war,[60] and destined to be the forerunner of the *Official Records* of a later date. *The Bold Soldier Boy and Union Volunteer* was a weekly newspaper of evanescent existence which sprang into being with the first call for troops and shortly afterwards was heard of no more.[61] P. T. Barnum, seeing a chance to combine good business and patriotism, offered a New York ex-alderman $1000 to sing the Star Spangled Banner daily at his museum for four weeks.[62] But besides this outward display there was also the more concrete patriotism in the form of contributions meant to be valuable to the soldiers. Donations of money, flags, arms, uniforms, patent medicines, Bibles, undershirts, and especially tobacco, as well as the service of women in sewing uniforms, were gratefully recognized by the soldiers. One New York colonel

[58] *New York Tribune*, April 30, 1861.
[59] Illustrations in *Harper's Weekly*, vol. 6 (March 1, 1862), pp. 135-137.
[60] Frank Moore, ed., *The Rebellion Record*, 12 vols. (New York, 1861-1868). This is the original *Rebellion Record*, and should not be confused with the *Official Records*, which are sometimes cited under the same title.
[61] *New York Tribune*, April 20-27, 1861.
[62] *Ibid.*, April 18, 1861.

listed thousands of dollars worth of such donations to his regiment alone.[63]

All of this enthusiasm was at the disposal of the states or of the federal government according as either or both were able and willing to make use of it. The tardiness of the government in grasping the situation left the states to take the initiative, not only in the raising of troops but also in organizing, training, equipping, and in all ways fitting them for the field. It was only when they were sent to the front, or to some camp of rendezvous outside the state, that they might really be said to have been under federal control, and even then the authority of the state governments followed them in matters relating to appointment of officers.

This advantage was first gained through the call for militia. The militia law left the men solely in the control of the states until they were sworn into the service of the United States. With the duty of raising, equipping, and training was coupled the privilege of selection of all officers from major-generals to corporals. In the apportionment of the first quotas New York and Pennsylvania were asked for two major-generals each and Ohio for one. The states were also asked to supply seventeen brigadier-generals. In all 3,549 commissioned officers were assigned in this one call:[64] one man in twenty of the total quotas – a splendid chance for political favoritism, and a taste to stimulate the appetite for a larger portion.

The calls for the first three-year men were, as before, for regiments,[65] not for a stated number of troops, thus

[63] *Ibid.*, June 1 ,1861.

[64] *Official Records*, series iii, vol. 1, p. 69.

[65] *Ibid.*, pp. 203-204.

again giving the governors the privilege of appointing all officers from colonels on down. The War Department seems to have made no distinction in this matter between militia and United States soldiers, and so the militia system of state control was grafted onto what was supposed to be a national army.

This situation was recognized and legalized by the act of congress of July 22, 1861. This act, providing for the creation of a volunteer army of 500,000 men, expressly provided that "The Governors of the States furnishing volunteers under this act shall commission the field, staff, and company officers requisite for the said volunteers. . . ." [66] The same method of organization was provided by the supplementary act passed three days later [67] and thereby the system became permanent. The principle of state rights, as applied to the raising of the army, had prevailed. The federal government might call for the troops and assign the quotas, but the states would raise the men, organize the regiments, and, to a great extent, control their destinies. The results of this triumph will be estimated in the following chapters.

The fact of the triumph is incontestable and the reasons are apparent. The weakness of the federal administration in the time of crisis had thrown the responsibility of defending the Union upon the states. The war had been in progress for nearly three months before President Lincoln had a congress in session. He then requested at least 400,000 men [68] and got permission to raise half a million. Advantage was taken of this to

---

[66] *U. S. Statutes at Large*, vol. 12, pp. 268-269.

[67] *Ibid.*, p. 274.

[68] Richardson, *op. cit.*, vol. 6, p. 26.

assign quotas of a little over 600,000 men, and the states responded by furnishing 700,000.[69] Contrast this with the feeble recruiting efforts of the federal government. The President had on May 3, called for ten regiments or a total of about 22,700 men. This, as legalized by act of July 29, provided for a regular army of about 42,000 men [70] but so incapable was the federal government in raising troops through its own efforts that by December, when the volunteers already exceeded 640,000 the total of the regular army was barely in excess of 20,000.[71] Scarcely two regiments had been recruited, and for some time previously certain recruiting officers had gone for weeks without doing any business at all.[72] Nor was any degree of success to be achieved, for this branch of the Union forces, throughout the war. In spite of all efforts of the federal government, later to be described, the goal established in May and July of 1861 was never reached.

Numerous reasons might be presented to explain the superiority of the states in recruiting: the influence of local and state bounties; popular election of officers; the desire of volunteers to be organized in units with their acquaintances – all of which inducements would draw recruits away from the regular army to the advantage of the volunteer army. But, behind all these facts, lies the stronger reason, that state rights had so strong a hold upon the minds of both of the major political parties, that they could conceive of no other

[69] *Official Records*, series iii, vol. 1, pp. 383-384.

[70] *U. S. Statutes at Large*, vol. 12, pp. 279-281; *Official Records*, series iii, vol. 1, p. 154.

[71] Count of Paris, *op. cit.*, vol. 1, p. 288; *Official Records*, series iii, vol. 1, p. 699.

[72] *New York Tribune*, October 21, 1861.

way to create a large army, than by turning the work over to the agency of the states. There were plenty of republicans in congress, who were willing to denounce their opponents for state-rights doctrines, but their actions in legislation did not correspond to their professions, as later evidence will show. The fact that congress turned over to the states the whole work of recruiting and organization, and this without any voiced opposition, goes to show the hold of the state-rights theory on the popular mind.

Nationality was a common word in 1861. Horace Greeley could write with exalted fervor of "the majestic development of Nationality" occasioned by the firing on Fort Sumter,[73] but the shoutings and enthusiasm which he translated into nationalism are better understood as the expressions of sectional and state pride or patriotism and of class interest. The historian George Bancroft had good reason in October, 1861, to urge upon the Massachusetts soldiers that they "Cease to be men of Massachusetts, men of New England, men even of the North – be Americans." [74] The same advice was needed by the mass of the northern people; but nowhere was it more badly needed than in the counsels of congress and of the federal administration. Four years of blundering warfare did not teach the lesson thoroughly to the majority. It is little wonder that in the beginning there was an almost complete reliance on the states.[75]

[73] *Ibid.*, April 17, 1861.
[74] *Ibid.*, October 10, 1861.
[75] Note on the delay in convening congress:
The standard political biographies of Lincoln defend both the small number of troops called for and the postponement of the convening of congress. For instance in J. T. Morse, *Abraham Lincoln* (Boston, 1897), vol. 1,

pp. 291-292, are the words: "July 4, 1861, the Thirty-seventh Congress met in extra session, and the soundness of the President's judgment in setting a day which had at first been condemned as too distant was proved. In the interval, nothing had been lost which could have been saved by the sitting of Congress; while, on the other hand, the members had had the great advantage of having time to think soberly concerning the business before them, and to learn the temper and wishes of their constituents." The reasons for the delay are defined as desire to give himself and circumstances time to work out "definite conditions, which certainly did not [then] exist. . ." dread of the conclaves of the lawmakers, and the wish to give Kentucky time to hold a special election for choosing members for that session, *ibid.*, p. 254.

The transparency of most of this argument is clearly apparent. The only statement worthy of second consideration is that concerning Kentucky. The North has long misjudged that state as to her stand in 1861. Without doubt at least 70% of the citizens of that state were loyal to the Union, but they resented armed invasion from either camp. Every election held during the year showed this overwhelming Union majority. In the election of June 30, for representatives to congress the vote was 92,460 to 37,700 in favor of the Union men and only one secessionist representative was elected out of ten. This vote is representative of all plebicites held during the year. If the call for militia to suppress insurrection would not cause this loyal majority to change to the secession flag, neither would an early session of congress to consider further war measures. The one thing Kentucky wanted was immunity from invasion and from aggression. This Lincoln very wisely granted. Finally, as to the election for representatives, this was postponed by Governor Beriah Magoffin to the last available moment. The call was not issued till May 3, and nearly two months were provided for the campaign. There is no particular reason why this election could not have been held much earlier if congress had been called to meet say some six weeks earlier. *Cf.* "Kentucky," in *American Annual Cyclopaedia and Register of Important Events of the Year 1861* (New York, 1867), pp. 396-397; R. M. McElroy, *Kentucky in the Nation's History* (New York, 1909), pp. 500-546; N. S. Shaler, *Kentucky, a Pioneer Commonwealth* (Boston, 1895), pp. 239-256.

As to the size of the volunteer force called out, the chief defenders and apologists are Nicolay and Hay, *op. cit.*, vol. 4, pp. 77-78. They condemn "eleventh-hour critics" for questioning this policy. They point to the limited armament of the country, the lack of equipment and supplies, and the almost bankrupt condition of the treasury. All these conditions certainly called for legislative consideration. But these authors avoid mentioning reasons for the deferring of the extra session of congress. Certainly the country was no better prepared to equip an army on July 4 than it had been two months earlier. Evidently feeling that other explanation was necessary, the authors proceed to declare that scarcely a spark of war feeling had been felt in the North even after the firing on Fort Sumter. "Faith seemed gone and patriotism dead." This statement is grossly false as all the evidence of the period indicates. They themselves admit that "Twenty-four hours later [after the call] all this was measurably changed. . ." but they give no explanation for this strange revolution of feeling. "Even that number [75,000]," they assert, "appeared a hazardous experiment – an immense army, a startling expenditure." They omit mention of the fact that New York alone was eager to furnish 30,000 of them, for two years instead of three months, and arm and equip them herself out of her $3,000,000 appropriation. They fail to note the hundreds of thousands of volunteers whose services were refused.

Feeding and Clothing the Volunteers

Feeding and Clothing the Volunteers

JUST as the states were entrusted with the recruiting and organization of the regiments for the army so, in like manner, they had to assume the responsibility of providing for the needs of the soldiers, until mustered into the service of the United States. The activities of states, corporations, and individuals in raising funds for this purpose has already been mentioned. Even for so small a force as 75,000, the Secretary of War was compelled to admit that the United States was not in a position to furnish camp equipage and clothing as rapidly as they were needed. Accordingly he advised the governors to furnish the material and present their bills. Though admitting that "clothing is sometimes issued to volunteers," he intimated that, since the soldiers received a monthly allowance for clothing in addition to their pay, it was up to them or to the states to see that they were provided with uniforms.[76] The official correspondence of the period is replete with pleas from the governors to the War Department for everything from tincups to stables, and replies from that fountain head of chaos, courteously requesting said governors to help themselves and present their bills for payment.[77]

It was not the intention that the state governments should be finally responsible for all such costs. The

---

[76] *Official Records*, series iii, vol. 1, p. 132.
[77] For example see *ibid.*, pp. 132, 177.

War Department simply confessed its inability to handle the situation and let it be understood from the first that the states would be reimbursed. Nor were its promises unfulfilled. Though the states assumed the risk of recovering these costs from the federal government, they were not the losers thereby. Congress, in its first rush of military legislation, made provisions for repaying to the states "the costs, charges, and expenses properly incurred by such State[s] for enrolling, subsisting, clothing, supplying, arming, equiping, paying, and transporting its troops. . . ." [78] The phraseology of the act itself shows the wide range of responsibilities which the governors were called upon to assume. Almost a month earlier, July 1, 1861, Secretary Cameron had estimated that $10,000,000 were due the states for advances already made. An appropriation act of February 25, 1862, set aside another $15,000,000 for the same purpose. [79]

It is not to the discredit of the state governments that this abdication of authority on the part of the War Department resulted in confusion, graft on a wholesale basis, and untold hardships to the soldiers. The states did what they could. They purchased by contract and in the open market, at home and abroad, all manner of articles necessary for the armies. [80] Legislatures were liberal and governors were zealous to hasten the work of organization. The result was that army contract business produced a windfall of profit to the omnipresent profiteer. The situation would have been bad enough if the federal government alone were in the market, buying up the scanty stores of the manufac-

---

[78] *U. S. Statutes at Large*, vol. 12, p. 276, act of July 27, 1861.

[79] *Ibid.*, p. 345.

[80] G. B. McClellan, *McClellan's Own Story* (New York, 1887), p. 42.

turers and merchants. But the result produced by a
score of states bidding against each other and against
the federal government, was nothing short of deplor-
able.

The need for food, clothing, and shelter was immediate and urgent. Arms and ammunition might be
supplied in more leisurely fashion, but food and clothing, especially food, must be had at once. Accordingly
the first scandals concerning the army contract business
were in connection with contracts for beef and clothing,[81] and then in practically every line of military
supply. An army of lobbyists, contractors, and speculators at once "hurried to the assault on the treasury, like
a cloud of locusts. . . . They were everywhere; in the
streets, in the hotels, in the offices, at the Capitol, and
in the White House. They continually besieged the
bureaus of administration, the doors of the Senate and
House of Representatives, wherever there was a chance
to gain something." [82] In a similar way, the same performance was repeated in practically every state capital.

Through haste, carelessness, or criminal collusion,
the state and federal officers accepted almost every offer
and paid almost any price for the commodities, regardless of character, quality, or quantity. The type of
clothing, food, and munitions thus supplied will be
considered separately, but, as an index to the kind of
product commonly supplied the following, by comparison with numerous other accounts, does not seem
exaggerated: "For sugar it [the government] often got
sand; for coffee, rye; for leather, something no better
than brown paper; for sound horses and mules, spav-

[81] *New York Tribune,* May 25, 28, 31, *et seq.*
[82] Trobriand, *Army of Potomac,* p. 135.

ined beasts and dying donkeys; and for serviceable muskets and pistols, the experimental failures of sanguine inventors, or the refuse of shops and foreign armories." [83]

War contractors became proverbially and notoriously rich. The $50,000,000 spent by the government in the first few months for arms alone went to enrich a dozen or more contractors. Poor men became rich and rich men became richer in a day. It was commonly reported that one man made two million dollars in a single year. Some made fortunes with practically no outlay or exertion of their own. Some received contracts at exorbitant figures and then sold them at a liberal discount to sub-contractors, thus making comfortable fortunes without turning a hand or a dollar or devoting any appreciable time to the process. Others made more, at slightly greater exertion, by filling contracts as poorly as possible. "The quality of the article they heeded little, provided it bore the name and the semblance of the thing, and could be had for almost nothing. . . ." [84] It is a notorious fact that many of the greatest fortunes of today had their origin in Civil War contracts. Many a millionaire who later sought so frantically to achive respectability through alliance with foreign nobility might well have inscribed "Shoddy" as the legend on his costly coat of arms.

Necessity, haste, and carelessness can explain the acceptance of a great many of these contracts and a very great deal of inferior goods. But a large amount of blame must go to a horde of government-paid officials who, either through criminal negligence or criminal

[83] Robert Tomes, "Fortunes of War" in *Harper's Monthly Magazine*, vol. 29 (July, 1864), p. 228.
[84] *Ibid.*, p. 228.

collusion, permitted or encouraged this robbing of the government treasury and cruelty to the American soldiers. The connection of General John C. Fremont and Secretary Simon Cameron with this sort of business is already widely known.

The army of lesser officials, inspectors and so on, who permitted such graft, came in for their full share of public censure at a time when General Fremont was considered a vicarious martyr – but few of them were ever punished. Accused inspectors passed the blame on to those letting the contracts, the latter blamed the contractors, and the contractors in turn contended that they furnished goods according to specifications.

An incident involving the state officers of New York and other prominent men is typical of such shifting of responsibility. A contract had been let to a firm known as Brooks Brothers for 12,000 uniforms which were delivered at a net price of $9.50 a uniform. They proved to be entirely unsatisfactory, of inferior material, strange and outlandish cut, and ingenious construction; sometimes pocketless, buttonless, or otherwise devoid of necessary entity.

An outcry arose at once, directed against the inspectors including George Opdyke, a prominent republican politician and later mayor of New York. They promptly replied that their only duty was to see that the materials in the uniforms equalled that in the samples which had been submitted to the contractors, and that the workmanship was good. If the uniforms were bad, they contended, it was due to the samples and not to the inspectors. Their arguments were not altogether convincing but they at least started a controversy of several weeks' duration, as to who was responsible for the malfeasance or neglect, a dispute which settled nothing and satisfied nobody. The state officers, responsible for letting the contract, presented an imposing brief of approximately 15,000 words, heatedly refuting the imputation of the inspectors that they had been in collusion with the manufacturers. There matters rested. Brooks Brothers had the money, the soldiers had some rags, and the public had its attention diverted by other scandals.[85]

Such wide publicity was gained by this complicity of public officials in the early contract business that one of the very first acts of the extra session of congress in 1861 was to institute an investigation of the existing practices and conditions. On motion of Charles H. Van Wyck of New York, July 8, 1861, a committee was appointed for this purpose by the speaker of the House of Representatives. This committee, headed by Van Wyck, held almost continuous meetings in various parts of the country from that time until July 10, 1862, taking testimony until late in April of 1862.[86]

The committee discovered an astounding amount of illegal and fraudulent activities, in some instances calling into question the honor or good judgment of men high in the political and military councils of the country.

The Department of the West, under Fremont, was found to be especially irregular in its operations. In one instance a consignment of 25,000 castoff and worth-

---

[85] *New York Tribune*, July 8, 15, September 5, 1861.

[86] The other members were Elihu B. Washburne of Illinois; William S. Holman of Indiana; Reuben E. Fenton of New York; Henry L. Dawes of Massachusetts; William G. Steele of New Jersey; and James S. Jackson of Kentucky. The report of the committee to congress was made in two large volumes totalling over 2700 pages, "Government Contracts," in *House Reports*, 37 Cong., 2 sess., *report* no. 2.

less Austrian muskets was purchased for $166,000, which figure represented a total loss to the government.[87] On another occasion 5000 Hall carbines were purchased by Fremont, through Simon Stevens of Pennsylvania. In June, 1861, the Ordnance bureau of the War Department itself had sold these same guns to Arthur M. Eastman of Manchester, New Hampshire, at $3.50 each. At a cost of from 75 cents to $1.25 Eastman had altered these arms and sold them to Stevens for $12.50 each. The latter then immediately sold the entire lot to General Fremont for $22 each, "General Fremont probably laboring under some misapprehension as to the nature of the purchase of the arms."

Various points were raised by this transaction. In the first place the committee found that the War Department had no business to sell the arms, and especially at such a price, at a time when it was buying worthless Austrian muskets at $6.50 each. Yet the order for their sale, which was private, was signed by the Secretary of War, on recommendation of the Ordnance bureau. In the second place it was scarcely consistent with the usual conception of honesty that such guns should be bought back in a few weeks' time at more than six times the sale price.

Stranger yet 790 of these guns had already, before the war, been condemned and sold by the War Department at a merely nominal price. Then later, in April, 1861, Alexander Cummings, as agent of the War Department, bought them back for $15 each. Two months later they were included in the number sold to Eastman for $3.50 apiece. Then in August, 1861, they were

---

[87] *Idem*, part i, pp. 38-40.

bought back with the rest at $22. The Committee reasoned in this case as follows: "Whether buying or selling, the liberality of the government is equally striking! General [James W.] Ripley [Chief of Ordnance] is a gentleman of large experience and inexorable in the performance of his public duties. The arm had been rejected from the public service as practically worthless years ago, and in his judgment no alteration could improve it; if so, the re-purchase of the arm is without possible excuse; if otherwise, the original sale of the arm is utterly indefensible." [88] It was further brought out in the testimony that J. Pierpont Morgan advanced the funds and collected the profits.[89] In the last phase of this transaction Stevens or Morgan was attempting to make $49,000 on $60,000 worth of material, which at any other time would have been totally worthless.

The same story was repeated in the purchase of general army supplies. Regardless of statute requirements that contracts be let only after advertisement for bids, "either through corrupt motives, or from a want of reasonable prudence," such mandate was thoroughly ignored and purchases were made by what was called "requisitions." In this way certain favored companies were given contracts running into tens of thousands of articles of all kinds of soldiers' clothing and equipment. The firm of Child, Pratt, and Fox at St. Louis during the Fremont regime in 1861 "furnished, from time to time, ordinary army supplies to the value of over $800,-000, apparently without the price of a single article being previously determined." The bookkeeper of the

---

[88] *Ibid.*, pp. 40-41.

[89] *Ibid.*, pp. 42-52. Robert Dale Owen and Joseph Holt later determined that Stevens was the actual contractor, *idem*, part ii, p. lxiv.

firm testified that the ordinary profit was about 40 per cent.[90]

The use of irresponsible agents in the making of government purchases extended even to the Secretary of War. In April, 1861, Secretary Cameron employed Alexander Cummings, editor of *The World*, to direct the buying of supplies in New York City. Cummings was not especially fitted for the work, whereas there were expert army officials in the city at the time who were eminently qualified for such superintendency. The authority was by order of Cameron to be jointly divided between Cummings and Governor Edwin D. Morgan. Shortly afterward (May 4, 1861) the governor delegated his power to a relative and business partner, George D. Morgan. "Governor Morgan seems to have regarded this extraordinary appointment as a franchise, subject to be transferred at pleasure." In his new capacity George D. Morgan made purchases up to $25,000 in a thoroughly irresponsible manner during the short time he was connected with Cummings.[91]

A fund of $2,000,000 was left at the disposal of the couple, subject only to nominal oversight by a committee of reputable citizens. A strange era of spending resulted. The sum of $21,000 was expended for *linen pantaloons and straw hats*. The firm of Benedict and Hall received a contract for 75,000 pairs of shoes at $2.20 a pair, which were worth much less. A member of the firm testified that Cummings received no pay from them for the transaction but that the contract was let to them in return for the kindness of an occasional temporary loan of $500 or $1000. Along with other

---

[90] *Idem*, part i, pp. 53-54.
[91] *Ibid.*, pp. 55-57.

peculiar army supplies purchased by Cummings were large quantities of Scotch ale, London porter, selected herring, and 23 barrels of pickles. Without being bound by oath or bond, Cummings spent $250,000 during the summer of 1861. Even if honest he was thoroughly incompetent; his sole qualification being that he was a friend of Simon Cameron.[92]

The same recklessness was often displayed by the War Department itself. A contract for 10,000 cattle at eight cents a pound was let to a favored company (Sibley, Tyler, Laughman, and Dyer) who immediately sublet the contract to another firm (Williams and Allerton) at $6\frac{1}{2}$ cents a pound, and made $32,268.17 by the deal without so much as risking a dollar. This sum and numerous others like it could have been saved the country simply by obedience to the law relating to advertising for bids.[93]

Of larger significance was the fraud in connection with the building of the fortifications at St. Louis in 1861. A contract entered into on September 25, 1861, between General Justus McKinstry, acting under special orders from Fremont, and E. L. Beard gave the latter individual the responsibility for constructing "all the fortifications." The questionable part of the deal lay in the fact that the fortifications were already nearly completed by day labor of St. Louis working men, under supervision of an army officer. The astounding feature of the business was that Beard actually received $151,000 for the work between August 29 and September 6, 1861, or from three to four weeks before the contract was let, and that he received the last installment on

---

[92] *Ibid.*, pp. 63-68.
[93] *Ibid.*, pp. 68-69; *testimony*, pp. 158-160.

October 3, or only eight days after the date of the agreement. "All the amounts were paid upon the direct personal order of Major General Fremont, with the exception of the first ten thousand dollars" which was paid by an indirect order.[94]

It was only due to the vigilance of the quartermaster, Major Robert Allen, that another $60,000 was not turned over to the contractor. Practically all of the $171,000 was profit, for the actual cost of construction of at least half of the fortification was paid from a separate fund. By liberal estimate Beard spent no more than $60,000 on the work thus clearing $111,000 even in spite of the interference of Major Allen. The responsibility for the letting of the contract was placed by the House Committee solely upon Fremont. The whole deal was all the more reprehensible since every dollar of the money "was diverted from a fund specifically appropriated for another purpose," namely for subsisting, clothing, and transportation of troops. This fund was "in utter contempt of all law and of army regulations, as well as in defiance of superior authority, . . . diverted from its lawful purpose," and turned over to Beard. At the same time laborers on the fortifications had much trouble in securing their pay and soldiers in the department were in want of necessary articles of clothing.[95]

Such dealings were repeated almost time without number. It was found by the committee that in the buying of beef, "when a conscientious officer refused to pass cattle not in accordance with the contract he was superseded by one who had no conscientious scruples in the

[94] *Ibid.*, pp. 73-76.
[95] *Ibid.*, pp. 76-83.

matter. . . ." [96] In the purchase of horses and mules in Missouri the most unblushing frauds were perpetrated. It became impossible, in 1861, to sell the animals except through middle men and go-betweens. These favorites bought the beasts at the smallest price possible and sold them always at the maximum allowed by the government. The buying of horses became so profitable that everybody who could get into favor with the proper authorities abandoned other pursuits in consequence. When ordinary profits were insufficient it was found that animals originally branded as cavalry horses at $119 could be re-branded as artillery horses at $150. A certain James Neil, a branding iron "artist," acquired a certain "standing of precarious pre-eminence" in this kind of work. As a result of such practices, in October, 1861, a board of survey found only 76 out of 411 cavalry horses, sent out from St. Louis, fit for service. Five were dead and 330 were *undersized, under and over aged, stifled, ringboned, blind, spavined, and incurably unfit for any public service.* These very horses cost eleven dollars each more than the regulation maximum of $119. The government could not get out of the situation at a loss of less than $40,000.[97]

One of the most alarming situations disclosed by the testimony taken at St. Louis was that many thousand dollars were paid out upon vouchers totally or partially false. Justus McKinstry, then major and assistant quartermaster, is especially named as being guilty of such forgeries.[98] The $800,000 worth of business han-

---

[96] *Ibid.*, p. 69.

[97] *Ibid.*, pp. 83-88, 98-99.

[98] *Ibid.*, pp. 99-101. McKinstry received the rank of brigadier-general on September 2, 1861. Frederick Phisterer, *Statistical Records of Armies of United States* (New York, 1893), p. 270.

dled by Child, Pratt, and Fox was tendered them chiefly through the activity of McKinstry, who paid them
sometimes as much as 55 per cent. higher than market
price. By their own confession the company made at
least $280,000 from the transactions. "This firm would
buy of its neighbor across the street, and then sell at
the most extravagant advance to the quartermaster the
very articles which that official had refused to purchase
from those who made or furnished them. . . ." When
McKinstry was on one occasion removed from his
office, the junior member of the firm went to Washington
and personally secured the re-appointment of the quartermaster.[99] Moreover it was discovered that Child,
Pratt, and Fox "contributed $200 toward the presenta-
tion of a service plate to Mrs. McKinstry, which cost
over $3,000, and to which contractors were told, by
those soliciting contributions, that if they did not contribute they 'would have trouble in collecting their
dues from the government.' He [Fox] also contributed
$300 towards the horses and carriage presented to Mrs.
[Jessie Benton] Fremont, had a brother-in-law in the
quartermaster's office under McKinstry, and a brother
a contractor to furnish horses for that department, in
whose behalf he procured of McKinstry twenty-five
dollars on each horse more than the original contract
price." [sic].[100]

Such dealings as those discovered by the Van Wyck
committee, in addition to the corruption of public
morals due to the commonly known practice of purchasing immunity through dividing the spoils with the
legislatures, officials, and magistrates, must have done

---

99 "Government Contracts," loc. cit., part i, pp. 106, 112-113.
100 Ibid., p. 113.

much to prepare the way for the petrifaction of public conscience in the post-war period – for the Tweed Ring, the Carpet Bag regime, and the scandals of the Grant administration.

An illustration of the popular attitude toward contractors and officials alike is shown by a cartoon of the day. Three inspectors and three contractors are draped about a room in varying degrees of indolence. In the foreground are cigars, a bottle, and glasses, presumably furnished by the contractors. One inspector is assuming the attitude of inspection of a garment, while the other two are frankly drinking and listening to the inducements of the contractors. The following conversation occurs.

First Contractor: "There sir! examine that blanket Sir! What could be better than it to protect our volunteers.– It is 2 feet 4 inches Square.– I'll allow 20 per ct – if they are passed. Oh! about the shoes? I admit we have used a leetle wood in the soles!"

First Inspector: "Ahem!! I'll pass 'em."

Second Contractor: "I assure you sir! the texture of this stuff [a pair of trousers he is holding] is fine,– very fine – in fact! Just the thing for our Volunteers. The sewing you observe is open – for the purpose of ventilation!!!"

Second Inspector: "Beautiful – how cool it will be for our brave fellows."

Third Inspector: "50 percent did you say? let 'em rip." [101]

Crude as this portrayal is it is borne out in its essential features by the official reports of the time. The cartoon itself was used to illustrate a surgeon's report

---

[101] *Harper's Weekly*, vol. 5 (August 10, 1861), p. 512.

POPULAR CONCEPTION OF THE CONTRACT SYSTEM AND ITS VICTIMS

As illustrated in a contemporary cartoon

of the conditions in the ranks of the New York troops. Examples equally as bad were to be found on every hand. In Pennsylvania $2.50 pants were contracted for at $5.00 a pair. Lower bids were submitted but were rejected due to the influence of notorious politicians.[102] Bids for a big beef contract ran from $3.90 to $8.30 a hundred pounds on foot and here again economy was sacrificed for the profit of the hungry vultures.[103]

A special committee appointed by the War Department, after Edwin Stanton's accession, to investigate contracts for arms found that the manufacturers of Colt's revolvers had been receiving $25 for a revolver that would ordinarily sell in the open market for $14.50 and had made in the course of a year $325,500 in excess profits through the sales. The indication of official corruption in this connection is shown in the fact that the Remington company had been offering for many months a revolver at least equally as good, for $15, and could get contracts for only 5000 of them, while the Colt company received contracts for 31,000 at a price ten dollars higher. Even such worthless things as sabres which, for ornamental purposes, would be expected to cost $4.12 had been selling for $8.50 [104] and apparently no effort had been made to check the practice until the appointment of this commission headed by the courageous Colonel Joseph Holt. It was estimated that this commission saved the government hundreds of thousands of dollars on contracts already confirmed besides annulling many other worthless ones.[105]

The chances for swindling were plentiful, due to the

[102] *New York Tribune*, May 28, 1861.
[103] *Ibid.*, May 31, 1861; "Government Contracts," *loc. cit.*, part i. pp. 68-69.
[104] *Official Records*, series iii, vol. 1, p. 927; vol. 2, p. 192.
[105] *New York Tribune*, March 17, April 21, 1862.

enormous size of the contracts as well as to the constant competition among states, and between the states and the federal government. One of the many proposals for bids from the state of New York alone was for items including the following: 135,000 pounds of bacon, 2063 barrels of mess pork, 67,500 pounds of shoulders, an equal amount of hams, 1719 barrels of mess beef, 250 barrels of beef tongues, 800,000 pounds of pilot bread, 3000 bushels of white beans, and split peas, rice, hominy, coffee, tea, sugar, candles, soap, salt, molasses, and dried apples in like proportions. Three deliveries of such quantities were called for during the month of December, 1861, alone. At the same time the Quartermaster-general's office for the state called for army clothes in unlimited quantities.[106] The state of Pennsylvania let a contract for 850,000 yards of army cloth at a total cost of over $1,300,000 to a single firm in November, 1861.[107]

By the end of the first year of the war the federal government had spent nearly $50,000,000 [108] for subsistence and a like sum for quartermaster's supplies; and for the whole war the Commissary-general of Subsistence drew upon the treasury for over $369,000,000[109] and the quartermaster-general accounted for over $678,000,000 in his department. This latter included some $240,000,000 for transportation.[110] But, after deducting operating expenses and all other incidentals,

---

[106] *Ibid.*, November 12, 1861.

[107] *Ibid.*, November 26, 1861.

[108] *Official Records*, series iii, vol. 1, p. 681; vol. 2, pp. 787-788; vol. 5, p. 1039, for tables of expenses. The latter citation contains totals.

[109] *Idem*, vol. 5, p. 1039.

[110] Compiled from the quartermaster-general's reports, *idem*, vol. 1, p. 681; vol. 2, pp. 787-788; vol. 3, p. 1120; vol. 4, pp. 876-877; vol. 5, pp. 251-252.

the total contract business of these two branches of the War Department totalled for the war something like three quarters of a billion dollars. If to this be added the nearly $163,000,000 spent by the Ordnance bureau [111] and a considerable portion of the cost of transportation, which was handled by contract, it is fair to state that the army contractors handled at least a billion dollars of government money during the war, and from all the evidence, by conservative estimate, retained a half of it.

Profiteering even on this scale seems small to the present generation, so familiar with the pestilence of profiteers of 1917-1918 and since, but considering the wealth, population, industrial conditions, and available resources of the two periods even the World War does not present a larger degree of profiteering activities than did the Civil War. As for official corruption the utmost efforts of a hostile congress in 1919-1920 failed to discover anything to compare with the conditions of 1861-1865.

But the worst results of the contract graft were not the added costs to the government, but the robbing of the soldiers and the deprivation, suffering, and unnecessary casualties which were visited upon them because of the kind of food, clothing, and supplies they received. If the food was inedible the soldier had either to suffer from eating, or from not eating, or else resort to the sutler and spend his pay for food. If his clothing dropped to pieces during a rain he had to draw more, often of the same kind, and, when his clothing allowance of $3.50 a month [112] had been exhausted, any addi-

---

[111] *Idem*, vol. 2, p. 850; vol. 3, p. 931; vol. 4, p. 799; vol. 5, p. 140.

[112] Earlier the sum had been as low as $2.50 a month, *idem*, vol. 1, pp. 153, 234; *U. S. Statutes at Large*, vol. 12, p. 269.

tional clothing came out of his regular pay of $13 a month. If his clothing allowance was not all used up the balance went to the soldier in the form of additional pay. Accordingly, in any instance, the sins of the grafters were visited upon the soldiers and there was but little recourse except futile complaint.

The degree of hardship inflicted upon the soldiers must be considered separately, in connection with the separate problems of the supplying of food, clothing, shelter, and arms. But first it should be noted that, as the war progressed and public indignation against the contractors and officials waxed stronger, more and more preventive measures were adopted and the way of the transgressor became more difficult. The outcry began almost with the beginning of the war. "How anybody but fiends," said the *Tribune*, in May, 1861, "can, for lucre, willfully palm off upon the Government, sleezy [*sic*] and rotten blankets, and rusty and putrid pork . . . passes comprehension." [113]

The cartoonist of *Harper's Weekly* very early began the portrayal of the fat contractor and the ragged soldier.[114] "Want Beefsteak?" asks the contractor of the hungry-looking, bedraggled soldier, "Good Gracious! What is the World coming to? Why, my Good Fellow, if you get Beefsteak, how on earth are Contractors to live? Tell me that."

The same edition repeats an extract from Admiral Charles Napier's dispatches stating that, "After we had hanged a few contractors [in the Crimean War], I am bound to say that the quality of beef served out to the troops improved amazingly." A "hint for General Mc-Clellan" accompanied the extract, in the form of a

[113] *New York Tribune*, May 25, 1861.
[114] *Harper's Weekly*, vol. 5, July *et seq.*

caricature of a contractor on a gibbet, counterbalanced with bags of money.[115] Referring to an exceptionally bad batch of cattle, which a contractor had picked up from the offscourings of the Chicago stock yards, the *New York Tribune* aptly describes them as "fag ends of small lots of scalawags which had been rejected by the speculators and Jew brokers." If the government accepted such stock the writer felt that no less a punishment should be dealt out than that "the inspectors ought to be sentenced to eat them. . . ."[116]

The popular indignation and the constant propaganda of publicists were not without effect. The contractors and officials overdid the thing. They reveled in a saturnalia of graft for a few months, but, by the beginning of the new year, the federal government began to revive from its torpor and to take action. The commission to investigate munitions contracts, and its work, have already been mentioned. The existence of state committees of inspection has been indicated. But, as long as the states were allowed to contract freely for army provisions, no hope could be entertained of even approaching the elimination of dishonesty.

This practice received a check early in 1862. The report of the congressional investigating committee, December 18, 1861, made public and confirmed earlier suspicion of many of the worst aspects of the business. The succession of Stanton to the office of Secretary of War, January 20, 1862, was a further step toward reform. Almost at once a closer surveillance over the activities in the states was felt.[117]

---

[115] *Ibid.*, pp. 528, 531.

[116] *New York Tribune*, July 22, 1861.

[117] The *Official Records* are very meager in their reports of War Department activities for early months of 1862. Newspaper reports relate

Congress also took a hand in limiting the abuses. Largely as a result of the findings of the Van Wyck committee acts were passed and approved June 2 and July 17, 1862, carefully limiting and circumscribing the methods of contract letting. Besides a number of provisions calculated to make bidding open and competitive and contracts ironclad and written, there were clauses designed to check the graver abuses of fraud and corruption. Contracts were not to be sublet; all contracts were to be reported to congress; and finally contractors were made subject to military law and court-martial in case they were indicted for fraud.[118]

While such acts as these tended to put the contractors on their guard, the measures fell far short of putting a stop to corrupt practices. As late as 1863 and 1864 Charles A. Dana, who was then assistant Secretary of War intrusted with the letting of contracts, found that the utmost care had to be exercised to discover and prevent frauds. Cleverness of swindlers was met by cunning of investigators. Peter H. Watson, another assistant Secretary of War, is said by Dana to have become quite an expert in detecting fraud.

A good example of his success was the uncovering of attempted swindle on the Quartermaster-general's bureau, in the matter of feed for horses and mules. The contract called for a mixture of oats and corn at a fixed ratio and the contractors, by changing the proportions, greatly increased their profits. Influential

---

annulling of contracts and threats of criminal action. See *New York Tribune,* January 20, February 17, 1862. The Van Wyck committee was credited with performing wonders in the way of cleaning out nests of contractors. In one instance Secretaries Cameron and Welles and other lesser individuals are pictured as rats, with the bull terrier, Van Wyck, killing them. *Harper's Weekly,* vol. 6 (March 1, 1862), p. 144.

[118] *U. S. Statutes at Large,* vol. 12, pp. 411-412, 596.

persons in Philadelphia including the president of the
Corn Exchange were involved in the swindle. One of
those interested returned $33,000 to the government and
another returned $32,000. The latter then demanded
that the contractors, who were under arrest, should be
liberated and have their papers and funds returned to
them.

Watson influenced President Lincoln to refuse this
demand, whereupon the culprits got no less a personage
than Senator David Wilmot of Pennsylvania to come to
their aid. On the continued refusal to let the men go,
Wilmot abandoned persuasion and resorted to vitupera-
tive language, but the men were held until the whole
matter was cleared up. Then, in one of those moments
more creditable to his generosity than to his judgment,
President Lincoln recommended their release.[119]

Stricter auditing of accounts, as inaugurated by Stanton, and the cancellation, early in 1862, of contracts for
foreign goods,[120] were further steps in the right direction. The latter act is comprehensible only when it is
understood that the imports, chiefly arms, were the
cast off junk of the armories and armies of Europe and
were imported not so much because of their cheapness
as because of the need to supplement the domestic supply. The increased output of American factories had
by that time made such superaddition no longer necessary. This made it possible that the average quality of
the goods could be improved by the restriction.

Thus, by one method or another, as government inspection became more and more strict, it became in-
creasingly more difficult for the bucket shop speculators

[119] C. A. Dana, *Recollections of Civil War* (New York, 1898), pp. 162-
164.
[120] *Official Records*, series iii, vol. i, pp. 869-870.

to prey upon the country. Accordingly they gradually turned to speculation upon the stock market [121] and left the government contract business more to the few great companies which were able to stand the strain or evade the restrictions. This by no means put a stop to unreasonable profits, but it tended greatly to raise the standard of the goods furnished; to check official collusion with contractors; and to limit the worst abuses of the contract business.

The recovery of national prestige in fiscal matters was much earlier and more complete than in any other branch of military affairs but it was far too late to prevent the conditions next to be described.

Food, though the first thing required for all soldiers after enlistment, did not furnish the greatest attraction for the contractors. There were plenty of scandals, in the early months of the war, in connection with the letting of beef contracts, but these were soon forgotten in the rush of the later contracts for clothing and munitions. It was in the very nature of the thing that the latter should form a more fertile source of profit for the speculators than would the articles of food. The camps of rendezvous in the early period of the war were all relatively small, and so the commanders usually found but little difficulty in furnishing or supplementing the food supply from the immediate neighborhood.

A large part of the army ration, as fixed by law, was made up of salt or fresh beef and either flour or bread,[122] the latter generally coming in the form referred to either as crackers, hard tack, or pilot bread. Such commodities as tea, coffee, and sugar had usually

---

[121] Tomes, *loc. cit.*, p. 229.

[122] *U. S. Statutes at Large*, vol. 12, p. 289, act of August 3, 1861.

to be received from headquarters, but it was a poor community in the '6os which could not supply the necessary amount of beef and bread for three or four regiments. Local patriots found profitable markets for their produce at the numerous training camps but, if as Shylocks they demanded their pound of flesh, at least they gave flesh in return.

The soldier might reasonably complain of the quality of much of his food but he usually got plenty of food of some kind, which is more than can be said oftentimes of his clothing. Undoubtedly there were privations but most of the harrowing tales of starvation and putrid food, told by the soldiers, relate to experiences in the field where, cut off from commissary stores and with no opportunity to forage, they had to take whatever was at hand, however undesirable, or do without. This situation certainly was not generally true in the places of rendezvous and in the training camps.

Undoubtedly many army units were well fed over a long period of time but, naturally, the cases where this was not true were the ones to receive the greatest attention. Some of the first companies in the rendezvous camps of the West lived on the fat of the land. Occasionally there was a scarcity of food, especially of potatoes. But, on the other hand, eggs were sometimes sold at six dozen for a quarter.[123] Wilson's Zouaves, containing probably as high a percentage of criminals and hardened vagabonds as any regiment in the army, were, during their first days of organization, billeted for the night on mattresses in a hotel, "eating chowder and hot soups, sent in by the neighboring restaurants –

---

[123] Upham, "Arms and Equipment for Iowa Troops," in *Iowa Journal of History and Politics*, vol. 16, p. 47.

comforts not enjoyed by them for many days previous to enlistment." [124]

Another New York regiment on gathering at the train in Philadelphia, for transportation to Washington, received orders for each man to provide himself with three days' rations. "A mountain of bread was already piled up in the station," said one of the soldiers. "I stuck my bayonet through a stout loaf, and, with a dozen comrades armed in the same way went foraging about for other *vivers*." Anything in the shops seemed to be at their disposal. [125]

Lest too bright a picture of benevolence might be inferred from the preceding statements it is well to look at the other side of the question. The first burst of generosity quickly subsided as more and more soldiers appeared, and the novelty of the state of war gave way to grinding monotony. Also, from the beginning, those who had things to sell believed in getting all that was possible for their produce, and none may accuse them of infidelity to their beliefs. The War Department had early opportunity to complain of exorbitant prices for subsistence. Commissary officers in the West were paying from forty-five to fifty cents a day for each man for rations the real value of which would range from fourteen to twenty cents. Accordingly they received orders (October 26, 1861) to cut this amount to nineteen cents a day for uncooked rations and, where possible, to fourteen cents. A maximum for board and lodging, where such was necessary, was set at forty cents a day. [126]

Even at such prices the food was often far from

---

[124] *New York Tribune*, April 22, 1861.

[125] Theodore Winthrop, "New York Seventh Regiment," in *Atlantic Monthly*, vol. 7 (June, 1861), p. 746.

[126] *Official Records*, series iii, vol. i, pp. 586, 596-597.

desirable. "Salt horse," an especially detested article of food, was described by one of its victims as being usually a "half-de-saltpeterized, half washed, half cooked article. . . ." This salt beef was sometimes supplanted by fresh beef but was more often "only varied with saltier and fatter pork." [127] To a newspaper man, who had a natural aversion to pork, it seemed that "its unclean stench crowds one's nostrils at every hour of the day as its smoke rises from a hundred huge frying pans – its scrofulous, greasy, foul-looking slices cover every platter – it reposes in superlative nastiness in every barrel!" [128] Butter was often of variegated hue, distinctive odor, and titanic strength, but when "seasoned with a liberal sprinkling of curses" [129] it was found to be edible if not exactly palatable.

But unpalatableness of army food was not its most objectionable feature. Too much salt meat and insufficiency of vegetables was a frequent cause of scurvy. This led to various governmental and private efforts to correct the evil. The governor of Iowa in the second year of the war sent out a rush call for "potatoes, onions, tomatoes, beets, poultry, . . . eggs," and canned fruits to be forwarded through his own officers to the Iowa soldiers in the field. The Sanitary Commission and other philanthropic societies were asked to contribute through this agency.[130] Soldiers' Aid Societies did much to help in this respect in 1862 and 1863. One appeal at this time was made for "potatoes, onions, cornmeal, dried fruit, eggs, butter, cheese, kraut, cranberries,

---

127 G. Haven, "Camp Life at the Relay," in *Harper's Monthly Magazine,* vol. 24 (April, 1862), p. 631.

128 Wilkie, *The Iowa First,* p. 69.

129 *Ibid.,* p. 7.

130 B. F. Shambaugh, ed., *Messages and Proclamations of Governors of Iowa* (Iowa City, 1903-1905), vol. 2, pp. 502-504.

dried rusks, beer, ale, horseradish, pepper, spice, dried berries, pickles, ginger snaps, soda crackers, codfish . . . " and other things calculated to add variety to the soldiers' diet.[181] But all this benevolence and foresight on the part of officials and citizens represented only an infinitesimal part of the supplying of the soldiers with food. Foraging and the army sutlers were the regular refuges for the weary victims of "salt horse" and pickled pork.

With all the resources that soldier life develops it was never as easy for the soldier to find clothing for himself as it was food. The primitive industrial conditions of the period did not permit of rapid adaptation to war-time requirements. There was no large body of laborers trained for the making of uniforms. Furthermore, the state of the market was such that, in any event, proper materials for soldiers' clothing could not be obtained in quantities sufficient to make the private manufacture of uniforms practicable on a large scale. The contractors were left in undisputed possession of the field and the army was largely at their mercy. When the supply of clothing was small or of inferior quality the soldiers had no alternative but to accept what was offered. There were no auxiliary sources for clothing as there were for food.

The deprivation of the soldiers in the matter of clothing was largely the result of four causes: shortage of supply; poor methods of distribution; inferior materials and workmanship; and the wasteful methods of the soldiers themselves. The last point will be discussed in connection with the daily life of the soldiers, but it is well to mention here that, inasmuch as the careless

[181] Upham, *loc. cit.*, p. 47.

OFFICIAL UNIFORMS FOR PRIVATES AND NON-COMMISSIONED OFFICERS

As prescribed by the federal government. Reading from left to right: (1) Sergeant-major, Artillery; (2) Sergeant, Infantry; (3) Private, Infantry; (4) Corporal, Cavalry; (5) Private, Light Artillery; (6) Great Coat for all Mounted Men

habits of the soldiers were largely the result of poor organization and worse discipline, the responsibility ultimately rested upon the government, as in the other cases.

The problem of shortage of supply was of more than temporary duration. With each increase in the size of the army the same perplexity was met anew and not until past the middle of the war did the War Department feel that it had the matter of supply fairly in hand. "By the fall of 1863," says Dana, "the army was pretty well supplied; still, that year we bought over 3,000,000 pairs of trousers, nearly 5,000,000 flannel shirts and drawers, some 7,000,000 pairs of stockings, 325,000 mess pans, 207,000 camp kettles, over 13,000 drums, and 14,830 fifes." [132] In the fall of 1861 the pressure was especially great. The army had just been increased by half a million men and the War Department was forced to admit its inability to keep up with the demand.

The quartermaster-general felt sure that the ragged condition of the soldiers was a retarding factor in the securing of enlistments. One hundred fifty thousand uniforms, he stated on October 22, would be insufficient to supply the calls already urgent. A week later he was still more uneasy about the prospect, or the lack of prospect, of sufficient clothing for the remainder of the half million men, soon expected in the training camps.[133] Nearly a year later the governor of Ohio was complaining that his troops were approaching the stage where they would soon be destitute of all kind of supplies.[134]

Yet, at the time when the shortage was most acute,

132 Dana, *op. cit.*, p. 162.

133 *Official Records*, series iii, vol. 1, pp. 582-583, 608-609.

134 *Idem*, vol. 2, p. 355.

in the fall of 1861, the manufacturers and contractors in America objected to the government purchase of some $800,000 worth of uniforms abroad. Reports went out that the sum to be spent ranged anywhere from $25,000,000 to $60,000,000. The Boston Board of Trade was led to register official objection to such foreign buying, in a long memorial to the War Department. The government was assured that, by December 1, the factories in this country would be able to furnish 400,-000 suits of uniforms every six weeks. Picture then the "dismay, distress, and ruin among the people" that would be caused by the closing down of these factories, due to foreign purchases.[135] Apparently neither the promises nor the fears were realized, for shortage continued, labor became increasingly scarce, and exorbitant prices continued prevalent.

In the meantime various and sundry means were employed to keep the army supplied. The activities of the various governors were naturally the most productive of results. Contributions and the patriotic labor of many women were helpful in many instances, and, on occasions, even the soldiers had to be relied upon to supply themselves. In the first call for troops, when several states were called upon for only one regiment each, the equipping of the troops was relatively simple. On occasions the colonel of a regiment or the captain of a company received instructions to attend to the matter himself, and present his bill. General Grant did his first administrative work for the Union army, in the capacity of a private citizen, by superintending the manufacture of the uniforms for the Galena company. Governor Yates had instructed the company to uniform

---

[135] *Idem*, vol. i, pp. 582-586.

itself, and, with great efficiency, the whole process was completed by a local contractor [136] in less time than the goods could have been supplied from Washington or Springfield, even if anything had been on hand at the capitals for distribution. The governor of Iowa, later in the year, arranged with a local contractor for three thousand uniforms including every necessary article of clothing, and received the goods within thirty days.[137] The governor of Pennsylvania, before the war had progressed a week, let a contract for ten thousand suits of clothing and three thousand blankets and spent money so lavishly that the state appropriation of half a million dollars was destined to but a month's existence.[138]

Promptness of execution in these early contracts does not imply perfection of product nor must it be inferred that such speed was universal. For instance, the quartermaster of the First Minnesota Regiment had great difficulty in supplying his men. It was April, the weather was cold, and prompt supply, especially of blankets, was imperative. Without funds, and in a restricted market, he did his best, but even then he could not escape the censure of a public which failed to realize the difficulties in his way.[139] The governor of Iowa, in a similar situation, sent a personal representative to Chicago to buy cloth for fifteen hundred uniforms, expecting the women of the state to volunteer for the manufacture. Nothing but the strongest and most durable cloth was to be accepted. But the material selected, the

---

[136] Chetlain, *Recollections of Seventy Years*, p. 72.

[137] Upham, *loc. cit.*, p. 38.

[138] *New York Tribune*, April 20, 1861.

[139] *Annual Message of Governor [Alexander] Ramsey to Legislature of Minnesota, January 9th, 1862* (a pamphlet in Iowa State Historical Library, Saint Paul, 1862), pp. 27-28.

best to be had, was described as "very poor, thin, sleazy, gray satinett, half cotton and half wool, only fit for summer wear." [140]

When their own efforts were not sufficient the governors did not hesitate to call for volunteer assistance. "Articles of clothing, shirts and drawers," said Governor Kirkwood, "never come amiss – in fact use can be found for them at all times." [141] Though such donations were sometimes solicited, they frequently came without any previous urging. A striking example of such generosity is shown in the case of a Boston company, every member of which was presented with a full uniform, even to socks and India rubber blankets. [142] Even an express company had a spell of generosity. When the first winter came on and found the army blanketless, it offered to carry free of charge all blankets that might be donated to the army. [143]

But probably the most highly appreciated of all the donations was that of the labor of the women. The garments they made were often of weird design and workmanship, but the patriotic spirit they displayed more than outweighed any lack of skill. Volunteering of such help began with the first calls for militia. [144] Soldiers' Aid Societies were organizing to make uniforms, as well as various kinds of accessories, useful or otherwise, which it was thought might add to the comfort of the soldiers. A group of two hundred forty-eight women in Dubuque, Iowa, worked for nine days at the manufacturing of uniforms for two companies, and, from the

---

[140] Byers, *Iowa in War Times*, p. 45; Upham, *loc. cit.*, p. 30.
[141] Shambaugh, *op. cit.*, vol. 2, p. 504.
[142] *New York Tribune*, May 24, 1861.
[143] *Ibid.*, October 5, 1861.
[144] *Ibid.*, April 23, 1861.

testimony of the recipients, they amply showed in cut and in fit the evidences of amateur work and haste in construction.[145]

The knitting of socks for soldiers became very common but never reached the proportions arrived at during the World War. This may be largely accounted for because of the lack of government coöperation. There were proposals made for the government to supply the yarn and let the women do the work,[146] but they came to naught. This however did not prevent the socially elect from starting a fad of knitting. Even Newport displayed her social preëminence by bristling with knitting needles. At society functions knitting, at least for a time, supplanted all other forms of diversion, except perhaps gossip, and every woman carried her knitting with her wherever she went. Naturally their hands, more adept at juggling tea cups and shuffling cards than at more menial pursuits, were but little skilled at the work and the result was that, to the observer, some stockings seemed all leg, others all feet, still others peculiarly deformed at the ankle, and, accidentally, some of perfect design.[147] But, undoubtedly, most of the articles of clothing donated to soldiers during the war were sent directly to the individual soldiers by their relatives at home, and were merely in addition to the regular supplies, instead of substituting for them. Even such contributions, as will later be shown, were as often as otherwise either thoroughly useless or else merely helped to burden down the already overloaded soldier.

---

[145] Upham, *loc. cit.*, p. 31; Wilkie, *op. cit.*, pp. 21-22.
[146] *New York Tribune*, October 22, 1861.
[147] *Ibid.*, November 9, 1861.

At no time in the North was it necessary for the soldier to furnish as much of his own equipment as in the Confederacy, but there is one notable exception, namely, blankets. The shortage of this article, already mentioned, was still acute as the second winter of the war approached. With no prospect in view of being able to meet the demand, the War Department was forced to advise volunteers and drafted men to bring with them a good stout woolen blanket apiece, of the regulation military size, eighty-four inches by sixty-six inches, and of five pounds in weight. Since all clothing, blankets, and shoes were charged against their clothing accounts, and no soldier furnishing his own blanket was required to draw one, it was urged that it was to his interest to supply himself, and avoid the discomfort of having to do without till supplied through the regular channels.[148] Aside from this official action, the soldier frequently supplied himself with such garments and shoes as he had with him when reaching the rendezvous, or from the omnipresent and ever-willing sutlers.

Inefficiency in distribution was oftentimes as annoying in its effects as the total lack of the needed articles. This inefficiency began in the individual army units and extended all the way up to the War Department. The War Department with nothing to distribute at the beginning of the war was, of course, temporarily powerless. Yet there is no evidence that its officers gave any direction to the supplying of the troops in the states. Frankly the problem of supply was regarded as a local matter, and the only directions from the Secretary of War were: equip your troops and present your bill. Even as late as August, 1862, the governor of Ohio had occasion to complain of great negligence on the part of

---

[148] *Official Records*, series iii, vol. 2, p. 483.

the quartermaster-general in supplying camp equipage and clothing.[149]

The justice of this complaint is shown by the fact that the report of the quartermaster-general, dated just two days later (August 13), showed stocks of clothing equalling or exceeding 600,000 in the items of coats, trousers, underwear, and pairs of stockings, and over 500,000 pairs of shoes. He himself admitted that "the stock on hand is extraordinarily large. . . ."[150] With all this stock on hand and the levies from the draft not yet in camp the governor had to continue to say of his soldiers that "from present indications they will [soon] be out of everything." In this connection it was sometimes felt that favoritism was shown to the governors, and thereby to the soldiers, of various states. For instance Iowa soldiers were certain that the officials "recognize[d] the difference between Hawkeyes and Suckers" and complained that they got but scant attention from the Quartermaster's department until the needs of Illinois were supplied.[151] Certainly Governor Yates of Illinois was sufficiently insistent in his requests and profuse in his advice to the administration, from the President on down. It would not be surprising if such persistence did have some effect upon the ready response of the Quartermaster's office. There were certain other personal and party reasons why Illinois might be favored, but, whether or not these had any influence, it is a significant fact that Secretary Cameron rarely refused a request from Governor Yates.[152]

As examples of inefficiency in distribution in the

---

[149] *Ibid.*, p. 355.

[150] *Ibid.*, pp. 371, 373.

[151] Upham, *loc. cit.*, p. 37. *Cf. ibid.*, p. 18; *Official Records,* series iii, vol. I, pp. 163, 186.

[152] For example see *Official Records,* series iii, vol. I, p. 985 (index),

army camps themselves, the following instances are typical. An Iowa regiment in Missouri, just before the battle of Springfield, was in rags – and not even many of them – due to the abrupt collapse of the trashy clothing first supplied. Uniforms for the whole regiment had been ordered and shipped to Quincy, Illinois, for transshipment to the field. But there they were halted. Two other Iowa regiments who happened to be in the neighborhood "kindly hypothecated them for the freight on their own uniforms" and nothing was being done to correct the abuse.[153] Clothing, when reaching the troops, was often distributed by depositing it "in a pile on the parade ground, and each company commander [was] directed to march his men to the place, where they were supplied. Company officers made no requisitions and the quartermaster took no receipts."[154]

The uniforms of the army in 1861, supplied under these conditions, were as motley in hue as they were insecure in texture. Three regiments from the same state had no less than five distinctive colors of uniforms: blue, gray, black and white striped, dark blue with green trimmings, and light blue.[155] The uniform of one of these regiments is described in detail as consisting of "a light blouse with green collar and patent leather belt, dark grey pants without stripes except in case of officers, a black felt hat turned up at one side and fastened by a tin bull's eye, the size of a sauce plate, which displays the red, white, and blue."[156] Wisconsin fur-

---

"Illinois, Governor of, Correspondence, War Department," and the references there cited. Especially good examples are in *ibid.*, pp. 163, 186.

[153] Wilkie, *op. cit.*, p. 95.

[154] Byers, *op. cit.*, p. 496.

[155] Upham, *loc. cit.*, pp. 37-38.

[156] Wilkie, *op. cit.*, p. 14.

CAMP SCENE, 1861, SHOWING ACTUAL "UNIFORMS" OF PRIVATES

nished light gray trousers, mixed gray blouses, and light colored hats, which looked very splendid until worn for a few days.[157]

Where the soldiers themselves were allowed to assert their individuality, the selection was generally that of the zouave uniform: baggy breeches, turbans, fezzes and brilliant red color, as well as individual adaptations which would have made the Algerian soldiers look modest in comparison.[158] These gaudy uniforms, gradually diminishing in their glory, were used till worn out and supplanted by the regulation blue. Yet, in spite of this outlandish display of color, it should be mentioned in favor of the American soldiers that even the officers did not resort to the helmets, bearskin hats, breastplates, and lace of the European officers.[159]

Even this wide variance of design and color would not have been so unendurable if the Confederate troops had not been likewise attired. The result of two such strange hordes meeting in battle was bewilderment. It was difficult to distinguish friend from foe and fatal blunders resulted.[160] When the troops came together on thickly wooded fields the confusion was so great that it was a regular occurrence for Union soldiers to fire on each other. This happened so frequently that orders were soon issued, both East and West, forbidding issuance of uniforms of any color other than the regulation light and dark blue. Thereafter, as fast as uniform clothing could be provided, the other clothing was with-

[157] Hinkley, *Third Wisconsin Infantry*, p. 6.

[158] *Harper's Weekly*, vol. 5 (June 8, 1861), p. 353. See picture.

[159] Trobriand, *op. cit.*, p. 83; *Harper's Weekly*, vol. 6 (March 1, 1862), pp. 135, 137.

[160] *Harper's Weekly*, vol. 5 (September 7, 1861), p. 562.

drawn from service.[161] Steps in this direction were taken early in the year 1862 [162] and, by the following winter, the army for the first time might technically be said to have been uniformed.

Shortage of clothing is easily explained; inefficiency of distribution might reasonably be expected as one of the natural blunders of a non-military state, in preparation for a great war; eccentricity of color and design can be forgiven; but the substitution of shoddy for genuine cloth was a crime against civilization, if not against the statutes. From the descriptions of the shoddy furnished during the first year of the war, it must certainly have exceeded in rottenness anything since produced, 1917 and 1918 not excepted. A serious magazine article describes it as "a villainous compound, the refuse stuff and sweepings of the shop, pounded, rolled, glued, and smoothed to the external form and gloss of cloth, but no more like the genuine article than the shadow is to the substance. . . ." [163] Another writer describes it as "poor sleezy stuff, woven open enough for seives [sic], and then filled with shearmen's dust." [164] The blankets were equally bad, frequently being only about a third the size of the regulation blanket, so rotten that one could poke his finger through them, of such light and open weave as to protect neither against cold nor rain, and addicted to falling to pieces without previous warning.[165] The *New York Tribune*, after examination of a sample blanket, was convinced that it was made "of horse hair and broom corn." [166]

---

[161] *Official Records*, series iii, vol. 2, p. 803.

[162] *New York Tribune*, February 18, 1862.

[163] Tomes, *loc. cit.*, pp. 227-228.

[164] *New York Tribune*, May 1, 1861.

[165] Trobriand, *op. cit.*, p. 136; *Harper's Weekly*, vol. 5 (August 10, 1861), p. 512; *New York Tribune*, May 1, 1861.

[166] *New York Tribune*, November 22, 1861.

The accuracy of these descriptions can best be checked by comparison with the testimony of the soldiers and of their witnesses. "Soldiers, on the first day's march or in the earliest storm, found their clothes, overcoats, and blankets, scattering to the winds in rags, or dissolving into their primitive elements of dust under the pelting rain." One day they had brand new uniforms. The next day they were practically naked.[167] A Wisconsin regiment, ten days after it had been supplied with bright new uniforms, had to be furnished again with blue overalls, in order that the soldiers might with decency be seen upon the streets.[168] Not a man in the Iowa First, it was predicted, would "run from a lady or the enemy. For very shame's sake they would not dare turn aught but their faces to either." It was half seriously doubted whether "the children of Israel looked half as ragged . . . after their forty years tramp in the wilderness. . . ."[169]

Elsewhere, even colonels were seen riding about on horseback in dressing gowns and slippers, and, in the Army of the Potomac, men were required to mount guard without trousers.[170] The quartermaster-general himself admitted that sentinels walked about Washington "in freezing weather in their drawers, without trousers or overcoats," but he attributed this to lack of supply rather than to collapse.[171] Still other soldiers resorted to stratagem to avoid the worst embarrassments just described. A regiment in Missouri got in the habit of making flour sack aprons and wore them behind in

---

[167] Tomes, *loc. cit.*, p. 228.

[168] Hinkley, *op. cit.*, pp. 6-7.

[169] Wilkie, *op. cit.*, pp. 65, 84.

[170] *Harper's Weekly*, vol. 5 (August 10, 1861), p. 512; *New York Tribune*, July 17, 1861.

[171] *Official Records*, series iii, vol. 2, p. 803.

lieu of sufficient covering of different nature. When General Nathaniel Lyon discovered the masquerade he ordered one of these camouflages removed but immediately, on detecting his error, ordered it replaced.[172] Others, still more ingenious, cut up their overcoats at the beginning of winter to make "the more necessary articles – pantaloons," while still others secured the uniforms of the Missouri secessionists or "butternuts." [173] Such was the shoddy of Civil War fame and such were its effects upon the soldiers.

The first and many later supplies of shoes were equally as bad as the clothing. Regardless of the weather there is no part of a soldier's personal equipment of more importance than his shoes. In the summer, when a breech clout or barrel would, in an emergency, substitute for other clothing, the soldier on the march must be not only shod but correctly shod if he is to keep up with the procession. In winter, overcoats, underwear, or both could be sacrificed more readily than shoes. Yet, in spite of these well known facts, the supply of durable, well-fitting shoes was, during the first eighteen months of the war, about as irregular as the supply of clothing.

There was no lack of knowledge as to the importance of good shoes and there was plenty of warning in regard to the matter, before the war was even fairly inaugurated. As early as April, 1861, the most widely read newspaper in America contained a letter from an ex-army surgeon who had served in the British Army during the Crimean War, telling of the overwhelming importance of well-fitting shoes.[174] Only a few weeks later

---

[172] Upham, *loc. cit.*, pp. 30-31.

[173] Chester Barney, *Recollections of Field Service with Twentieth Iowa Infantry Volunteers* (Davenport, 1865), pp. 107-108.

[174] *New York Tribune*, April 30, 1861.

came the warning that good feet were of more importance even than a good stomach, and that an infantryman
should be ready to "march twenty or thirty miles without feeling a pang or raising a blister." [175]
Such knowledge and admonition must have made but
scant impression upon the contractors and inspectors.
Leather was as easily imitated as cloth, and the result
was that some shoes went to pieces the first day they
were worn,[176] while the average life of a pair of contractors' shoes was estimated at from twenty to thirty
days.[177] At one time two hundred fifty men in a western
regiment were barefooted, or nearly so, through necessity, and only twenty-five men in one of the companies
were able to do camp duty for want of shoes. The shoes
of the rest of the regiment were said to have been beneath the contempt of beggars.[178] For lack of shoes
many soldiers bound pieces of rawhide to their feet,
and it is to be inferred that others had plenty of raw
hide without binding it. Several of the men in the Sixth
Iowa Volunteers marched with General William T.
Sherman to Knoxville barefooted.[179] It is hard to find
anything humorous in a situation such as this, but even
the soldiers were able to smile at the magnanimity of
a general who ordered that each man of a barefooted
regiment be supplied with two pairs of shoes each, at
a time when the quartermaster, probably to the general's knowledge, had no shoes at all to issue.[180]
Important as shoes were there were plenty of instances where the absence of any shoes was preferable

[175] Winthrop, *loc. cit.*, p. 753.
[176] Upham, *loc. cit.*, p. 41.
[177] Trobriand, *op. cit.*, p. 136.
[178] Wilkie, *op. cit.*, pp. 94-95; Upham, *loc. cit.*, p. 40.
[179] Upham, *loc. cit.*, p. 41.
[180] Barney, *op. cit.*, p. 100.

to the kind of foot wear issued. "If you find a foot soldier lying beat out by the roadside," said an old campaigner, "five to one his heels are too high, or his soles too narrow, or too thin, or his shoe is not made straight on the inside, so that the great toe can spread into its place as he treads." Moreover, he asserted in indignation, "A captain of a company, who will let his men march with such shoes as I have seen on the feet of some poor fellows in this war, ought to be garroted with shoestrings . . ." or at least be compelled to "wash the feet of the whole army of the Apostles of Liberty." [181] Some of the shoes blistered the feet of the soldiers so badly that they had to remove them and go barefooted. Many soldiers were thus observed with their shoes tied together and hanging across rifle barrels or attached to their knapsacks. But in these cases they were used to going barefooted,[182] and could stand the latter inconvenience more easily than the former. "Trust in God; But Keep Your Shoes Easy!" [183] became a motto of the soldiers.

The cost of such clothing to the soldier varied greatly from time to time but not in proportion to the quality. Often the poorest material cost as highly as the best. The most superior army uniforms from Europe cost no more than the fragile substitutes of the most conscience-less contractors.[184] Cost to the United States on staple articles of clothing ranged as follows for the entire period of the war: hats, from $1.62 to $2.18; caps, from $0.35 to $1.04; trousers, from $2.05 to $5.89; shirts, from $0.45 to $3.01; underdrawers, from $0.37 to $1.90;

181 Winthrop, loc. cit., p. 753.
182 Barney, op. cit., pp. 109-110.
183 Winthrop, loc. cit., p. 753.
184 Official Records, series iii, vol. 2, p. 804.

shoes and boots, from $1.45 to $4.83; overcoats, from $6.50 to $16.11; and rubber ponchos, from $1.87 to $5.60.[185]

The cost to the soldier was about the same as to the government. A soldier's diary for November, 1861, shows the price of a coat, $6.71; of an overcoat, $7.20; pants, $3.03; shoes, $1.96; two shirts, $1.76; wool, double blankets, $2.96; hat, $1.55; two pairs of underdrawers, $1.00; two pairs of socks, $0.52; a cap, $0.60; and a leather collar, $0.14; making a total of $27.43 for a complete outfit, exclusive of those accoutrements paid for directly or ultimately by the government. The cost of similar articles was about the same a year later.[186] Pants, coats, and shoes alone came to about $15.00,[187] and one regiment reports that its whole outfit of hat, blouse, pants, and shoes cost only $8.00, an amount which the durability of the articles proved to be entirely too high.[188] Considering that the clothing account, as fixed by law, totaled only $42 a year, the soldier had to exercise some care, especially during the rigors of marching or battle, if he avoided overdrawing his allowance or buying from the sutler out of his slender monthly wage.

With conditions existing such as those described, the question naturally arises: what did the War Department do to remedy these abuses, and with what results? Stricter regulation of the contract business and inspection of the goods tendered have already been considered. Another thing to be attended to was to see that the

[185] *Idem*, vol. 5, p. 286.

[186] A. G. Downing, *Downing's Civil War Diary* (Olynthus B. Clark, ed., Des Moines, 1916), pp. 16, 90.

[187] Upham, *loc. cit.*, p. 33.

[188] Wilkie, *op. cit.*, p. 14.

soldiers were supplied promptly, and with the proper articles. The development of this branch of administrative work was as gradual as was the supervision of contracts. The quartermaster-general admitted that, at the beginning of the war, the organization of the department did not furnish enough experienced officers to handle the necessary business and hence the state contracts were necessary.[189] It is furthermore a significant fact that this department and others as well, throughout the war, made repeated declarations of the inadequacy of the office force at their command.[190]

Seemingly, throughout the war, it was the practice never to anticipate an administrative need and prepare for it, but always to wait till an emergency arose and then wait the tortuous legislative and executive processes to remedy it. Nevertheless the bureau got into the work and probably did it as effectively as was possible under the circumstances. At least clothing of some sort or another was supplied. It was much better, said its chief, to supply inferior clothing to the soldiers than to let them go about in a semi-nude condition in the winter time. Probably, after all, he was right in saying that his department was unjustly criticized for the conditions of 1861.[191] It could scarcely be blamed because the President chose to consider the Civil War a local rebellion which could be handled by executive action. If there had existed and had been in operation a definite war program, and if congress had been hastened into session to help, doubtless the inadequacy of the Quartermaster-general's bureau, in addition to scores of

---

[189] *Official Records*, series iii, vol. 2, p. 802.
[190] See *idem*, vols. 1-5, reports of various administrative bureaus.
[191] *Idem*, vol. 3, p. 803.

other awkward situations, could have been very largely avoided or more rapidly remedied.

The growing efficiency of the department is fairly depicted in the gradual improvement in conditions and the ability thoroughly to handle the situation after the autumn of 1862. The ban on state contracting early in 1862 was the first definite announcement that the department was able and determined to attend to its duties. Even before this step, one very important abuse had been partially remedied. By general order of August 15, 1861, camps of rendezvous were established and recruiting officers were required to muster each soldier as recruited and send him to the nearest camp.[192] Thus all soldiers recruited in that way were in a position to draw clothing at once. This did not apply, however, to companies and regiments that continued to be raised purely by state authority, and it was not until December, 1862, that permission was given to governors to muster men by companies rather than by regiments in order to facilitate distribution of clothing and supplies.[193]

In anticipation of the state draft, careful provisions were made in August, 1862, for the prompt supply of all necessary clothing, equipment, food, and transportation as soon as troops were accepted.[194] But the greatest foresight was displayed by the Provost-marshal-general's bureau when, in anticipation of the federal draft, it issued a circular, May 23, 1863, requiring that drafted men, when presenting themselves at district headquarters, were to be at once "put in uniform and

[192] *Idem,* vol. 1, p. 412.
[193] *Idem,* vol. 2, pp. 882, 934.
[194] *Ibid.,* pp. 482-484.

supplied with one knapsack, haversack, canteen, and blanket." Even a "knife, fork, spoon, tincup, and tin plate" were to be supplied at the same time.[195] Thus, two years after the war had started, for the first time a really efficient and simple method of distribution had been created.

In purchasing, the Quartermaster-general's bureau did not develop as much efficiency as in distribution, and the development was a slower process. This has an easy explanation in that distribution was purely a departmental matter, whereas buying brought the department directly in contact with the contractors. Even though unconsciously, the quartermaster-general yielded more or less to this pressure. Arguments such as those of the Boston Board of Trade were very insidious in their tendency to cause the War Department to make all of its purchases in the United States. "Keep your money at home and help American labor," was as potent an argument then as ever.

Yet, if the truth were told, much of the contractors' goods were bought abroad. So potent was the argument of the commercial interests that the quartermaster-general actually apologized, in his report of 1862, for making an extensive purchase of excellent goods in Europe. He had bought material equal to the best supplied to European armies and at prices no higher than the shoddy of America. The total equipment for each soldier, including not only a complete uniform but every other necessary piece of equipment, except arms and ammunition, even to shelter tents and cartridge boxes, cost only $50.00 and was admittedly of the best.[196]

---

[195] *Idem*, vol. 3, p. 221.
[196] *Idem*, vol. 2, p. 804.

It was evidently felt necessary to give all this justification for purchasing foreign goods directly instead of through middle men, and there is no evidence of an equal repetition of the offense. One may well agree with his statement that a comparison of the United States with France showed that there was "much to learn in this country in the economy of war." [197]

In the closing months of the war the reports declared that there were no longer many complaints received of defective material or workmanship. Some contractors and inspectors were still under investigation for peculation. The continued presence of fraud was admitted, but, with the rigid care that was being exercised it was felt that, in amount, it was being held to a minimum. [198]

[197] *Ibid.*
[198] *Idem,* vol. 4, p. 886.

The Problem of Munitions

The Problem of Munitions

AS LONG as North and South continue, even in a tolerant or friendly mood, to discuss the various merits of the contending sections in the great civil conflict, it will continue to be a sore spot in the Northern memory, as well as a source of joy to the South, that the Union was compelled to raise something like two soldiers for every soldier in the South,[199] in order to defeat the Confederacy. The southern opinion is that, even with these odds, the ultimate victory of the North was due more to the success of the blockade than to the victories of the armies. In other words it took the sheer numbers of the Union army to offset the efficiency and

---

[199] No conclusive figures on the total number of enlistments in the Confederate army have ever been compiled. There seems to be very little basis for the old legend that the number was so small as 600,000. Yet this estimate has very recently been defended by C. B. Hite in "The Size of the Confederate Army," in *Current History*, vol. 18 (May, 1923), pp. 251-253. T. L. Livermore, in his *Numbers and Losses in the Civil War in America 1861-65* (Boston, 1901), p. 63, arrives at an estimate of about 1,200,000. A census office employee, as early as 1892, estimated the number as high as 1,500,000, see A. B. Casselman, "Numerical Strength of the Confederate Army," in *The Century Illustrated Monthly Magazine,* vol. 43 (new series vol. 21, March, 1892), p. 795. More recently he has increased his estimate to 1,650,000, Casselman, "How Large Was Confederate Army?," in *Current History*, vol. 17 (January, 1923), pp. 653-657; Casselman, "Did the Confederate Army Number 1,650,000?," *idem*, vol. 18 (August, 1923), pp. 846-850. The debate between Hite and Casselman represents the extremes of estimates of persons doubtless influenced by sectional pride. But, even if Casselman's figures be accepted, the Union forces of 2,898,304 were approximately double the total strength of the Confederate army. See also R. H. McKim, *Numerical Strength of Confederate Army* (New York, 1912), an estimate of 601,980 men.

natural advantages of the smaller Confederate army,
fighting on its native soil and for its cherished traditions,
while the initial advantage, greater efficiency, and increasing power of the Union navy decided the issue.
Without endeavoring either to prove or to disprove this
proposition the following pages may cast some further
light upon the reasons why the North, with all her superior industrial development and easy contact with the
outside world, in addition to her greater population and
wealth, required four years of warfare to bring the
South to terms.

As to inherent fighting ability no distinction can be
drawn between the Union and the Confederate soldiers.
In leadership the South undoubtedly had the advantage, for well known reasons, at least during the first
two years of the war. In everything else the North had
the advantage, and had only herself to blame if she did
not use it to bring the war to a speedy close. While most
of the errors of the North can be traced to a lack of
nationalism, expressed in the form of state-rights fetich-
ism, the mistakes having to do with the arming of the
federal troops were due to sheer stupidity, expressed
in the failure of the War Department and the chief
military men to recognize the importance of certain
revolutionary inventions in war-making machinery.

The South, due to its almost purely agricultural pursuits, could work no revolution in fire arms herself and,
due to lack of recognition abroad coupled with the
tightening of the Northern blockade, could not have
imported them in large quantities even if the markets
had been open to her. Without any such disadvantages
to labor under, the North was free to choose any type
of weapon it wanted. The choice was not the highest

type of arm then to be obtained, but the traditional muzzle-loading musket of the American Revolution, altered only by the addition of the percussion cap and rifling. These were just such guns as the South was able to obtain, and in the use of them the South probably had a shade the advantage.

Yet it was possible, and it would have been practically as easy, to supply all but the first hundred thousand, and even some of them, with a high-grade type of breech-loading rifle, using copper cartridges with percussion cap included – rifles that could have been loaded with a couple of simple motions and fired with three times the rapidity of the weapons actually supplied. Within a year every man in the army then in existence could have been so equipped and at no time thereafter would there have been any shortage of such weapons. If the military authorities had so chosen they could have supplied whole regiments, brigades, divisions, or corps with efficient repeating rifles before which no enemy of twice their number, not similarly equipped, could have stood battle.

If the half a million men raised in 1861 [200] had been armed with these modern weapons, carefully trained in their use, and taught the art of shooting, so rare among soldiers, it is reasonable to suppose that by the spring of 1862 the Union army would have been in a position to crush the rebellion before the approach of another winter, to have saved from two to three years of additional warfare and all the complications and miseries they brought forth, and have left the South as well as the North in a far better condition than they

---

[200] The total of men and officers on December 31, 1861, was 527,804; present for duty, 477,193, *Official Records,* series iii, vol 1, p. 775.

were to be in three years later, when the Confederacy was finally starved to submission. This is not a statement merely of what might have been but of what could have been, if only a few men of vision had supplanted the time servers who were determining the military policy. The following account of the arming of the Union soldiers will present the evidence in proof of these assertions.

At the beginning of the war there were enough muskets and rifles of one kind or another in the possession of the United States to have equipped half a million soldiers but to have done so would have exhausted the supply. The common opinion that Secretary John B. Floyd had, before his resignation, looted the arsenals of the North and sent the whole available supply South is largely without foundation. Undoubtedly Floyd had done his best to favor the South in the distribution of arms, but even when Secretary Cameron tried to make a case of "bad faith" against him, his figures failed to show that the Union suffered very greatly by the transactions. The statement that 273,567 stand of muskets and rifles were in slave territory at the beginning of the war [201] is misleading. He included in this list nearly 110,000 which confessedly were in Missouri, Maryland, and the District of Columbia, thus leaving in secession territory less than 165,000 stand of such arms in comparison with a total of more than 446,000 in regions practically inaccessible to the Confederacy.[202] Of the arms in the South something like 115,000 had been transferred thither by Floyd [203] shortly before his resig-

[201] *Ibid.*, p. 322.
[202] Compiled from Cameron's figures, *ibid.*, pp. 321-322.
[203] *Ibid.*, p. 39.

nation, thus giving color to the notion that he had practically stripped the North of such material, but falling
far short of proving the same. Whatever the early problems of the Ordnance bureau may have been, shortage
of arms of the usual kind for the first soldiers was not
one of them.

The situation in the states was somewhat different
and varied from place to place, being seemingly worse
in the West than in the East. For instance the governor
of Iowa was certain that there were only about 1500
old army muskets and 200 rifles in possession of the
state. So precious were these that the militia companies
rarely saw them and if they wished to hold a parade
they had to give bond to the state to insure their safe
return before they could even borrow them.[204] The governor of Indiana asserted that good, bad, and indifferent
his state had only 2,500 small arms in all whereas 20,000
were needed.[205] It was the governors of these two states
who sent the most frantic calls to Washington for arms
in April and May, Indiana for fear of Kentucky and
Iowa for fear of Indians.[206] Both governors were need-
lessly alarmed. They probably could not understand
why Ohio should receive 18,000 guns and Illinois 21,-
000 while Indiana had trouble in getting 5000 and Iowa
could scarcely get enough for a couple of regiments.[207]
Probably nobody else could explain it satisfactorily.
These governors needed only a little patience to wait
until the War Department deigned to consider their

204 Upham, "Arms and Equipment," in *Iowa Journal of History and Politics,* vol. 16, pp. 5-6.
205 *Official Records,* series iii, vol. 1, p. 126.
206 Byers, *Iowa in War Times,* p. 47; Upham, *loc. cit.,* pp. 8-9; *Official Records,* series iii, vol. 1, pp. 102-103, 108, 116, 158, 163, 186.
207 *Official Records,* series iii, vol. 1, pp. 127, 186.

needs. After all their soldiers had many things to be supplied with and many things to learn before guns would be an absolute necessity. Furthermore no state had to wait long for a supply of weapons.

But such guns! Only about eight in a hundred were rifled, the rest being smooth-bore muskets. More than half of all of them had been originally made as flint-lock guns and were only recently altered to percussion. Over 24,000 guns late in 1859 were still unaltered from the flintlock type.[208] Many of the altered guns were almost worthless. Several thousand had been sold by the War Department in December, 1860, for $2.50 apiece[209] and, from the description by the soldiers, the remainder were, we may judge, far inferior to the type of gun to which they were accustomed. The rifled-out muskets were said to be "so light, that their barrels would spring after the rapid firing of a dozen shots."[210] A less reverent observer thought it would be "a master stroke of policy" to allow the Confederates to steal the whole lot of altered flintlocks that were sent to a regiment. They were, he said, "Infinitely more dangerous to friend than enemy [and] will kick further than they will shoot. . . ." Rusty, cumbersome, and antiquated, they were alternately provocative of merriment and of exasperation.[211]

Not all guns were as poor as the majority of the made over stock. The latest model of the Springfield rifle was considered by the Ordnance bureau as equal to any rifle in the world, special comparison being made to the Enfield, which was copied much after the American

---

[208] *Ibid.,* p. 1.

[209] *Ibid.,* pp. 3-4, 7.

[210] Hinkley, *Third Wisconsin Infantry,* p. 89.

[211] Upham, *loc. cit.,* p. 18.

model.[212] As far as muzzle-loading rifles were concerned this statement is probably not greatly exaggerated, but many soldiers at the time preferred the Enfields.[213] The better rifles were especially prized because they could handle the minié bullet. This relic of a bygone age was of the usual elongated shape but hollowed at the base for a distance of about a third the length of the bullet. When fired, the gases forced the lead into the riflings of the gun barrel thus insuring a snug fit and the certainty that the bullet would follow the rifling. The minié bullet was rendered still more efficient by the fact that the cartridge was fastened to the base of the bullet, the whole incased in a paper cover, and then placed in the barrel and rammed down.[214] Minié rifles were highly prized by the soldiers but they were limited in number and the supply was soon exhausted.

The paucity of good guns, in all the accumulation of rust in the arsenals, was soon revealed, and this led to a demand for a largely increased supply. Even before the war, when the regular army was constantly below 20,000, it had been the policy of the government to keep a store of muskets reaching nearly 700,000, and even that amount was not considered large.[215] With the country at war and the actual state of the munitions disclosed, the demand for an augmented reserve was almost immediate. There were three principal means of increasing the supply: first, by amplifying the productive capacity of the government armories; second, by contracts with private manufacturers and jobbers;

212 *Official Records,* series iii, vol. i, p. 264.
213 Upham, *loc. cit.,* p. 21.
214 *Harper's Weekly,* vol 5 (August 3, 1861), p. 495.
215 *Official Records,* series iii, vol. i, p. 33.

third, by importation from abroad. All three methods were employed though, through necessity, in the reverse order.

In the first anxiety to arm the troops, purchasing agents of all kinds and varieties swarmed in the European markets. They included not only those authorized by the War Department or by state governors, but private adventurers, unauthorized army officers, and meddlesome foreign ministers as well. The states, largely through pride in wishing to see their soldiers well armed and soon, entered the open market first. By June 1, New York alone was advertising for bids on 10,000 minié rifled muskets and 2,000 minié rifles, with all their accompanying appurtenances, in addition to a proportional amount of all the other munitions and appliances that would be found necessary for a mixed force of twelve or fifteen regiments of infantry, cavalry, and artillery.[216] By the middle of August a purchasing agent for the War Department found that all the private munitions manufacturers of Brimingham and London, with one exception, were working to fill contracts for Ohio, Connecticut, and Massachusetts.[217]

Even earlier than this, excitable Americans abroad had determined that the salvation of the Union depended on their efforts. The Minister to Belgium, Henry S. Sanford, was, by May 12, so disappointed because he had not been commissioned to purchase arms that he confessed to a temptation to buy the whole surplus supply of Belgium and ship it over, on his own authority.[218] Sometime previous to this, John C. Fre-

[216] *New York Tribune,* June 1, 1861.
[217] *Official Records,* series iii, vol. 1, p. 418.
[218] *Ibid.,* p. 247.

mont, with no authority other than his own will, had
made foreign contracts for munitions for the Department of the West. Yet, these purchases secured the approval of Mr. Sanford, and our representatives to England and France, Charles Francis Adams and William
L. Dayton respectively, took upon themselves the authority to draw upon the United States Treasury to pay
for them. Cannon and shells to the amount of $75,000,
and 10,000 rifles at a total cost of $125,000 were thus
secured.[219] The men concerned in these irregular transactions were too prominent to permit of scandal at that
time and, at the instance of the President himself, the
War Department accepted the drafts and the incident,
except for a report to the House of Representatives,
was closed.[220]

The effect of such indiscriminate buying and competition between private, state, and federal officials was
greatly to enhance the price of the articles most in
demand. This practice was all the more reprehensible
since the ultimate cost fell upon the federal branch of
the government, which could just as well have furnished the whole supply, more expeditiously, and at a
much lower price, if acting alone. That this condition
was allowed to exist is merely another reflection upon
the laxity of national authority at the time – a further
evidence of the strength of the state-rights doctrine in
the North. Realizing the situation, after the damage
had already been done, the Secretary of War requested
the several governors to withdraw their purchasing
agents from the arms markets, assuring them that the
War Department would supply them quicker and more

[219] *Ibid.,* pp. 538-539, 360-361, 293.
[220] *Ibid.,* pp. 308-309; *House Exec. Doc.,* 37 Cong., 2 sess., *Doc.* no. 67.

cheaply than they could themselves.[221] The admonition was unnecessary. The urgent need for arms was past and governors in general had ceased their efforts. Only one governor, Morgan of New York, bothered himself to justify the practice. He replied that the Enfield rifles, of which he had ordered 20,000 in June, were ordered because of the failure of the War Department to supply arms.[222]

Though not as quick as the states to begin operations in the open market, the War Department, when it started, easily outstripped them in the magnitude of its contracts. As early as the latter part of April the Lieutenant-colonel of Ordnance had contemplated foreign purchase of from 50,000 to 100,000 small arms.[223] No immediate action was taken but within six weeks definite proposals were made to the Secretary of War for increasing the stock of side arms and pistols and in the middle of June a request was made for private contracts for 100,000 of the latest Springfield-pattern rifles.[224] Shortly afterward some minor contracts were let to private manufacturers in America, but the action of congress in authorizing an addition of 500,-000 volunteers to the army brought the situation to a crisis. Cameron called upon congress for an additional appropriation of $10,000,000,[225] and, upon recommendation of President Lincoln, an agent was sent to Europe with funds to the amount of $2,000,000 for immediate purchases.[226] Accordingly Colonel George L. Schuyler

[221] *New York Tribune,* November 26, 1861; *Official Records,* series iii, vol. i, pp. 675-676.
[222] *Official Records,* series iii, vol. i, pp. 273, 698.
[223] *Ibid.,* p. 245.
[224] *Ibid.,* pp. 263, 278-279.
[225] *Ibid.,* p. 355.
[226] *Ibid.,* p. 702.

of New York was commissioned, toward the last of June, to purchase 100,000 rifled muskets, 20,000 cavalry sabres, 10,000 revolvers, and 10,000 carbines, with complete discretionary powers as to the prices to be paid.[227]

At the very beginning of his transactions Schuyler assumed responsibility for unauthorized contracts made by Dayton and Sanford,[228] then, after looking the situation over in Great Britain, began to purchase on a large scale on the continent. Since his orders were to buy for immediate delivery, he missed an excellent chance to secure the later output of the best factories in London and Birmingham at about sixty-five shillings a rifle, and as a result, this supply went to Confederate agents.[229] On the continent he sized up the situation pretty well, thoroughly understood the promiscuous buying and selling of the cast-off guns of the European armies,[230] and feared the possibility of receiving a liberal number of such relics. One lot, in particular, of 60,000 guns was accepted at the rate of $7.65 apiece subject to inspection.[231] No doubt the inspection was as careful as possible under the conditions, but the inspection force was entirely too small for effectiveness and the product was pretty bad.[232] Altogether he succeeded in spending the total appropriation and, before the first of December, had guns of one description or another, pouring into America on almost every ship. Some 37,000 of these were of the best Enfield pattern and about 48,000 were of the French official stock. These were secured at the

---

[227] *Ibid.*, pp. 355, 475-476.
[228] *Ibid.*, p. 419.
[229] *Ibid.*, p. 622.
[230] *Ibid.*, p. 486.
[231] *Ibid.*, pp. 598, 640, 742.
[232] *Idem*, vol. 2, p. 190.

rather moderate price of from $14 to $17 apiece.[233]
Many of the rest were practically worthless.

Beginning with October 14, a new policy was inaugurated, of trusting munitions contracts to the ministers of the foreign courts, the first instance being an
appropriation of $1,000,000 placed to the credit of
Sanford at Brussels.[234] Thereafter foreign purchases
pyramided and the ratio of worthless material was
greatly increased. By June 30, 1862, nearly 738,000
rifles, muskets, and carbines had been purchased abroad
at a total cost in excess of $10,000,000. Of all these only
116,740 were Enfields, 48,108 were of the French official type, and nearly all the rest were a nondescript con-
glomeration containing 170,255 from Austria, 111,549
from Prussia, 57,194 from Belgium, and 203,831 simply listed as other foreign rifles. Such articles as revolvers and swords were bought during the same period
in like proportions and with similar results.[235]

The surplus of arms in Europe is easily explained.
Twenty years before the outbreak of the Civil War,
Prussia, already looking toward military supremacy,
had abandoned the old type of musket for the improved
needle gun. These copper-cartridge breech loaders had
been given every known practical test during the in-
tervening years and their superiority was established.[236]
European states which had not adopted needle guns
had, at least, adopted the very best patterns of muzzle
loaders such as the Enfield and the French army rifles

---

[233] *Idem,* vol. 1, pp. 484-486, 567, 594.

[234] *Ibid.,* p. 575.

[235] *Idem,* vol. 2, pp. 855-856. The total cost of these guns, plus about
62,000 purchased in United States, was $11,167,448.10.

[236] "Rifled Fire Arms," in *Eclectic Magazine of Foreign Literature, Science, and Art,* vol. 53 (August, 1861), p. 560; article on "Small Arms," in
New International Encyclopaedia.

and, consequently, the market was flooded with cast-off guns of every description. Turned loose under these circumstances, "agents without either experience or credit, and sometimes unscrupulous, bought in every part of Europe, on account of the federal government, all the muskets they could pick up, without any regard to their quality or price." Consequently they gathered up from the German states, big and little, all the old-fashioned arms which those states were glad to get rid of at any price, to enable them to replace them with needle guns. "The refuse of all Europe passed into the hands of the American volunteers." [237]

In connection with this contracting an enormous amount of graft was discovered. A commission, composed of Colonel Joseph Holt and Robert Dale Owen, met in March, 1862, and rendered a report on July 1, covering 104 cases involving contracts amounting to fifty million dollars. This amount was larger than the total expenditures of the Ordnance bureau for the first year of the war, but, in view of the fact that many of the contracts were for future delivery, the amount does not seem unreasonable. Of this $50,000,000 the commission claimed to have saved the government a total of $17,000,000 by rejection of some contracts, curtailment of others, modification of some, and price reductions in many. It seemed that some of the contractors, who otherwise seemed honest enough, felt that, while "bound to respect the property of its individual citizens, the country, as a whole, is a fair subject of plunder. . . ." Men secured contracts and sold them to middlemen and both made huge profits. In one instance the amount paid to a middleman was reduced $580,000 by

---

[237] Count of Paris, *Civil War*, vol. 1, pp. 298-299.

the commission, by curtailment and in rates, and, in another case, an importer's bill was trimmed a million dollars in rates alone. The latter contract was for 188,-000 guns and 38,000 sabers, and the proposal for the amount of reduction came from the frightened importer himself. Since the reduction averaged nearly five dollars for each weapon it can merely be inferred what the intended profit must have been.[238] A single instance of such profits is to be seen in the notorious Department of the West under Fremont's supervision. Fremont was known to have paid $22.50 for Hall carbines which sold on the market, when new, for $17.50, but the ones which he bought were second handed and condemned and could be bought at public auction for less than six dollars. For Enfield rifles, liberally valued at $20, he paid $26.50. Colt's revolvers were worth $15 and by contract sold for $25, but brought $35 when bought by him. And as a final favor to the Colt company their carbines brought $60 and their rifles $65.[239] As a partial remedy for this latter type of abuse the War Department set a maximum price of $20 for Enfield rifles delivered in New York,[240] and the investigating commission cut the contract price on Springfields from $20 to $16.[241]

Aside from the abuses always to be expected from contractors, the War Department was guilty of various indiscretions, if not of actual fraud, which greatly added to the opportunities of the money-bag patriots. By act of March 3, 1809, the War Department was ex-

---

[238] See report of commission in, *Official Records,* series iii, vol. 2, pp. 188-190.

[239] *Idem,* vol. 1, pp. 538-539.

[240] *New York Tribune,* November 11, 1861.

[241] *Official Records,* series iii, vol. 2, pp. 191-192.

pressly prohibited from buying materials except by open purchase or by sealed bids previously advertised for.[242] This act was still valid but was ignored. Private contracts were made for large quantities for future delivery, with private individuals and with manufacturers, with little or no regard to market prices or economy.

This circumstance is rendered all the more questionable by the fact that some manufacturers could get contracts while others could not, even though offering the same product at a lower price. The case of the Colt and Remington revolvers has already been mentioned. There were plenty of similar cases of favoritism. One gun manufacturer, who had tried in vain to secure any business from the War Department, got orders for 200,000 guns from middlemen who, though unable to manufacture guns, knew well how to get contracts. Evidently both manufacturer and middleman made plentiful profits. Worse yet, the commission asserted, contracts could be secured by the unfavored companies if they hired the right persons to approach the War Department for them. One case is cited, though the names, for obvious reasons, were suppressed, where a United States Senator charged a manufacturer $10,000 for securing a million-dollar contract for him. In this case the usual five per cent. was shaved to one per cent. because of the vigilance of the commission. In another case a manufacturer of pistols had been assured by the officials that his pistols did not meet the army requirements, yet a short time afterward he secured a contract for thousands of them at $20 apiece. The magic that had performed the feat was a ten per

---

[242] *U. S. Statutes at Large*, vol. 2, p. 536.

cent. bribe to a go-between who secured the contracts for him.[243] It was for such business as this that the President was forced, tardily but gladly, to remove Cameron from the office for which he had never been qualified.

Even before this cabinet shakeup some definite efforts had been made to check the munitions graft. Combinations between manufacturers and importers of arms had the effect of artificially increasing prices. To check this the collectors of customs were ordered to deliver to the United States all arms and ammunition imported.[244] Maximum prices on standard articles had also helped some. But it was not until the legal method of advertising for bids was reverted to that munitions contracts came out into the open, where flagrant peculation was more difficult to indulge in. Furthermore the growing reliance on the domestic supply of munitions greatly simplified this phase of the work for the new Secretary of War.

Foreign purchases had been, from the start, intended merely as a temporary expedient. While immediate needs were being supplied from this source, great efforts were made to increase the output of the national armory and to stimulate private manufacture at home. The Harper's Ferry armory had been destroyed early in the war, leaving only the Springfield armory under national control. But the latter was capable of making only 800 muskets a month at the beginning of the war. By liberal appropriation and efficient management the

---

[243] *Official Records*, series iii, vol. 2, pp. 193-194. Further information on whole subject of the investigation is in *Senate Exec. Doc.*, 37 Cong., 2 sess., Doc. no. 72.

[244] *New York Tribune*, December 4, 1861; *Official Records*, series iii, vol. 1, pp. 702-703.

armory was so enlarged and improved with new machinery that, during the month of October, 1861, 6,900 were turned out and 10,000 were expected in December. With increased appropriations and facilities the officials were not disappointed in expecting to produce 200,000 guns in 1862.[245]

Private manufacture was stimulated to an even greater degree during the same period. Owing to the necessary changes to be made in converting the factories to a war time basis, the American manufacturers supplied the government with only a little over 30,000 rifles during the first year of the war,[246] but by the end of that time their facilities were so greatly enlarged that the total productive capacity of the United States became 700,-000 small arms annually. Furthermore there were resources for an indefinite supply and the Ordnance bureau was able to declare that the longer the demand continued the greater the resources would be developed and increased.[247] Nor was this mere idle boasting, for never again during the war was there a shortage of the best muzzle-loading guns, and at the end of the war there was a surplus of 1,195,572 rifles and muskets unissued by the Ordnance bureau,[248] in addition to all the serviceable weapons in use by the soldiers. These facts should be borne in mind when we come to consider the short-sighted policy of the military men.

The increasing supply of ammunition kept pace with the increasing number of weapons. The supply of saltpeter for gunpowder was ample from the start, and was

[245] *New York Tribune,* November 5, 1861; *Official Records,* series iii, vol. i, p. 702.

[246] *Official Records,* series iii, vol. 2, p. 855.

[247] *Ibid.,* pp. 852-853.

[248] *Idem,* vol. 5, p. 145.

replenished by purchases from Europe, Dupont, and the saltpeter deposits of Peru, California, New Mexico, and the available parts of Texas. By 1864 the Ordnance office felt that in case of necessity it could secure enough of this ingredient totally independent of Europe.[249] Even during the first year of the war the reserve stock of gunpowder increased from a little less than four million pounds in March, 1861, to twelve million pounds in June, 1862. Already, by the latter date the United States was independent of importation of manufactured powder.[250]

In the foregoing account it has been intimated that many of the weapons, especially those from Europe, were of very poor quality. Just how bad they really were can best be told through the testimony of those who knew best – the soldiers. The Austrian and Belgian guns were especially detested, and it will be remembered that over 170,000 of the one and 57,000 of the other had been purchased. Adjutant-general Lorenzo Thomas examined a consignment of 3000 of the Austrian guns and declared that only 500 of them could be used.[251] Such as were thought fit for issue to the soldiers were described by them as very heavy and clumsy, though rather short,[252] and they were so slow of fire as to endanger the life of the person using them.[253] General Grant testified before a congressional committee that the "men would hold them very tight, shut their eyes, and brace themselves for the shock." [254] Fortunate-

[249] *Idem,* vol. 4, pp. 582-583.

[250] *Idem,* vol. 2, p. 853.

[251] *Ibid.,* p. 430.

[252] W. F. Scott, *Story of a Cavalry Regiment, 1861-1865* (New York, 1893), p. 25.

[253] Upham, *loc. cit.,* p. 22.

[254] "Government Contracts," in *House Reports,* 37 Cong., 2 sess., *report* no. 2, part ii, p. 1.

ly many of the soldiers had the "hardihood or ingenuity to 'lose' them," [255] and when this happened they had at least an even chance to be supplied with something better.

The Belgian rifles were worse, if possible, than the Austrian. They were of uneven calibre, some had crooked barrels, and many of the locks were out of repair. The soldiers "called them 'pumpkin slingers' and pronounced the crooked barrels adapted to shooting around hills." Finally the barrels were so brittle as to be easily broken into pieces.[256] The Vincennes rifle was described as having an irregular bore causing the bullets to fit too tight and then too loose. The locks were of soft iron, the bayonets impractical, and the rifling shallow and useless.[257] Some soldiers in the early months received no fire arms but a revolver and a pair of horse pistols and the revolver was apt to be of an impractical type such as the Starr revolver. This was a five shooter using paper cartridges and percussion caps and it "caused more fear in the regiment than it ever did among the enemy. Its shot was very uncertain, its machinery often failed to work, and it had a vicious tendency to go off at a wrong moment." [258]

Iowa troops in the first year of the war were equipped with Austrian muskets, Prussian muskets, Belgian rifles, Harper's Ferry muskets, Spencer's carbines, Sharp's carbines, Colt's revolvers, navy revolvers, Whitworth rifles, Colt's revolving rifles, Minié rifles, besides some of the other varieties of less known weapons. The twenty-fourth regiment, which was known

---

[255] Scott, *op. cit.*, p. 63.

[256] Upham, *loc. cit.*, pp. 22-23.

[257] J. A. Beaver, "The Colonel's Story," in *The 148th Pennsylvania Volunteers* (J. W. Muffly, ed., Des Moines, 1904), pp. 73-74.

[258] Scott, *op. cit.*, p. 25.

from the professions of its soldiers as the Temperance Regiment, very appropriately drilled for two months with wooden swords and guns:[259] such weapons had at least the temperance virtue that there was no kick to them.

Such was the kind of arms that reached the soldiers, in spite of the fact that the government officials knew that thousands of the imported guns were useless and that most of them could never be issued.[260] In view of what the soldiers received we can only conjecture the state of the thousands of guns rejected at the start. Because of the great variety of guns in use, much care had to be exercised to avoid hopeless confusion. The better muskets were kept for soldiers doing guard duty. The rest were sorted according to calibre and kind of ammunition required, and were so distributed as to come as nearly as possible to having each regiment supplied with weapons using a uniform ammunition. Then gradually the most worthless were thrown away until after a time the better kind of arms was substituted for them all.[261]

The providing of artillery was a much simpler matter in the mobilization of the army than was the question of the supply of small arms. The Civil War was primarily an infantryman's war, and, though the artillery played an important part, especially in siege operations, the question of supply was never acute. There were only 7,892 cannon issued to the army during a period of over five years from 1861 to 1866, whereas during the same period over 4,000,000 small arms were

259 Upham, *loc. cit.*, pp. 20, 24.
260 *Official Records*, series iii, vol. 2, p. 191.
261 Count of Paris, *op. cit.*, vol. 1, p. 299.

issued.[262] Important changes were in progress at the time both in the methods of manufacture and in the structure and mechanism of cannon, but it cannot be shown that the War Department did not take advantage of these changes as rapidly as their success justified them in so doing.

The principle of rifling, as applied to cannon, was just coming into prominence in 1861. Breech-loading cannon had been known from very early times [263] and there were various types of breech-loading cannon in existence or being experimented with at the time of the Civil War. None of them, however, were very successful, with the possible exception of the Whitworth gun, produced in England.[264] Among the most important achievements of American inventors at the time was that of Captain T. J. Rodman, who devised a method of hollow casting and internal cooling, which greatly reduced the danger of flaws from cooling in the manufacture of large guns. By this improvement cannon of fifteen-inch calibre were made, which proved to be successful, and before the end of the war cannon of twenty-inch calibre were being experimented with.[265] Such an achievement was considered as something stupendous at the time. Many people considered that these

---

262 *Official Records,* series iii, vol. 5, p. 1042.

263 See article on "Artillery," in *Encyclopaedia Britannica,* eleventh edition.

264 Described in detail in *Harper's Weekly,* vol. 5 (June 15, 1861), p. 381 (August 10, 1861), p. 510.

265 Detailed description of the gun and its manufacture will be found in Count of Paris, *op. cit.,* vol. 1, pp. 302-303; *Harper's Weekly,* vol. 5 (March 30, 1861), pp. 204-205; vol. 6 (August 23, 1862), pp. 535-537, (September 6, 1862), p. 561; vol. 8 (November 19, 1864), p. 749; "Heavy Ordance," in *Report of Joint Committee on Conduct of War,* 38 Cong., 2 sess., vol. 2. pp. 1-2 of the section, and testimony.

inventions had brought cannon to the point where further improvement was practically impossible. The following extract needs no comment: "In looking at a monster gun of the present day, with its missile warranted 'good at five miles,' we can scarce restrain a smile when we think over the many awkward forms and impotent changes artillery has undergone before it arrived at its present perfection. . . ."[266]

This enthusiastic praise of cannon just barely beginning to evolve from the mediaeval pattern may be forgiven since the writer was describing the best cannon of which he had any knowledge. As much cannot be said of the Ordnance officer who boasted that "the U. S. muskets as now made have no superior arms in the world."[267] Colonel James W. Ripley was in a position to know and he alone was to blame if his prejudice prevented him from admitting that there were various types of breech-loading rifles in existence, and some of them repeating rifles, which had all the accuracy and power of the Springfields as well as the advantage of a much greater rapidity of fire.

The principle of breech loading was an old one and was, by 1861, gaining wide recognition. The adoption of the needle gun by the Prussian army has already been mentioned. Hardly a man in the army or War Department could have been ignorant of the fact that the cru-

---

[266] F. L. Sarmiento, "The Artillerist," in *Harper's Magazine*, vol. 24 (March, 1862), p. 545. Further comments on and descriptions of common guns of the period may be found in "Heavy Ordnance," *loc. cit.*, pp. 2-7, *et seq.*; J. T. Headley, "Early Cannon," in *Harper's Magazine*, vol. 25 (September, 1862), pp. 593-607; "Rifled Ordnance," in *Eclectic Magazine*, vol. 53 (July, 1861), pp. 395-404; *Harper's Weekly*, vol. 5 (August 10, 1861), p. 510; Count of Paris, *op. cit.*, vol. 1, pp. 306-307; *New York Tribune*, March 13, 16, 26, 31, 1863; *Official Records*, series iii, vol. 5, p. 142.

[267] *Official Records*, series iii, vol. 1, p. 264.

saders sent into Kansas by the New England Emigrant
Aid Society had been armed with Sharp's rifles, because of their greater efficiency. Such breech loaders
as the Colt, Hall, Sharp, and Burnside were declared
before the Battle of Bull Run to be favorites in private
hands though not yet adopted by the army.[268] Even a
man who objected on general principles to the use of
breech loaders in the army, himself being an expert
rifleman, said of the latest pattern of the Colt's rifle
that, "we have never known an instance of a premature
discharge of either of the chambers. . . . In reply to
the common assertion, that much of the explosive force
must be lost by escape of gas between the chamber and
the barrel, we simply state the fact that we have repeatedly shot through nine inches of solid white cedar
timber at forty yards. . . . This is good enough for any
ordinary purpose of hunting or military service . . .
and for our own use, against either man or beast we
should ask no better weapon." [269] Yet this was not merely a breech loader; it was a repeating rifle of the revolver type now long since discarded.

Even such primitive breech loaders as the Sharp and
the Hall were highly prized by those who were fortunate enough to possess them. The Hall rifle deviated
from the old muzzle loaders in that a section of the
barrel, just long enough to hold the cartridge, was detached from the rest of the barrel and fastened to the
stock by a hinge. Into this section the prepared cartridge, made of paper, and the ball were inserted. The
slide was then closed and the gun was fired with a per-

---

268 *New York Tribune,* June 2, 1861.
269 H. W. S. Cleveland, "Rifle Clubs," in *Atlantic Monthly,* vol. 10 (September, 1862), p. 306.

cussion cap the same as any ordinary gun. This was the oldest practical breech loader in existence and had been known for more than forty years before the Civil War.[270] The Sharp's rifle was an improvement upon the same principle yet did not use a metallic cartridge.

The objections to guns of this type were that there was an escape of gas at the joining of the two barrel sections, that the mechanism was liable to derangement, that the barrel required frequent cleaning, and that they were more expensive.[271] Yet, in spite of these objections they were the most highly esteemed weapons used in the early part of the war. Colonel H. Berdan of the United States Sharp Shooters, when advertising for sharp shooters for his regiment, offered as a special inducement that he had 1,400 new Sharp's rifles and 900 Colt's rifles for their use.[272] An Iowa company, armed with the Sharp's rifles boasted that they would "strike a man at eight hundred or one thousand yards every time. . . ."[273] Even those armed with the more primitive Hall carbines found that they were called to the front to bear the hottest of the firing, whenever they went into battle.[274] Union guns and United States carbines are also described as being "breech loaders, of simple mechanism and easily carried, but they required a paper cartridge and a percussion cap, and had to be recharged for each shot." Yet, when armed with them the soldiers immediately showed greater efficiency.[275]

No account of even these hybrid breech loaders rates

[270] Scott, op. cit., p. 63; "Small Arms," loc. cit.
[271] Harper's Weekly, vol. 5 (August 3, 1861), p. 495.
[272] New York Tribune, January 17, August 27, 1862.
[273] Wilkie, The Iowa First, p. 88.
[274] Scott, op. cit., p. 63.
[275] Ibid., p. 183.

them as anything but superior to the best of muzzle loaders, yet they were the poorest breech loaders on the market at the time. The copper cartridge, containing ball, powder, and cap, already an old favorite in Prussia, was coming into popular favor in America and was relegating to the past all forms of guns which were fired on any other principle.

Even a military man, who had an ingrained prejudice against anything but the old-style guns, reporting to General Ripley, was forced to admit that the Ballard carbine using the copper cartridge was "the very best breech-loading carbine that has been presented to me for trial." [276] His reservation is evident, but, comparing his statement with those of the users of the paper-cartridge breech loaders, it is evident that a high compliment was unwittingly paid to the weapon. The manufacturers of this gun themselves admitted that it was "universally acknowledged to be the nearest to perfection of any breech-loading rifle ever made." [277] Perhaps for single shooters they were correct but when they included all breech loaders they took in too much territory.

Before the close of 1861 General Ripley had made an adverse report [278] against what was later to be the most coveted rifle in the Union army and the one most feared by the Confederates. This was the Spencer rifle which was described by the Count of Paris as "an excellent arm, the use of which became more and more extended in the Federal army. The butt is pierced, in the direction of the length, by a tube containing seven cartridges, which are deposited successively, after each

[276] *New York Tribune*, August 4, 1862.
[277] Advertisement in *Harper's Weekly*, vol. 6 (April 12, 1862), p. 239.
[278] *Official Records*, series iii, vol. i, pp. 733-734.

fire in the chamber, replacing in turn those which, when discharged, are thrown out by a very simple mechanism. This magazine, entirely protected, is very easily recharged. Many extraordinary instances have been cited of successful personal defence due to the rapidity with which this arm can be fired, and some Federal regiments of infantry which made a trial of it were highly pleased with the result." [279] The rifle was loaded "by throwing down a lever which threw out the shell of the old cartridge, and throwing the lever back the new cartridge is forced into the gun ready for firing." [280]

The chief weakness of the gun was the possibility of magazine explosions, of which there were said to have been some cases,[281] but, even if this were true it does not seem to have injured the popularity of the weapon. Troopers could fire it fourteen times a minute while mounted and still faster when on foot.[282] Nothing could stand before its tremendous fire. From the time troops were supplied with it they not only won their engagements but they expected to win. Some regiments "even acquired a sort of habit of looking upon every approaching fight as 'a sure thing.' And there was a corresponding disheartenment on the part of the rebel cavalry," who began to show a distinct unwillingness to fight against such odds. The story became popular that the Confederates "were saying that the Yankees had now made a gun that they loaded on Sundays and fired all the week." [283] Another sentiment was

[279] Count of Paris, *op. cit.*, vol. i, p. 300.

[280] E. J. Copp, *Reminiscences of War of Rebellion* (Nashua, N. H., 1911), pp. 431-432.

[281] Scott, *op. cit.*, p. 283.

[282] Upham, *loc. cit.*, p. 27.

[283] Scott, *op. cit.*, pp. 283-284.

that "It is no use for us to fight you'ens with that kind of gun."[284]

In spite of the enormous success of these copper-cartridge guns, both single shooters and repeaters, the military men found plenty of opportunity to oppose them as long as possible, and it was not until nearly the end of the war that the Ordnance bureau, under a new chief, was converted to their advocacy. In December, 1861, the chief of Ordnance had denied contracts to the Spencer company and to the Henry company, which produced a similar rifle, on various grounds. They were objected to because they required a special kind of ammunition, because they could not be loaded with powder and ball like ordinary muzzle loaders, and because the stocks might get crushed while the bearers were riding on horse back. Then too the government had already ordered 73,000 breech loaders which would cost $2,250,000 and that was considered enough.[285]

Reserving comment on the general objections to a later paragraph, it may be observed here that if 73,000 breech loaders had been contracted for at that time they were of the old paper-cartridge, percussion-cap kind, that they were slow in delivery, and that they formed merely a part of the hodgepodge of arms contracted for, during that year, so many of which had to be rejected. It is a significant fact that in a report of the department nearly seven months later only 8,271 breech-loading rifles were listed out of a total of over 757,000 guns which were purchased up to June 30, 1862.[286]

The reluctance of military men to give credence to

---

[284] Upham, loc. cit., p. 27. For illustrations of rifles, revolvers, and ordnance see Atlas to Accompany the Official Records of the Union and Confederate Armies (Washington, 1891-1895), plate number 173.

[285] Official Records, series iii, vol. 1, pp. 733-734.

[286] Idem, vol. 2, p. 855.

the value of these arms until actually forced into accepting them is almost astounding. For instance, twenty years after the adoption of the needle gun in the Prussian army the statement appears that "if all the Prussians say about the needle gun be true, they have the best rifle in the world; but we think that, had its merits not been counterbalanced by grave disadvantages, we should have heard more about it in this country." [287] Then, military writers in general contended "that soldiers in action fire too fast already, and that it is only adding to the evil to give them the means of firing four or five times as fast by placing breech loading guns in their hands." [288] In seeking objections to the Henry and Spencer repeating rifles, General Ripley found the further weaknesses that the spiral feed spring might wear out, that the fulminate might explode at improper moments, that distribution of ammunition might be made more complex, and that they were too expensive. [289]

Nobody today would question the supremacy of the breech-loading rifle in its present improved form. The following comparison is intended to show that, even in its more primitive form, the breech loader of 1861 was the logical gun for universal use in the army. The actual performance of the two opposite types of weapons is the best criterion to their value.

The general objections to all kinds of breech-loading guns can be classified under five heads: (1) the diffi-

---

[287] "Rifled Fire Arms," *loc. cit.*, p. 561.

[288] *New York Tribune*, June 2, 1861. Two very illuminating articles, showing both an admiration for new weapons as well as serious doubts as to advisability of adopting them for the army are: Cleveland, "The Use of the Rifle." in *Atlantic Monthly*, vol. 9 (March, 1862), pp. 300-306; Cleveland, "Rifle Clubs," *loc. cit.*, pp. 303-310.

[289] *Official Records*, series iii, vol. 1, pp. 733-734.

culty of supplying the guns with ammunition; (2) the delicacy and intricacy of the weapons, which might result in easy derangement of the mechanism or be difficult for the soldiers to handle; (3) danger of explosion of magazines in the repeating rifles; (4) the greater cost of the weapons; (5) waste of ammunition by the soldiers, due to rapid firing. Some of these objections were mere subterfuges or fanciful arguments produced to justify prejudices, while the others were imaginary bugaboos which shortly, but not soon enough, had to give way before the proved superiority of the weapons.

Little need be said concerning the first objection. It was first used in 1861 when, as has been already shown, practically every kind of small fire arm in existence, from horse pistols and squirrel rifles to a very few breech loaders, were being issued to the army. In those early days it was a fortunate regiment which did not get its ammunition mixed up because of the various calibres and makes of guns to be supplied. To have supplied copper cartridges to certain regiments would, from the start, have been as simple a matter as to supply them with minié balls. When the odd and antiquated weapons were abandoned for an improved type, it would have been as practicable to have substituted first-class breech loaders as to supply the Springfields that were given the preference. Clearly the ammunition difficulty was purely imaginary.

As to the delicacy and intricacy of the weapons, the difficulties as spelled out on paper sound much worse than those actually experienced. What could be more delicate than the Belgian rifles whose barrels could be broken by striking them across a pine board? What mechanism could be more easily deranged than that of the Austrian rifles, whose locks were made of soft iron and whose springs were too weak to explode the fulminate? But it is unfair to compare the Spencer, Colt, Henry, or Ballard rifles with the junk of 1861. Even the paper-cartridge breech loaders were described by their possessors as "of simple mechanism and easily carried" and even the Hall carbines were preferred to the muzzle loaders.[290]

The number of motions required to load the clumsiest breech loader were fewer and the danger of exposure was much less than in the ramming process of charging a muzzle loader. With the Spencer rifle seven cartridges could be hastily slipped into a steel tube and this be inserted in the stock of the gun, while another soldier was tearing the cartridge for a muzzle loader, and getting his ramrod out. Then, with the simple process of lowering and raising a lever, the gun would be recharged until the seven shots had been fired. The mere fact that two such magazines of cartridges could be fired by a cavalryman in a minute is sufficient proof that in intricacy of management the repeating rifle was not to be compared with the muzzle loader with its paper cartridge, torn by the teeth, its separate bullet and wadding, rammed down with a ramrod, its percussion caps, and its difficult cleansing.

As to the fancied difficulty that the spiral spring in the magazine might weaken with wear, the triviality of exchanging it for a new one would be as easy as supplying a muzzle loader with a new ramrod for one that had been lost. Furthermore, any of the repeaters could be fired as single-shot guns if necessity should

---

[290] Scott, *op. cit.*, pp. 183, 63.

demand it. As for the escape of gas from the apertures, such apertures were not to be found in the copper cartridge rifles, whose barrels were all in one piece. The sole exception was the Colt revolving rifle, which carried its cartridges in a revolving chamber like any ordinary revolver. Even of this gun an expert rifleman, who had a complex against repeating rifles in the army, said, as before stated, that it would shoot "through nine inches of solid white cedar timber at forty yards. . . ." [291]

The same writer, speaking of the Ashcroft rifle, said that it was equal in performance in all respects to the best muzzle loader, that it was simple, solid, and strong, accurate and precise. The force of explosion caused a perfect closure of the joint, yet the breech was as easily removable as the cocking of a gun. "We have in the course of experiment fired the gun three hundred times, and have since seen it fired five hundred times, without once wiping or cleaning, and the working of the joints was as easy and the shooting as good at the last as at first." [292]

The absolute ridiculousness of the argument that breech loaders were too intricate may be seen when their performance is compared with that of the old favorites, the muzzle loaders. These obsolete incumbrances were almost totally unmanageable in the hands of an excited soldiery. A reliable army officer stated that of 27,574 muskets collected from the field, after the battle of Gettysburg, 24,000 were loaded, 12,000 contained two charges each, and 6000 were charged with from three to ten loads each. One musket had in

[291] *Cf. ante,* p. 129.
[292] Cleveland, "Rifle Clubs," *loc. cit.,* p. 308.

it 23 loads, each charge being put down in regular order. "Oftentimes the cartridge was loaded without being first broken, and in many instances it was inserted, the ball down first." [293] In the excitement and confusion of battle the frightened or excited soldier was unlikely to realize that his charge had not exploded and would continue to reload until the ramrod informed him of his error. With even one unexploded charge in a gun it was useless for immediate use and the extrication of several dead charges was an interminable task. Such a condition was impossible with the breech loader which had to be emptied before the next charge could be inserted.

In spite of fears to the contrary, the records do not show that the magazine explosions were of any appreciable frequency. From the comparative size of the two it is a mathematical certainty that the chance of an enemy bullet penetrating the magazine of a repeating rifle would be smaller than of its penetrating the ordinary cartridge boxes of the soldiers, and it would be difficult to prove that the effect would be any more disastrous. Warfare has never been placed in the same class with checkers as a harmless pastime, and, where bullets are flying so thick or so close as to penetrate the magazine of a rifle, the death of a soldier could scarcely be attributed to the kind of a gun he carried. Furthermore, if the evidence is to be relied upon, whenever repeating rifles were used by Union forces the enemy, without any reflection upon their courage, were chiefly concerned in seeking cover rather than returning the fire. "There have been several instances," said

[293] T. T. S. Laidley, "Breech-Loading Musket," in *United States Service Magazine*, vol. 3 (January, 1865), p. 69.

an authority, "where a single regiment, armed with breech-loading, self-capped rifles, has held in check a whole brigade armed with the ordinary musket. . . ."[294]

It seems strange that the mere cost of the improved weapons should have been argued as an objection to them. If they cost twice as much as muzzle loaders they were at least three times as efficient. Measured not by the number of the guns but by their effectiveness the breech loaders were the cheapest guns used during the war.

But speaking of rapidity of fire brings up the principal argument of the reactionaries, namely that soldiers fired too rapidly as it was and that fast-shooting rifles would merely encourage them to waste more ammunition. For instance it was estimated that the Austrians at Solferino used 272 pounds of lead to kill each man.[295] As a matter of fact the soldiers did waste their ammunition. The Ordnance office reports show that over ninety million pounds of lead, nearly thirteen million pounds of artillery projectiles, and twenty-six million four hundred thousand pounds of powder were issued to the army during the war.[296] There are no very satisfactory figures as to the total number of Confederates killed, but in the Union army the total of those killed in battle and dying of wounds afterward was only slightly over 110,000.[297] If the Confederate killed be taken at about the same number then it took in excess of nine hundred pounds of metal and two hundred forty pounds of powder to kill each man. Probably three

[294] *Ibid.*, p. 69.
[295] *New York Tribune*, June 2, 1861.
[296] *Official Records*, series iii, vol. 5, pp. 1042-1043.
[297] *Ibid.*, pp. 664-665.

hundred pounds of lead and eighty pounds of powder were used for each man wounded only to the point of temporary disablement.

Yet this does not adduce an iota of argument against the use of more efficient weapons, but it does cast a serious reflection upon the effectiveness and the kind of training that the soldiers received. The alleged experts confused rapid firing with poor aiming. The latter rather than the former was the thing to be corrected. The remedy for this, said a contemporary, "lies in thorough discipline and practical knowledge of the use of the gun; and the soldier will be more likely to take time for aiming, if he knows he can be ready to repeat his shot almost instantly." [298]

The argument of the military men was that, if a soldier wasted ten pounds of lead in a given time with a muzzle loader, he would waste twenty pounds in the same length of time with a gun firing twice as fast, therefore, in battle the muzzle loader is the preferable weapon. The same argument applied in a different way would be: If one man wastes ten pounds of lead in a given time with a muzzle loader two men would waste twenty pounds in the same length of time; therefore one man in battle is preferable to two men. One of the strange paradoxes of the war is that the North, in its hysteria, used every means from bribery to force to increase the shooting power of its army by the addition of more men and yet, at the same time, refused, until too late, to increase the shooting power by means of more effective weapons in the trained hands of the veterans.

The final proof of error on the part of the War Department is that it was forced by conviction, before the

---

[298] Cleveland, "Rifle Clubs," *loc. cit.*, pp. 306-307.

end of the war, to adopt for future use the very type of weapon which it had sought so long to avoid. The growth of this conviction was slow and painful. During the first two years of the war, contracts for the best type of breech loaders were constantly refused. Only a few here and there were accepted. The manufacturers of the Henry repeating rifle were even told that their weapons could not be accepted unless the company would arm a whole regiment with them at its own expense, and keep them supplied.[299]

Yet even these few better guns eventually received recognition, but it was not until 1864 that they were purchased even in moderate quantities. The change of leadership in the Ordnance bureau (September, 1863) seems to have been beneficial. The new chief, General George D. Ramsay, in a report made in August, 1864, showed that a total of 33,652 repeating rifles and carbines, chiefly of the Spencer type, and 15,051 single-shot, copper-cartridge guns had been purchased since the beginning of the year, and that 78,100 repeaters and 11,850 single shooters had been contracted for, to be delivered in monthly installments until August, 1865.[300] Of these guns, probably 100,000 were in the hands of the Union soldiers by April, 1865, when the war ended. Most of these guns were, in the beginning, bestowed upon the cavalry, and by the winter of 1864-1865 most of them, especially in the Southwest, were supplied with Spencer carbines.[301] The results thoroughly justified the act.

By December, 1864, the Ordnance office was thor-

---

[299] *Official Records*, series iii, vol. 2, pp. 412-413.
[300] *Idem*, vol. 3, p. 1199; vol. 4, p. 593.
[301] Scott, *op. cit.*, p. 369.

oughly convinced. "The experience of the war has shown," said the chief, "that breech-loading arms are greatly superior to muzzle loaders for infantry as well as for cavalry. . . ." Therefore he recommended that a board be appointed to meet at the Springfield armory to "examine, test, and recommend for adoption a suitable breech-loader for muskets and carbines, and a suitable repeater or magazine carbine, and that the arms recommended by the Board may, if approved by the War Department, be exclusively adopted for the military service." [302] Finally, when the war was all over, it was announced that a speedy plan was at hand for converting into breech loaders the million Springfield muskets and the half million foreign or captured guns still unissued.[303] It is now a certainty that this process of conversion of old arms and manufacture of new breech loaders could just as easily have begun in 1861 as in 1865, if men of brains and foresight instead of stereotyped automatons had been in the proper positions of influence and command.

The inventive genius of the Civil War period went far beyond the simple improvements in small arms described above. Rifles with telescopic sights were used to a limited extent by sharp shooters as early as the Peninsular Campaign, and with deadly effect. In expert hands they were infallible at three-quarters of a mile and would do good service at a mile. So accurate were they that the rifleman, even at a distance, could select the "particular feature of his [the enemy's] face, or

---

[302] *Official Records*, series iii, vol. 4, pp. 971-972. The Chief of Ordnance at this time was Brigadier-general Alexander B. Dyer, the man who had done more than any other to bring the Springfield arsenal to its high state of efficiency during the war.

[303] *Idem*, vol. 5, p. 143.

which button of his coat" should be the target. Their
use at Yorktown has been attributed as the reason why
negroes were first used to man the fortifications. One
of the wartime stories was that "At Edward's Ferry,
on the twenty-second of October [1861], seventy
men . . . repelled a charge of fifteen hundred of the
enemy and drove them from the field, with the loss of
more than one hundred killed, while not one of their
own men received a scratch." Yet the gun was hooted at
by military men, when a New York company armed
itself with them. Indeed for practical field work the
gun would have been an encumbrance because of its
weight. Weighing from thirty to thirty-two pounds it
might better be described as a species of light artillery.
Yet such a gun, used behind breastworks by sharp-
shooters, should have received more attention than was
actually accorded it.[304]

Other inventions of the period remind us strongly
of the more highly-perfected instruments of modern
warfare. Poison gas, liquid fire, machine guns, and sub-
marines of more or less primitive type were known even
during the earliest months of the war. The attempts of
the Confederacy to produce a practicable submarine
undoubtedly stimulated the effort to perfect that form
of naval auxiliary in later years. The man-driven craft
of 1861 [305] was the lineal grandfather of the modern
super-submersible.

Poison gas, though evidently not used, was known.
"Carcasses," "smoke balls," and "suffocating balls," as
they were called, were "shells with several fuse holes,

---

[304] Cleveland, "Use of the Rifle," *loc. cit.*, pp. 300, 304; Cleveland, "Rifle
Clubs," *loc. cit.*, p. 307; *Harper's Weekly*, vol. 5 (October 5, 1861), p. 625;
vol. 6 (May 10, 1862), pp. 289, 299.

[305] Illustrations in *Harper's Weekly*, vol. 5 (November 2, 1861), p. 701.

from which horrible fumes, vapors or flames rush forth, blinding and suffocating all around." Their purpose was "to drive an enemy from mines or galleries, or to clear a breach in a fortress." [306] The attitude of American soldiers toward such methods of warfare is shown in the reply of General McClellan to an inventor of an incendiary shell, from which liquid streams of fire were guaranteed to "spread most fearfully in all directions." McClellan replied that "such means of destruction are hardly within the category of those recognized in civilized warfare. Kindred inventions have been made in Europe, but I do not think they have been employed in modern times. I could not recommend their employment until we exhaust the ordinary means of warfare." [307]

Of ordnance, both light and heavy, the product of the American inventor was large. Some of the inventions were valuable and many were useless. In dealing with these weapons the trouble with the War Department was that no thorough system was used in testing and trying them before rejection or adoption. Every inventor of influence or patronage "could easily manage to have a few of his guns recommended to the principal of some foundry, who was generally his partner. A few shots fired in the neighborhood of the factory were deemed sufficient to determine the strength of the guns; and, if chance favored them, the piece was immediately received and added to the diversified assortment which already existed in the Federal artillery." [308] Among the inventions tried out was a repeating cannon built on the revolver principle and guaranteed to fire a shot every

[306] *Ibid.* (August 10, 1861), p. 510.
[307] *Official Records*, series iii, vol. 1, p. 606.
[308] Count of Paris, *op. cit.*, vol. 1, p. 301.

five seconds, but it proved to be more dangerous to the users than to the enemy and it was soon abandoned.[309] Perhaps the most impractical of all weapons submitted was a gun that was lighter than its own projectile:[310] the recoil of such a gun could better be imagined than described.

Some inventors even resorted to the catapult principle and tried to substitute centrifugal force for gunpowder. Two such guns are reported, both built on the same principle. The one receiving the most publicity was built in Baltimore and intended for the Confederate army. It was known alternately as the Baltimore steam gun, the Winans steam gun, and Dickenson's revolving gun. The curiosity looked like a cross between a prehistoric monster and a steam tractor, weighed over three tons, and was about the size of a fire engine. A musket barrel, whirling at 1600 revolutions a minute on one end as a pivot, was fed from a hopper and released the balls at an orifice in the surrounding drum. It was supposed to hurl three hundred, two-ounce balls a minute. Its range was not over a hundred yards and its aim was not accurate. Captured by the Union army, after the Baltimore riot (April, 1861), this gun was properly looked upon as a mere curiosity, though some preferred to think it would revolutionize warfare, and, from its very destructiveness, prove the means and medium of peace.[311] The McCarty rotary gun, very similar to the Winans gun, was subject to the same weaknesses as its prototype, in that its shortness of range rendered it too easily disabled by the enemy.[312]

[309] *Ibid.*, p. 305; *New York Tribune*, October 29, 1861.
[310] Count of Paris, *op. cit.*, vol. 1, p. 305.
[311] *Harper's Weekly*, vol. 5 (May 25, 1861), p. 331; *New York Tribune*, May 1, 11, 15, 16, 1861.
[312] *New York Tribune*, June 20, 1861.

In a totally different class from the fantastic fabrications just mentioned were the machine guns of the Civil War of which one was to become world famous. The conception of a rapid-firing small artillery was an old one but it could not be very well worked out until the invention of the metallic cartridge. The evolution of the machine gun was the most distinctive contribution of the United States to military science, yet again, it must be confessed, the War Department did not recognize the value of the invention until the war was over.

One such gun, known as the "coffee mill," was described by the Count of Paris as "a large rampart gun, whose open breech was surmounted by a funnel [hopper], which was filled with cartridges; these cartridges were composed of solid steel tubes containing the charge, which were successively dropped into the open space of the breech by means of a crank; a hammer, moved by this crank, struck a percussion-cap placed at the bottom of the cartridge, and caused the discharge; after this discharge the tube fell into a box, from which it was taken to reload. This machine fired one hundred shots per minute, and threw ounce balls, with great precision, to a distance of seven or eight hundred meters. . . ." It was operated by a sort of pump-handle arrangement and was aimed while firing. It could be drawn by one horse and operated by two men. It is said that President Lincoln himself tried it out and recommended its adoption, but it was not used during the war, and the machines were afterward sold as old iron for $8.00 apiece.[313]

Of more certain and unquestionable value was the invention by Richard Jordan Gatling, which was

---

[313] Count of Paris, *op. cit.*, vol. 1, pp. 305-306.

known, and is still remembered, as the Gatling gun. The first of these guns was made at Indianapolis in 1862, and, pursuant to its custom, the War Department consented to buy a few of them. Twelve were manufactured and were used by General Butler in the East. This first model of the Gatling gun fired two hundred fifty to three hundred shots a minute.[314] To use it in battle, according to the report of soldiers, "they would hitch a horse to the gun, start on a gallop, turn a crank, and the bullets flew almost as thick as hail, mowing down the rebel lines." [315] That this description is true in substance is shown by the later performances of the gun. But in spite of its demonstrated effectiveness the gun created no immediate impression on the Ordnance officers. Yet immediately after the close of the war, the Gatling gun in an improved form was adopted by the United States for the army.[316]

Thus the cycle of treatment of metallic cartridge guns was completed. The Gatling gun, like the repeating rifle, was appreciated only when it was too late for it to be of any use. If the remissness of the War Department can be condoned at all, it will be on the score that among so many freakish inventions it was difficult to state in advance just which weapons would prove successful. But the use of this argument opens the way for the final indictment of the "experts." *No proper system of examination and testing was ever developed.* If as much attention had been paid to proper investigation of weapons, including exhaustive trials of their strength

---

[314] "Richard Jordan Gatling," in *Appleton's Cyclopaedia of American Biography* (New York, 1887).

[315] F. G. Stidger, ed., *Treason History of Order of Sons of Liberty. . .* (Chicago, 1903), p. 21.

[316] "Richard Jordan Gatling," *loc. cit.*

and efficiency, as was expended in listening to the importunities of favorites and distinguished intermediaries no great difficulty would have been experienced in discovering the outstanding mechanical achievements of the war. If the Navy Department had been as conservative as the War Department, the *Monitor* would not have appeared to check the depredations of the *Merrimac*; in all likelihood the blockade would have been seriously interfered with, if not entirely broken, and the Confederacy would have been given a new lease of life, in which case a negotiated peace could have been the only logical conclusion of the war.

The Evolution of Discipline

The Evolution of Discipline

CONSERVATISM in the matter of ordnance supplies was equalled only by gross neglect to provide ample facilities for effective discipline. Even though the army was supplied with the most efficient weapons obtainable, yet it would be impotent without able leadership, careful training, and rigid discipline. Good arms and flawless discipline are the two inseparable prime requisites of any military force regardless of its size. The efficiency of a battalion of police in dispersing a mob, many times its size, is a fair example of the superiority of good arms and effective organization and discipline over mere brute force and numbers. Patent as this fact is and has always been, the United States violated its most fundamental tenets in the Civil War. She poured out her wealth and wasted her resources in roundabout and extravagant ways of increasing the size of the army, while neglecting proper armament and training of the soldiers.

In the training as well as in the arming of the soldiers the mistakes were very largely the result of a lack of capable leadership in important federal offices. Unwillingness of ordnance officers and other military men to adjust themselves to changing conditions prevented the adoption of modern weapons. An excessive case of state-rights prejudice and misapplied democracy on the part of a preponderating number of federal civil officers made proper training and discipline of the soldiers well-nigh impossible. There were those at the time who realized the errors that were being made and wished to see them corrected, but they were not in positions of power, and democracy, perhaps fortunately, does not lend itself to the rise of dictators. The reasons for the early triumph of the state-rights principle in the creation of the army have already been explained. The effects of this triumph on discipline remain to be shown here.

No very definite plans for training the soldiers were devised by the War Department at any time during the war. In the call for the three-months militia one to three designated cities in each state were assigned by the Secretary of War as places of rendezvous,[317] but these selections seem to have been more to get the militia assembled at easy points for transportation, than to prepare for any definite training. In fact but very little training could be expected of troops who were to remain in the service only ninety days. With the call for the first few regiments of three-year volunteers, a slight improvement was made in the directions for assembling and training the recruits. The governors were asked to assemble the men at rendezvous which were to be camps of instruction, each camp to be large enough to accommodate from four to eight regiments. Well-drained spots close to fuel, water, food, and transportation facilities were recommended, but the governors were allowed to select the spots and to arrange for the training. Yet by autumn it was hoped that the volunteers would have acquired "discipline, habits of obedience, and tactical instruction. . . ."[318]

---

[317] *Official Records*, series iii, vol. i, p. 69.
[318] *Ibid.*, pp. 229-230.

Another step was taken, after the call for 500,000 volunteers, to provide camps at such places as New York, Elmira, Harrisburg, and Cincinnati under charge of officers of the regular service, to which soldiers should be sent as soon as mustered.[319] On the surface this looks like direct federal control over the training of the volunteers. In fact, it applied only to those troops which were not connected with any state organization but were recruited directly by the United States. Such troops were very few in number as compared with those raised by the states, and hence the influence was but small. As long as the soldier had the privilege of choosing the organization in which he would enlist, there was no federal supervision of training until the completed regiments went to join the army at the front or at the concentration camps at army headquarters, such as at Washington, Cairo, or St. Louis. Not until the structure of the volunteer army was complete and the practice of creating new organizations was ended did the incoming volunteers or conscripts, as a rule, receive adequate training. Then it was through actual experience in the ranks with veterans, instead of in any formal training camps.

Poor as the provisions were for camps, the federal government could still have taken the one most necessary step to provide proper training and discipline, if it had only chosen to supply the army with the proper type of officers. The value to an army of well trained and able officers can scarcely be overrated. There can be no quarrel with the statement of a Union officer that good officers make good troops and bad officers make bad troops. "An officer who knows his business can

---

[319] *Ibid.*, p. 412.

make good soldiers out of almost anything, give him but a fair chance." [320]

A good officer has to have not only the courage and ability to lead his troops into the thick of a fight: he must be a master of his profession and that vocation is no more easily mastered than that of the surgeon, the lawyer, or the master of finance. A clerical blunder or an error in judgment on the part of an officer may cause the loss of life of thousands of soldiers. It was blundering that caused the surprise of the Union army at Shiloh, the attack on Kenesaw Mountain, and the disaster at Cold Harbor. But these blunders, on the part of otherwise capable officers, though more widely known than many others, represent but a small part of what the soldiers had to suffer through incapable leadership from captains on up the line to major-generals.

Bravery and military genius are indispensable qualities of the officer, but it is application to detail which determines whether or not these inherent qualities are to avail in the critical moments. The life, health, and efficiency of the soldiers as well as the welfare of their families are dependent on the foresight and business habits of regimental commanders. A single error in an ordnance requisition may send a body of troops into action with insufficient ammunition and subject them to the mercy of the enemy. "One wrong spelling in a muster-roll may beggar a soldier's children ten years after the father has been killed in battle." [321]

Such mastery of intricate detail could not be acquired without a rigid course in special training intended for

---

[320] T. W. Higginson, "Regular and Volunteer Officers," in *Atlantic Monthly*, vol. 14 (September, 1864), p. 355.

[321] *Ibid.*, p. 354.

that purpose. Either a West Point training or else long experience in the army were imperative as a part of the equipment of a first-class officer. In raising an army of a million men it was clearly impossible to furnish officers of such training for all positions, yet it would have been possible to have appointed all the general officers and their aides and at least the colonel for each regiment from the more than eleven hundred commissioned officers in the regular army. Of the more than fifteen thousand privates and non-commissioned officers [322] remaining, a large majority would have proved valuable as captains, lieutenants, and sergeants; not that they were especially trained for this work but they were familiar with army life and discipline, knew how to take and execute orders, and could adapt themselves to the change in rank much more readily than could a person who had never before worn military uniform.

To have supplied officers in this way would have necessitated the breaking up of the regular army, but that would have been far preferable to the situation that arose as an alternative. It was the opinion of no less an army organizer than General McClellan that it would have been wise either to "break it up, as a temporary measure, and distribute its members among the staff and regiments of the volunteer organizations, thus giving the volunteers all possible benefit from the discipline and instruction of the regulars, or to fill the regular regiments to their full capacity and employ them as a reserve at critical junctures." [323] The number of trained officers, including those who, like Grant and McClellan, returned from civil life to tender their

---

[322] *Official Records*, series iii, vol. 1, p. 22.
[323] *McClellan's Own Story*, p. 97.

services, was sufficient to have filled all the more responsible positions in the army of half a million men raised in 1861. Had their services been thus employed and had promotions been based on merit, the supply of capable officers could have grown with the army, and at no time could the situation have become as bad as it was in 1861 and 1862.

The value of trained officers was a thing well known to everybody, however unpalatable the idea may have been to politicians and spoilsmen. During the first week of the extra session of congress Senator James W. Nesmith of Oregon declared the right of the army to have experienced officers.[324] Within two weeks after the firing on Fort Sumter the evils of the volunteer system were forecasted in a letter to the *New York Tribune*. The people know, said the correspondent, "that it takes long to organize an army – longer to discipline it to those qualities which make veterans and insure victories – longer yet to discover the true commanders from among the crowd of egotists, peacocks, and place hunters, with which the volunteer system is apt to oppress a great military movement." [325]

Even the Secretary of War had a faint glimmering of the responsibilities if not of the possibilities of the situation. He expressed his sentiments in a dispatch to the various governors, outlining his ideas and offering his advice as to the selection of officers. None should be appointed except such as were of undoubted moral character and patriotism, and who were of sound health. As to further qualifications no lieutenant should exceed twenty-two years of age, captains should be un-

---

[324] *Congressional Globe*, 37 Cong., 1 sess., p. 52.

[325] *New York Tribune*, April 29, 1861, a letter from Samuel Wilkeson to the editor, dated April 24, 1861.

der thirty, while the maximum age, at appointment, for majors, lieutenant-colonels, and colonels should be thirty-five, forty, and forty-five years respectively, unless they were West Point graduates or had a good knowledge of military affairs, acquired by service. The efficiency of the troops and the glory of their states were, he assured the governors, dependent upon the high moral character and intelligence of the officers.[326] If this dispatch reveals anything it shows the utter failure of Secretary Cameron to understand the problem of discipline. With such leadership in the War Department perhaps it was just as well that the governors were left the responsibility. Even state rights is preferable to incapable federal control.

The surrender to state rights left the whole problem of selecting regimental and company officers to the governors, but the state executives were not altogether responsible for the situation that resulted. No doubt if able officers had been at hand, they would have received appointments, but, with most of the officers held rigidly in the regular army, there were not many such to be had. Where they were to be found, they had no great difficulty in securing appointments, though it must be confessed that Grant was ready to give up in despair before he secured a colonelcy.[327]

Even old soldiers were in demand to teach the recruits the simpler duties of marching, loading, and firing guns. Such soldiers could become sergeants without dispute, "and if they could instruct in the movements of the platoon they were almost assured of the rank of commissioned officer." [328] But, when the supply of such

[326] *Official Records*, series iii, vol. 1, pp. 227-228.
[327] Chetlain, *Recollections of Seventy Years*, pp. 75-78.
[328] Trobriand, *Army of Potomac*, p. 63.

veterans was exhausted, the remaining officers would, on the average, have been as well fitted for their positions if they had been drawn by lot. Even the veterans were, in view of other considerations, destined for lieutenancies or non-commissioned offices, while less able men were elected to command the regiments and companies.

With many officers to appoint and few competent men to choose from, it was no doubt easy for the governor to convince himself that, since all citizens were on an equality, in that they were all ignorant of any military science, it was just as well for him to appoint the ones who "would produce the more agreeable consequences at the next election-time. . . ." [329] Consequently the army was treated like the civil service and the spoils system prevailed. Men were appointed according to their influence in the state, or in a certain section of the state, or according to their devotion to the party in power.[330]

If such political favorite were also successful as a recruiting agent so much the more reason for his appointment as an officer. The number of candidates for colonelcies, naturally the most coveted job, was regularly in excess of the number of regiments to be raised, and the governor was forced to refuse many requests. Men offering to raise regiments did so with the previous understanding that they were to receive colonels' commissions. They in turn made bargains with others to secure for the latter the commission of lieutenant, captain, or major in return for helping raise the regiment.

[329] Higginson, *loc. cit.*, p. 354.

[330] Francois Ferdinand Philippe Marie, Prince de Joinville, *Army of Potomac; organization, commander, campaign* (New York, 1862), p. 14; *Harper's Weekly*, vol. 5 (August 10, 1861), p. 499.

The prospective colonel was the entrepreneur of the enterprise and the captains were his staff of assistants. All the devious ways before mentioned were resorted to in the recruiting, and then the rewards came in the form of the proffered commissions.[331]

When the office was such that no political or social favorite chose to have it, or when the recruiting was such that no particular individuals could claim the honor of the offices in recognition of their services, another device was resorted to, which exemplifies probably the strangest misdirection of democracy the past can offer, outside of Russia in 1917. Such officers were elected by the soldiers themselves. This practice was widespread throughout the country and was recognized by both state and federal governments. Usually such elections were for offices below that of colonel and, where the election was valid and fair, the colonel merely reported the names of the men receiving the majority votes to the governor, and he issued the commissions without question.[332]

This system was actually made permanent by act of congress, July 22, 1861. Vacancies in the offices of the volunteer regiments were to be filled by no other means than election. Company offices were to be filled by the rank and file, and positions higher than captain were to be subject to the vote of the commissioned officers of the regiment.[333] Instances were known where even the colonels and other field officers were from the beginning elected either by the privates or by the line

[331] Joinville, *op. cit.*, pp. 14-15; A. F. Sperry, *History of the 33d Iowa Infantry Volunteer Regiment 1863-6* (Des Moines, 1866), p. 3.

[332] Shambaugh, *Messages and Proclamations*, vol. 2, pp. 469-470; Scott, *Story of a Cavalry Regiment*, p. 21; Chetlain, *op. cit.*, p. 73; Joinville, *op. cit.*, p. 14.

[333] *U. S. Statutes at Large*, vol. 12, p. 270.

officers,[334] but ordinarily the choicest offices were not left to such chance disposal. Quite frequently election was a mere formality anyway. Some companies were indifferent, but more often the decision of the volunteers was either set aside or, by steam-roller methods, the elections were fixed before hand. In such cases the vote of the soldiers was merely the ratification of the choices made by the interested persons.[335]

Strangely enough, the prevailing opinion at the beginning of the war was that these methods were as likely as any others to procure good officers. Most officials of the locality, state, and United States were elected, directly or indirectly, by the people, and the country had been governed reasonably well. Why should not election and the spoils system work equally well in the army? Brains and initiative were considered the only really essential attributes of officers. Technical skill would come as a matter of course. Any great leader of industry or finance could "give an average army-officer all the advantage of his special training, at the start, and yet beat him at his own trade in a year." [336] If a man were a success in his own chosen business or profession it was taken as a sure sign that he would also be successful as an officer. Hence men from all walks of life, with professional politicians represented in goodly numbers, were to be found in every grade of office from sergeant to major-general.

The great majority of officers thus selected ranged in ability from technical ignorance to gross incompetence and total incapacity to learn. Officers were as

---

[334] Chetlain, *op. cit.*, p. 73.

[335] Jones, *Army of Potomac*, p. 40; *Harper's Weekly*, vol. 5 (September 7, 1861), p. 562; *Downing's Diary*, p. 163; Joinville, *op. cit.*, p. 14.

[336] Higginson, *loc. cit.*, pp. 348-349.

ignorant as privates and many of them were "unfitted from their education, moral character, or mental deficiencies, for ever acquiring the requisite efficiency." [337] Of this latter class a careful Franco-American observer, himself an officer in the army, recites an instance of a New York merchant who paid $20,000 to raise a regiment of cavalry and was rewarded therefor by a colonelcy. Totally ignorant of his duties and indifferent as well, he spent his whole time showing off his uniform on Pennsylvania avenue and in the bar rooms of the big hotels. "He was present at all the receptions at the White House, at all the evening parties of the ministers, always most attentive to the wives of the high officials and of the senators. Radically incapable of commanding his regiment, much less of leading it into battle, but sustained by the double power of money and of political influence, he was nominated brigadier General, and appointed afterward to guard some empty barracks, in a post evacuated by the enemy. This was his share of glory, and, without ever having drawn his sabre from the scabbard, he returned home, to enjoy in peace the delight of being able to write the title 'General' upon his visiting cards." [338] Were it not that such officers as the one described frequently had more capable subordinates, their commands would have been in a wretched state indeed.

Perhaps a large majority of these misfit officers really wished and tried to do their best. None can say that they were afraid to fight or to die, but the complaint of one of the more efficient of them after three years of warfare was that they were slovenly and remiss in

[337] Trobriand, *op. cit.*, p. 63; *McClellan's Own Story*, p. 97.
[338] Trobriand, *op. cit.*, p. 89.

nearly every other department of military duty.[339] They were inclined to look upon the *Army Regulations* as antiquated and useless and were willing to admit that, if they could only have the opportunity, they could improve them wonderfully in a month or two. But those of them who eventually became capable officers, on leaving the service as scarred veterans, were equally as convinced that they were just beginning to master the wisdom these regulations contained.[340]

Such things as military tactics all but the most sluggish could eventually master; and there were plenty of books on the market, official as well as unofficial, to guide them in their study.[341] The trouble was that beyond such study the officers were indifferent. They did not intend to follow military life as a career. Their term was only from three months to three years, and at the end of that time they would be out in civil life again. For so short a time they did not care to master so carefully something they would never use again.[342]

Fortunately for the Union cause there were enough exceptions to the general rule of incompetence to provide a nucleus for spreading a modicum of discipline throughout the army. Thereby it was held together, even though no great heights of efficiency were attainable. On the one hand we have the declaration of the able organizer McClellan that many raw civilians, possessed of sufficient "pride, intelligence, and educa-

---

[339] Higginson, *loc. cit.*, p. 355.

[340] *Ibid.*, p. 350.

[341] Numerous works on military tactics were advertised in the leading newspapers and magazines of the period, Winfield Scott's *Tactics* in three volumes, and William J. Hardee's *Tactics* in two volumes, were the favorites, but books on various phases of military life were abundant, see *Harper's Weekly*, vol. 5, May 18, 1861, *et seq.*

[342] Higginson, *loc. cit.*, p. 352.

tion, soon became excellent officers; though these very men most keenly regretted their lack of a good military education in early life." [343]

On the other hand we have the conviction of one of the better class volunteer officers that "on the whole, no regiments in the field made progress so rapid, or held their own so well, as those placed under regular officers. And now that three years [of war] have abolished many surmises, and turned many others into established facts, it must be owned that the total value of the professional training has proved far greater, and that of the general preparation far less, than many intelligent observers predicted." [344] This statement, coming as it does from one who would naturally be disposed to say the best words possible for the volunteer officers, is all the more convincing for its frankness, especially since it confirms the prevailing opinion of military experts of the day.

The same officer proceeds to explain the advantages that the West Point training gave to its recipients. Like any other professional education it contained nothing that any intelligent man could not learn in later life but that did not preclude the benefit of learning it in advance. No lawyer would trust a cadet to try his cases, yet there was no hesitancy on the part of the lawyer to presume to know more than the cadet. The general

---

[343] *McClellan's Own Story*, p. 97.

[344] Higginson, *loc. cit.*, p. 349. Higginson, an early abolitionist, was colonel of a regiment of negroes in South Carolina, of which he left his impressions in his book: *Army Life in a Black Regiment* (New York, 1896). He was described by his superior officer as "an able and accomplished officer," *Official Records*, series iii, vol. 4, p. 1027. Governor Andrew of Massachusetts called him a "brave and chivalrous gentleman of high culture," *idem*, vol. 3, p. 424. *Cf.* also his biographical sketch in *Appleton's Cyclopaedia of American Biography*.

standard of professional earnestness was higher among the West Pointers than among the volunteers [345] in spite of the exceptions to the rule which might indicate the reverse.

Yet relatively an infinitesimal portion of the volunteer-army officers, except the generals, were West Point men, and many even of the generals were equally ill prepared. West Point men outside the regular army were pretty sure of receiving some sort of a commission, usually on the staff of, or in some other way subordinate to, the politically appointed colonels; but the persistence of the War Department in maintaining both a regular and a volunteer army made it very difficult for a regular-army officer to be transferred to the volunteers. The result was that captains or lieutenants of regulars often were better trained than brigadier-generals of the volunteers.

Even so famous a general as Philip Henry Sheridan found it difficult to break loose from the regulars and might have spent his career there as a subaltern, or at best as a colonel, if General Henry W. Halleck had not, according to Sheridan's word, taken the responsibility of confirming his appointment as a colonel of volunteers, without consulting the War Department.[346] How many other "mute inglorious" Sheridans remained submerged in the regulars throughout the war, due to the short-sighted policy of the War Department, cannot, of course, be known. It is interesting, however, to note that Sheridan was not elevated from his captaincy until the latter part of May, 1862, and then almost as a matter of chance, whereas, on the other hand, the civilian poli-

---

[345] Higginson, *loc. cit.*, pp. 351-352.
[346] P. H. Sheridan, *Personal Memoirs* (New York, 1888), vol. 1, p. 141.

tician Benjamin F. Butler had been a year earlier
created a major-general. The later army careers of these
two men make further comment unnecessary.

Such were the officers, but what of the men? Here, at
least, the government could scarcely be blamed. It was
not responsible for the quality of the men who responded to the early calls to arms. It had never been
the policy of the United States, and has not been since,
to maintain a large standing army – and there is much
to be said in favor of this attitude. But regardless of the
merit or demerit of preparedness as a national policy,
no one person or group of persons was responsible for
the lack of any great trained force in 1861. The situation was one of national scope and had merely to be
reckoned with and its ill effects counteracted. There
seemed to be no need for conscription in 1861, although
the system had its defenders, and it would have been
practically impossible to have passed a conscription act
at that time. The only alternative then was to take whoever came and make the best of them. The responsibility for this latter duty was clearly upon the shoulders
of the War Department officials and was, for the time
being, enough to absorb their attention, had they had
the desire and the capacity to deal with it.

The Count of Paris was convinced that the men who
responded to the first calls for militia were far inferior
to the three-year men who followed. He regarded them
as representing the unemployed classes of America,
who desired a three-months' summer outing at the expense of the government, and referred to some of the
regiments as the scum of the larger cities.[347] This judgment is undoubtedly harsh, but, in extenuation of it, it

---

[347] Count of Paris, *Civil War*, vol. 1, pp. 176, 178.

must be remembered that he was merely describing what he saw. Without question some of the militia regiments were thoroughly deserving of this description but it is equally certain that many of the three-months regiments were made up of men fully the equivalent in calibre of any produced by the war. Most of the evils which he attributed to the quality of the first volunteers can better be traced to the kind of training they received, or rather to the lack of training. Even the most illiterate negroes later became efficient soldiers when placed under capable officers. Therefore it seems that, after all, in considering the quality of the volunteers, the attributes most worthy of notice are those that pertained to their amenability to discipline.

The Wilson Zouaves were undoubtedly a hard lot of men but their fighting qualities were unquestionable. Their officers, including Colonel Wilson, were more responsible than the men for the lack of discipline that they to the last displayed.[348] It is an exceptional soldier who will not take advantage of a weak officer especially in a democratic country with as extensive a frontier life as the United States possessed in 1861. The worst that can be said of the volunteers as a class is that they were thoroughly untrained, even in the use of fire arms; that they had little conception of the tasks that lay before them; and that they had the traditional American attitude of ingrained opposition to the army type of discipline. None of these were ineradicable defects: time and experience were sufficient to cope with the second, and wise discipline would have dissolved the other two.

As to the bravery of the first troops, the dismal failure

---

[348] *New York Tribune*, May 1, 4, 1861; *Harper's Weekly*, vol. 5 (November 9, 1861), p. 705; Count of Paris, *op. cit.*, p. 176.

at Bull Run needs only to be checked by the brilliant
fight at Wilson's Creek in Missouri to show that cowardice was no essential trait of the militia. General
Lyon, with his dying words, expressed his admiration
for the work of the volunteers.[349] Even at Bull Run
the blunders were more those of the officers than of the
men.

A surprisingly large number of recruits, even from
the frontier states, were totally ignorant of the use of
firearms, but the most difficult trait of the men to be
inhibited was the one which, on all ordinary occasions,
was most harmless – their democracy. Observers, both
foreign and domestic, officers and privates, were agreed
on this point. The general criticism of the American
army by foreigners was that the soldiers were superior
to the officers. The officers could lead the men but
could not command them. To one volunteer officer the
reason for this was plain: "three years are not long
enough to overcome the settled habits of twenty years."
The weak point of the volunteer service was that the
soldier detested taking orders and the officer shrank
from commanding. The soldier would comply with a
reasonable order but he did so because it was reasonable, not because it was an order. If seemingly unfair
or trifling orders were issued, the officers found that
they had not soldiers but free and independent citizens
to deal with.[350]

To the privates it seemed that they were punished
for very trivial offenses. "To them, in their greenness,
the taking a bit of rest when on guard, some disorder of
dress on parade, leaving a horse once ungroomed, might

---

[349] L. D. Ingersoll, *Iowa and the Rebellion* (Philadelphia, 1866), p. 31;
Wilkie, *The Iowa First*, p. 109.

[350] Higginson, *loc. cit.*, p. 350.

be contrary to strict army regulations, but were not criminal, and the volunteers were not hireling soldiery, but free and independent American citizens. This spirit, the necessary result of American institutions, was hard to control in the army. Indeed it was never wholly controlled, though it was slowly subordinated to higher considerations, through that good sense which hard experience taught the volunteers. Gradually they learned the value, the necessity, of discipline." [351]

The American representative of the London *Times* was less charitable in his criticism. "It is hard to teach Americans discipline," he said, "Their regular army has been for the most part composed of Germans and Irish. The people are averse to obedience on principle; and even children, as I have observed, particularly in the North, are less manageable . . . than in the old fashioned country, where the fifth commandment is held in respect." Though his criticism was harsh, his conclusion checks with the rest, that every man felt himself sovereign and resented orders from officers. [352] Editorial comment in the *New York Tribune* admitted a measure of truth in his statement but expressed a hope that the condition would not be abiding.

Very little respect could be expected from such independent men for such inept officers – and as little was shown. They felt their equality or superiority to their officers and even the latter could sometimes sense and resent it. The ignorant officer was likely to attempt to disguise his lack of skill under a domineering exterior, and resentment rather than salutary effect was the result. But more often there was an easy familiarity be-

---

[351] Scott, *op. cit.*, p. 14.

[352] W. H. Russell, in *New York Tribune*, September 4, 1861.

tween officers and men which made rigid discipline impossible. Too often both officers and men came from the same neighborhood, to which they all intended to return. They had known each other and each others' peculiarities all their lives. The privates could not bring themselves to call by anything but his first name, or to salute with decorum, the village lawyer, undertaker, or livery-stable flunky, even if he were now a captain or a lieutenant.

On the other hand the politician, lawyer, or tradesman, if an officer, looked upon his men as clients, customers, constituents, or rivals. As such he did not wish to offend them in matters of discipline, and have the occasion remembered against him later in civil life.[353] As a foreign prince saw it the officer "is simply a comrade who wears a different costume. He is obeyed in everyday routine, but voluntarily. In the same way, the soldiers don't trouble themselves about him when circumstances become serious. . . . In the eyes of the greater number this title of volunteer does not signify the soldier who devotes himself generously and voluntarily to save the country or to acquire glory, but rather the well-paid soldier who only does what he wishes and pleases." [354]

This situation was rendered even worse by the system of election of officers. A premium was placed upon popularity rather than on ability. The candidate had to stoop to all the practices of the politician. Fortunately there were no babies to kiss, but there were truculent voters to be appeased, and the time-honored practices of rousing their interest and support had to be

---

[353] Higginson, *loc. cit.*, p. 350; Joinville, *op. cit.*, p. 15.
[354] Joinville, *op. cit.*, p. 16.

employed. But the officer, when elected, was, because of his closer contact with his constituency, more bound by his campaign promises than was the case of his brother politician outside the army. If the decision of the soldiers was ignored by the colonel the heritage of resentment made life miserable for the supposedly fortunate recipient of the commission. If the election were sustained the incumbent was bound by his promises. Either result was bad but still the soldiers clung to their right of election with dogged persistency. When gradually, by 1863, the system was changed to appointment and promotion for merit, the men were very unwilling to give up the practice.[355]

Whatever the mode of selection the attitude of the men toward the officers varied according to the conduct of the officers toward the men. The discomfiture of an officer was a treat to the privates, and the more important the officer the greater the fun. If the commanding general were thrown from his horse, the situation could be made more delectable only if his landing place were a mud-puddle.[356] A command from a corporal was considered as an impertinence and, if repeated, might even result in a reprimand from the offended person. Sergeants and corporals were mere necessary evils to facilitate drill and were obeyed or not according to the way the soldiers felt about it.[357] The sergeant pleading with his squad and the private patronizing his captain were even made the subjects for illumination by the popular cartoonists.[358]

---

[355] Scott, *op. cit.*, pp. 21-22; *Harper's Weekly*, vol. 5 (September 7, 1861), p. 562.

[356] *Downing's Diary*, p. 84; Sperry, *op. cit.*, p. 74.

[357] Jones, *op. cit.*, p. 46.

[358] See *Harper's Weekly*, vol. 5 (May 18, July 20, 1861), pp. 320, 464.

So numerous were the easy-going or inefficient officers that the occasional strict disciplinarian, even
though not personally obnoxious found himself in a
very trying situation. For instance a lieutenant-colonel,
who had the uncomfortable habit of denouncing incapacity wherever he found it, quickly became "the one
powerful man in the camp,– the most hated, feared, and
admired." Yet he received but little support from either
officers or men, was met constantly with as much difficulty and obstruction as could be put in his way, and
finally gave up the struggle and resigned. "But it had
already come about [by 1865] that he was spoken of in
the Fourth Iowa with great respect and admiration,
and with sincere interest in his career; for the volunteers had in the meantime learned something of sol-
diering." [359]

Merit of this kind was usually not recognized until
too late. A sentinel in the Missouri campaigns was arrested for killing his colonel, supposedly by accident,
though many thought it to be a murder. He was tried
and acquitted in spite of strong evidence of his guilt.
The animus ascribed was that the officer was very competent and therefore "among his soldiers he was fearfully unpopular. He was, however, a splendid disciplinarian, but this was something the volunteers did
not want. In their minds the colonel had been only a
petty tyrant, and not even wholly loyal. . . . More than
once his life had been threatened by soldiers who regarded themselves as having been badly treated by
him." [360]

With such officers and such men and the prevailing

---

[359] Scott, *op. cit.*, pp. 14-15.
[360] Byers, *With Fire and Sword*, pp. 26-27.

relationships between them, the matter of drill and other military training was largely a farce. The officers, if diligent, managed to keep just one or two jumps ahead of the men in the mastery of Scott's or Hardee's *Tactics,* the *Army Regulations,* and the *Articles of War.* Then, having learned a lesson, they went forth and showed their superior knowledge by teaching it to the soldiers, and reprimanding or punishing them for their mistakes.[361] "The struggles of the officers were of course continually reflected upon the men, and they were drilled and taught, formed and reformed, pulled and hawled, put through movements and evolutions more or less correct or incorrect, impossible or astonishing. . . . The blind led the blind, and often both fell into the ditch, though not always at the same time; and the vexation of an anxious officer was many times only the occasion for unfeeling amusement on the part of his pupils, thrown into confusion by his mistakes."[362]

Imagine the consternation of the colonel who, as a stimulus to his memory, had written all his orders for a drill on slips of paper, when his horse shied causing him to lose the handful of slips. He was at a total loss how to proceed further so simply called his line officers to him and told them to march their companies back to quarters. To make matters worse, not all of the line officers remembered the order for deploying a column, and so were obliged merely to dismiss the men as they stood.[363]

A parallel situation occurred when a company was approaching a large open ditch and the commander

[361] Jones, *op. cit.,* p. 44; *Harper's Weekly,* vol. 6 (August 23, 1862), p. 542.
[362] Scott, *op. cit.,* pp. 15-16.
[363] Jones, *op. cit.,* p. 45.

forgot what command to give and so called out "Look out for that ditch!" The men, not understanding the order, tried to emulate the Hebrews in their passage of the Red Sea but came nearer to repeating the drama enacted by their Egyptian pursuers.[364]

Sometimes even regular officers found themselves at a loss to know how much to expect of the raw volunteers. Consequently some of them relaxed in discipline to such an extent that their regiments got into a worse state than those of the volunteer officers. So much can be said for training without brains.[365]

On the other hand certain volunteer officers grew very adept at manipulating their men. When the books on tactics failed to give anything complicated enough for them, they would invent fanciful drills of their own.[366] But, in all the pretty capers that they learned to cut, or in the more stolid drill of the rest of the army, one will search in vain to find any great emphasis on rifle or musket shooting. Such a task does not seem to have been considered as a necessary part of the soldiers' training, though many, perhaps most of them were totally unversed in the use of firearms.

Many of the results of this lack of discipline were far from being of a harmless nature. Neglect of officers was responsible for much suffering and many disasters or near disasters. Even troops on guard duty, when near the enemy, were left without any adequate inspection during many hours of the night. Late in September, 1861, a more than usually zealous major, who was temporarily commanding the guard of a brigade near

---

[364] *Downing's Diary*, p. 16.
[365] Higginson, *loc. cit.*, p. 349.
[366] Jones, *op. cit.*, p. 42.

Washington, sent out an officer to make a report of conditions in the guard. "He stated in his report the next morning that he had entered the camps of twelve regiments, without being stopped, or even challenged, walking around freely everywhere with his men. In the sixty-second New York he had found seven sentinels asleep, rolled up in their blankets. Finally, what seemed hardy credible, he went into the deserted tent of the colonel of the Nineteenth Indiana, whence he carried off the flag of the regiment without anyone's being present to oppose it." Yet at that very time the Confederates were encamped only a short distance across the river from them.[367]

Another efficient and reliable officer writes, "I have ridden by night along a chain of ten sentinels, every one of whom should have taken my life rather than permit me to give the countersign without dismounting, and have been required to dismount by only four, while two did not ask me for the countersign at all, and two others were asleep." This was a regiment that had been in the service for almost two years and had just been detached from the old Army of the Potomac.[368]

So rampant was negligence that officers even gave it as an excuse to escape penalities for worse offenses. Thus a high officer was acquitted of the ruinous charge of false muster only by having witnesses swear that he was in the habit of signing all papers without looking at them. A lieutenant, tried for neglect of duty for allowing a soldier on important picket duty to be found with two inches of sand in the bottom of his gun, pleaded for mitigation of his sentence, that it had never

[367] Trobriand, *op. cit.*, pp. 87-88.
[368] Higginson, *loc. cit.*, p. 355.

been the practice in his regiment to inspect the guns of men on picket duty. And this was after three years of warfare.[369]

A commission inspecting conditions in the camps around Washington and Fortress Monroe and in the Army of the Potomac, in July, 1861, found such varied conditions that not even the shortage of clothing and supplies would explain them. While a majority of the camps were in good order, there was indescribable filth around others and no provision was being made for sanitation. Lack of clothing was easily accounted for but, when soldiers failed to change their underwear for six weeks at a time in the middle of the summer, their officers were directly culpable. In some regiments it seemed that there was collusion between colonels and quartermasters to cheat the men out of their allowances. Some men were getting full rations and others almost nothing while the officers were loafing around in Washington. At the same time other officers went to the opposite extreme of being too zealous in drilling and punishing men,[370] resorting to all the meaner forms of castigation for which the army was notorious, with the exception of flogging, which had fortunately been abolished shortly before the war.

Other problems of discipline were the direct result of insuppressible tendencies on the part of certain men, which would have severely taxed the abilities and patience of expert officers. Freed from the restraint of home, or never having known moderation, many soldiers were inclined to take possession of the cities where their regiments were quartered. Marching about the

---

[369] *Ibid.*, p. 354.
[370] *New York Tribune*, July 17, 1861.

streets, even Pennsylvania Avenue in Washington, without restraint, turbulent, and pillaging almost at will, they kept in turmoil the localities which they infested.[371] A woman from Yonkers, New York, wrote that the town was terrorized by the lawlessness of some of the recruits in a regiment quartered there. Rough loud talk in the streets, lack of respect for private property, and insults to women had roused the ire of the populace.[372] Colonel Ephraim E. Ellsworth, one of the early hero martyrs of the war, unable to quell certain violent spirits in his zouaves, was compelled to expel them from the regiment and turn them over to the civil authorities.[373] Without any deliberately evil intention a great many soldiers, otherwise lawabiding, were willing to take advantage of their liberties, under lax disciplinary conditions, and commit acts of minor vandalism.

Of a more serious nature was the effect of poor discipline upon the soldiers when under fire. The Prince de Joinville said of them that in battle the regiments would march against the enemy and fight bravely, but when they thought they had done as much as military honor required they would, by tacit agreement, all march off together.[374] No doubt the Prince was honest enough in his statement but the picture is far from accurate. An organization that would by tacit agreement *march* off the battle field sounds too much like a soldiers' soviet to apply to the volunteers of 1861 – they did not have that much organization among them. They might, as individuals, flee in terror or, as at Bull Run, discipline might be thrown to the winds, and colonels,

371 Trobriand, *op. cit.*, pp. 63, 78.
372 *New York Tribune*, June 6, 1861.
373 *Ibid.*, May 9, 1861.
374 Joinville, *op. cit.*, p. 16.

majors, and captains lead in the flight from the enemy. But this was no "tacit agreement": it was every man for himself and the devil take the hindmost.

Bull Run is the classic example of the breakdown of discipline in the Civil War. The nature of the collapse is well illustrated in the flight of a regiment known as the "First Regiment of Fire Zouaves" from New York. The fire department of New York City, hearing of their inglorious haste, made an investigation shortly afterward and found only 217 men in the camp at Alexandria, including twenty-five who were in prison for desertion. Twenty-five were in the hospital and 150 were straggling about in Washington, or between there and Philadelphia headed for New York. On the other hand the number of the regiment killed or taken prisoner at Bull Run was estimated at 220, though no doubt many of these were deserters. The excuse offered by the men for their precipitate flight was that they were deserted by their officers and had to shift for themselves. One soldier said he had been ordered to retreat at Manassas and never got the word to halt, so, like a dutiful soldier, he just kept on going. The regiment was so shattered by the experience that it had to undergo a thorough reorganization before being ready for the field again.[375]

Such cowardice as this was equalled only by the unseemly and almost indecent haste of the militiamen to hasten home at the very hour of the expiration of their three months' service. From the West came the news that "the time of the First Iowa Regiment will soon be out – the men in their intense anxiety to clasp to their bosoms their wives and children, and to taste the lager

---

[375] *New York Tribune,* August 9, 12, 13, 1861.

brewed in their native villages, refuse to continue in service for any material length of time beyond the three months for which they enlisted." [376] A similar comment on the eastern militia was preserved in a cartoon inscribed "an Affectionate Testimonial to The Pennsylvania Fourth, and to Varian's (N. Y.) Field Battery." In it an officer is represented as shouting to his men "Forward Boys! Show them your steel." But the fleeing soldiers reply "Thank ye Cap'n – We're off home the three months are up Hurrah!!" [377]

But it would be unfair to mention these particular organizations without stating that they are merely examples and fairly representative of the first volunteer troops. Even the career of the Wilson Zouaves, so widely noted for their desperate character and uncontrollable impetuosity, came to an ignominious climax only a few months after Bull Run when, taken by surprise, they escaped complete rout only by the arrival of re-enforcements. Here again lack of capable officers and discipline was to blame. Colonel Wilson himself received public censure for "the inefficiency and want of skill displayed in the action." He did not even arrive upon the scene until all was over. [378]

The culmination of such evils is disclosed in the worst crimes of the soldier: desertion, sometimes combined with treason, and mutiny. The problem of desertion during the war is deserving of a special treatise but, due to its connection with the problem of discipline, some mention must be made of it here. A total of 260,339 desertions from the ranks was reported for

[376] Wilkie, *op. cit.*, p. 85.
[377] *Harper's Weekly*, vol. 5 (September 7, 1861), p. 576.
[378] *Ibid.* (November 9, 1861), p. 705.

the period of the war, in addition to another 161,286 desertions for failure to appear when drafted.[379]

The first item, at least, is directly attributable to the laxity of discipline. The comment of a private concerning his own experience is illustrative of one of the reasons why there was one desertion for every eleven enlistments throughout the war. Speaking of conditions at Camp Curtin in Pennsylvania more than a year after the beginning of the war, he tells of the sentinels being armed with clubs and of soldiers coming and going as they pleased. "We rushed the guards to go bathing in the river, and we did duty generally when it was convenient." With apparently no feeling of shame he tells how he himself was absent on one occasion for three days on a visit to a neighboring town and, even after that extended visit, was not reported as a deserter.[380] If all such excursions had been reported as desertions, as they might have been, the total would have undoubtedly been far larger than that cited. But most of such desertions were never reported. A liberal estimate of the number of stragglers who returned voluntarily to the ranks is placed at twenty-five per cent. leaving nearly 200,000 actual and complete desertions.[381]

The return home of the militia regiments after Bull Run was thoroughly legal and, except in the popular sense, could not be termed desertion. Yet the refusal of many of these soldiers to re-enlist for three years or the war, especially at a time when the whole North was alarmed over the probable outcome of the war, was

[379] *Official Records*, series iii, vol. 5, pp. 109, 600.
[380] C. A. Ramsey, "Story of Headquarters Clerk and Sergeant Major," in *The 148th Pennsylvania Volunteers*, p. 336.
[381] *Official Records*, series iii, vol. 5, p. 109.

looked upon with extreme disapprobation by the loyal part of the population. It was thought that patriotic wives and sweethearts should spurn their men for such an inglorious homecoming,[382] yet there were daily reports of the return of such regiments, during the months of July and August. Individuals re-enlisted but companies and regiments seldom.[383] This is at least a partial justification of the harsh judgment passed by men who, like the Count of Paris, felt that the three-months militia were the poorest fighting material produced by the war. But viewed in the light of the execrable training they had received one is still left in doubt.

One unsalutary result of this exodus was mutiny in some of the remaining regiments. There were two or three cases of open revolt in the army about Washington and, had they not been promptly suppressed by the vigor of the newly appointed McClellan, the spirit would undoubtedly have spread much farther through the Army of the Potomac. The principal disturbance was in the New York Seventy-ninth, with lesser outbreaks in the Twenty-first and the Thirteenth. The trouble was over the length of service. These men had enrolled for three years or the war, understanding by that that the war would be over in a few weeks and that the "three years" phrase was merely a precautionary measure on the part of the government. But Bull Run disillusionized them and they felt tricked. Accordingly, when the militia began to return, they wanted to go also.

The Seventy-ninth was a regiment composed mainly of Scotch Highlanders who were good fighters but

---

[382] See cartoon, *Harper's Weekly*, vol. 5 (August 10, 1861), p. 510.
[383] *New York Tribune*, July, August, *passim*.

intractable in disposition. The officers were incompetent, and it seems that a large number of the men were drunk. Desertions had occurred until 140 of the men were missing at roll call. Then came an order for the regiment to march into Virginia, and it was met with refusal. No time was wasted in dealing with the insurgents. Colonel Andrew Porter was sent with a battalion, a squadron, and a battery of regulars, who drew up in front of the mutineers and prepared to mow them down if they did not submit. At once the rebellion collapsed. The ringleaders were arrested and put in irons and the rest of the men were marched into Virginia, according to previous orders. Thereafter the regiment did good service. After a month their colors were restored and the incident was closed.[384]

In another case a regiment was brought to order by transporting sixty-three officers and men to the Dry Tortugas to labor during the remainder of the war. Since neither regiment gave any further trouble after the initial display of discipline the judgment of Mc-Clellan may be sustained when he said, "I think the trouble arose rather from poor officers than from the men." [385]

For the improvement in discipline that began late in 1861, the experience gained in battles was largely responsible. The skirmish at Big Bethel, Virginia (June 10, 1861), was considered to have "emancipated us, cheaply enough, from the mischief of civilian brigadiers." [386] Bull Run certainly exhibited the weaknesses

---

[384] *McClellan's Own Story*, pp. 99-100; *New York Tribune*, August 17, 23, September 16, 1861.

[385] *McClellan's Own Story*, p. 100.

[386] *Harper's Weekly*, vol. 5 (August 10, 1861), p. 499. For report of the skirmish see *Official Records*, series i, vol. 2, pp. 77-104.

of a large number of colonels and minor officers and
led to a demand for a better system of selection of officers. "Better offend a thousand ambitious candidates
for military rank," said a critic, "than have another
flight led by colonels, majors, and captains." [387] A representative conclusion from the affair of Ball's Bluff
(October 21, 1861) was that the men were better as
soldiers than their officers were as leaders and commanders.[388]

The active agents in the improvement of discipline
were competent officers who, here and there, were able
to assert their influence and give something like real organization to their troops. First in the list of such organizers should be mentioned George Brinton McClellan.
McClellan's fame has long been eclipsed by that of more
illustrious leaders later in the war. His conceit undoubtedly lessened his effectiveness as a commanding general, and his policy of over preparedness and extreme
caution are perhaps rightly assigned as his chief blunders in the Peninsular Campaign. But, when compared
with his successors, John Pope, Ambrose E. Burnside,
Joseph Hooker, and even Halleck, he appears in a
much more favorable light. It is doubtful whether his
conduct after Antietam was any more remiss than that
of George G. Meade after Gettysburg. As a leader in
battle he will probably rank as one of the half dozen
greatest generals produced by the Union. But his fame
today would be much greater if he had been retained
for the duties for which he was best fitted, and had
never been given complete charge of the Army of the
Potomac in the field. Not even his enemies will detract

---

[387] *Harper's Weekly*, vol. 5 (August 10, 1861), p. 499.

[388] Trobriand, *op. cit.*, p. 125. For report of the affair see *Official Records,*
series i, vol. 5, pp. 289-372.

from his ability and work as an organizer or as an engineer, and, now that the political rancor of the sixties is but a memory, it is time for us to view McClellan more from the point of view of his constructive work rather than of his shortcomings.

When he took charge of the Army of the Potomac it was composed of about 50,000 infantry, an infinitesimal portion of cavalry, and a few batteries of artillery. This army was loosely organized, undisciplined, and both men and officers were swarming about the streets of Washington, with little or no regard to the proprieties of *Army Regulations*.[389] Immediately he undertook the work of reorganization. His first order was for the reconstruction of the general staff, in order to secure capable officers for directing the work that was to follow. His second order directed the return to their camps of the numerous officers and men who were "in the habit of frequenting the streets and hotels of the city," reminding them of the numerous duties that they owed to their commands.

To carry out this command he appointed Colonel Andrew Porter as provost-marshal in Washington, with orders to report for further instructions.[390] The results were immediate. Only a few days later an observer stated that Colonel Porter "has already begun his work by closing up the liquor saloons in the capital, around which much drunkenness and riotous conduct has existed for some days past."[391]

McClellan's own opinion of the value of his work is, of course, very favorable but as temperate as could be

---

[389] *Official Records*, series i, vol. 5, p. 11.

[390] *Idem*, vol. 51, part i, pp. 428, 430. Orders dated July 27 and July 30, 1861.

[391] *Harper's Weekly*, vol. 5 (August 17, 1861), p. 515.

expected. "With new troops," he said, "frequent reviews are of the greatest utility and produce the most excellent effect. Those I held did much towards making the Army of the Potomac what it became." His policy, he said further, was not to try to make an army of regulars out of the volunteers but simply to get them in condition to be handled on march and in the field, and to carry out orders. It was the "time and labor upon the organization and instruction of that army" that got it in shape so that its "courage, discipline, and efficiency finally brought the war to a close."[392]

In giving credit to the Army of the Potomac for winning the war, he fails to mention the influence of other men who succeeded him in leading and maintaining the organization of the army. Yet in statement of actual accomplishment, he is more moderate than some others, and his testimony checks well with the current observation of the time. Throughout the winter of 1861-1862 great progress was made in instruction, discipline, and organization in all branches of the service. There was constant drill by battalion, brigade, and division. At Tenallytown there was even that rarely reported activity, target practice.[393]

Camp Defiance at Cairo, Illinois, at first under command of Brigadier-general Benjamin M. Prentiss, was another of the camps which was favored with efficient control, and almost from the beginning. In spite of the extremely bad physiographical conditions at that point, the medical service was good, the hospitals well conducted, and the troops were kept in splendid condition and were well drilled. By early fall it was felt that they

---

[392] *McClellan's Own Story,* p. 98.
[393] Trobriand, *op. cit.,* p. 119.

were well prepared to take the field.[394] It was from this camp that Grant took the troops that distinguished themselves at Fort Donelson.

The process by which efficiency was attained was no doubt often painful to the volunteer officers. It included, in the words of one of these officers, having "some young regular army lieutenant ride up to your tent at an hour's notice, and leisurely devote a day to probing every weak spot in your command,— to stand by while he smells at every camp-kettle, detects every delinquent gun-sling, ferrets out old shoes from behind mess-bunks, spies out every tent pole not labelled with the sergeant's name, asks to see the cash balance of each company fund, and perplexes your best captain on forming from two ranks into one by the left flank. Yet it is just such unpleasant processes as these which are the salvation of an army; these petty mortifications are the fulcrum by which you can lift your whole regiment to a first-class rank, if you have only the sense to use them. So long as no inspecting officer needs twice to remind you of the same thing, you have no need to blush. . . . He may be the most conceited little popinjay who ever strutted in uniform; no matter; it is more for your interest to learn than for his to teach." [395]

In addition to developing the best talent of officers who had any to develop, it was equally essential to get rid of the hopelessly incompetent — and their name was legion. Horace Greeley, with his usual penchant for criticism as often wise as otherwise, came out in the *Tribune* just a day before Bull Run, recommending: (1) examinations for all officers; (2) transportation to

---

[394] Chetlain, *op. cit.*, p. 79; *Harper's Weekly*, vol. 5 (June 1, 1861), p. 350.
[395] Higginson, *loc. cit.*, p. 353.

training camp immediately after enlistment; (3) reservation of the right to place men in other regiments than those which they originally chose; and (4) making recruiting officers responsible for completing regiments they had started.[396]

Each of these items was aimed at a current abuse, and all were intended to allay excusable discontent. But the first is of special interest since it was just a step in advance of a provision of congress enacted two days later, and which may have been his source of inspiration. In the army act of July 22, 1861, provision was made for a military commission in each military department to examine all officers in volunteer regiments and remove all adjudged incompetent; no officer, however, was to be removed without the approval of the President.[397]

Orders for the execution of the law were promptly issued,[398] and within a month its effect was being seen. Many incompetent officers who realized their deficiencies resigned immediately rather than be humiliated by failure to pass a rigid examination. Any person failing to report for examination when summoned was considered as having vacated his position, thus rendering subterfuges very difficult.[399] When the board was appointed at Washington, two colonels and twenty-five other commissioned officers resigned from one division immediately after their summons. On November 1 was published a list of thirty-eight discharges, and a few days later a list of over one hundred "resignations,"

[396] New York Tribune, July 20, 1861.
[397] U. S. Statutes at Large, vol. 12, p. 270.
[398] Official Records, series iii, vol. 1, p. 349.
[399] Harper's Weekly, vol. 5 (August 17, 1861), p. 515.

mostly of captains and lieutenants, but reaching up in a few instances to major and colonel.[400]

This latter point is significant – the number of colonels either resigning or being discharged was remarkably low in comparison with officers of lower grades. The reason is apparent. Colonels, though no better trained than privates, were often of too much importance politically to be antagonized. There is, of course, no direct evidence that political influence was brought to bear in the trials, but considering the number of incompetent colonels who continued to retain their commands, the situation can scarcely be considered as a mere oversight.

The examination requirement was hailed as an improvement, as it undoubtedly was, but its indirect effect in discouraging indiscriminate appointments and acceptances seems to have been greater than its direct effect in dismissing or securing the resignation of those already in office. In an army so extravagant of officers as to create 2,537 generals, including those by brevet,[401] or one general for every battalion (on the present model) raised during the war, and with minor officers in proportion, it cannot be expected that a few hundred dismissals or resignations would work any revolution in the discipline, especially since the new appointees were not likely to be very greatly superior to those they superseded. The vacancies were required by law to be filled by election, so but little net benefit could be expected of the result.

These various influences all tended toward better

---

[400] *New York Tribune*, September 27, November 1, 16, 1861.

[401] Phisterer, *Statistical Record of the Armies of the United States*, pp. 247-316.

organization and discipline, but neither individually nor collectively were they capable of achieving anything like the machine like precision of regulars. The whole process toward better discipline was one of tardy evolution, directed to a certain extent and urged on very strenuously by pressure from above. A sprinkling of regular-army officers among the staffs and an occasional brigadier-general or colonel here and there, who had received West Point training, exerted an influence which gradually percolated down through the ranks and tended to give more and more coherence to the mass. Efficient colonels or generals, though compelled to select their staffs from civil life, were able to impart to them enough of technical knowledge of a practical nature to render them of great service to their organizations.

This instruction was largely of an informal character and might well have been supplied in officers' schools to many more men and with much less effort and waste of time, if anybody had had the foresight and energy necessary to initiate the project. The consequence of this failure was that, to the very last, organization and discipline were unevenly distributed. But the tendency, due to lessons of experience, was in the direction of betterment. As officers were removed by examining boards or by courts-martial, or as they were killed in battle, opportunities were created for supplying their places with better material. Soldiers learned to vote for, and officials learned to appoint, efficient and courageous officers, so that the service was gradually improved, though it never even remotely approached the French model of 1794.

Taking the ordnance service as a model, for so it was considered, an official said of it: "Every ordnance blank now contains a schedule of instructions for its own use, so simple and so minute that it seems as if, henceforward, the most negligent volunteer officer could never make another error. And yet in the very last set of returns which the writer had occasion to revise,– returns made by a very meritorious captain,– there were eight different papers, and a mistake in every one." [402]

In general the process of natural selection and survival of the fittest worked better in the lower grades of officers than in the higher. The law for examination of officers did not apply to grades above that of colonel, and consequently there was no easily-available instrument for dislodging them. As a writer in 1864 aptly expressed it, "Those who remain are among the senior officers in our volunteer army, in their respective grades. They command posts, brigades, divisions. They preside at court-martials. Beneath the shadow of their notorious incompetency all minor evils may lurk undetected. To crown all, they are, in many cases, sincere and well meaning men, utterly obtuse as to their own deficiencies, and manifesting all the Christian virtues except that of resignation." [403]

In its later phases discipline was rendered simpler due to the knowledge, gained through experience, that the safety and well being of all depended upon coöperation and efficiency. Through constant dealings with men imbued with the democratic trait of self assertiveness, the officers learned to give only proper orders and, through increased knowledge of the value of army dis-

[402] Higginson, *loc. cit.*, pp. 354-355.
[403] *Ibid.*, p. 354.

cipline, the men learned to inhibit their self assertiveness and obey all reasonable orders without cavil.[404]

Increasing the size of the army after the first year did not increase the problem of discipline. With the abandonment of the policy of accepting new organizations, all new recruits went to fill up the depleted ranks of old regiments. The operation of state and federal drafts disposed of the soldiers obtained in the same way. Thus the neighborhood "soviet" gave way to a more cosmopolitan organization less likely to be controlled by petty jealousies and rivalries. The incoming recruits fought by the side of seasoned veterans and therefore developed into soldiers much more rapidly than their predecessors had. Moreover, the later volunteers did not have to unlearn so much as those of 1861. The hilarious effervescence of the Spring of 1861 gradually gave way to a dogged determination to win the war at any cost. The levies after Bull Run no longer looked upon the war as a three-months' excursion or a military demonstration, hence they more readily learned to sink their individualism beneath the demands of the general welfare.

Of course these lessons were being learned by the men in the army perhaps even more thoroughly than by those outside. Nevertheless the late comers profited much and the army was benefited all the more because of their having learned this much before enlistment. Of the attitude of mercenaries and conscripts more will be said in a later chapter, but this much of a forecast can be made here: the conscripts almost universally and the *bona fide* substitutes generally made good soldiers

---

[404] Jones, *op. cit.*, p. 46; Scott, *op. cit.*, p. 16; *Harper's Weekly*, vol. 6 (August 23, 1862), p. 542.

as compared with the standards of the army at that time. "Good soldiers [in an absolute sense] they were not – indeed, they were scarcely soldiers – but they were honest in their desires to become such, and this was the surest way of attaining that end." [405]

As a result of this haphazard method of throwing the troops together and organizing them like a volunteer fire brigade, the army actually was, what it was sometimes called, an armed mob – and not very well armed at that. The fact that this state of affairs did not have disastrous effects upon the Union does not add any glory to the administration or to the War Department. It merely is a result of the fact that the enemy was fewer in numbers, as poorly armed, and nearly as badly organized as the North. It is a significant fact that the Union did not conduct one single creditable fight in secession territory during the year 1861, and the minor successes in Missouri and western Virginia were merely the results of local struggles between the secession and loyal elements of those communities.

In the year which elapsed between the beginning of the war and the active attempts to invade the Confederacy through Virginia and Tennessee, the Union had ample time to create an efficient fighting machine. Starting with the regular army as a nucleus, it could have been expanded, utilized as a training school for officers, and have supplied enough trained officers for every brigade to continue the superintendence, direction, and instruction of the novices. The army could have been thoroughly equipped with modern weapons and trained to a point of efficiency not to be achieved till many months later. West Point-trained soldiers could have

---

[405] Count of Paris, *op. cit.*, vol. 1, pp. 176-177.

been given the chance to advance and assume the positions of chief responsibility, and the Union would not have suffered in the meantime by reason of the dilution of the regulars. If they were kept intact for national defense it is notorious that they were not used. At Bull Run there was less than a regiment of them, and they not so distributed or situated as to allay the panic of the rest.

The only plausible conclusion is that the almost complete abdication of authority on the part of the federal government in leaving to the states the initiative in raising the first troops, left the government in the precarious situation where, to try to wrest this control away from the states again, would result in bitterness and political bickerings on too extensive a scale for the party discipline to endure. Having once made this initial mistake it was difficult to recover national control, and so another element was contributed to the prolongation of the war.

Daily Life of the Soldier

Daily Life of the Soldier

THE soldiers departing for camp or for the front in the spring of 1861 were heroes to all who beheld them. Enthusiasm abounded on every hand and none were more enthusiastic than the boys themselves. The excursion was ready to begin and each soldier was determined to return, after a brief summer's campaign, covered with glory, marked perhaps by wounds, and prepared to preëmpt the position of local story-teller so long monopolized by the veterans of the Mexican War or the few lingering survivors of the War of 1812. The conquest of the "Secesh," the "Chivalry," or the "Johnny Rebs," was to elevate the knight errant to fame and perhaps to fortune. The celebrations at their departure and the receptions along the line of their journey were well calculated to stiffen their resolution to fight valiantly, suffer hardships and privations, bleed, and maybe die in defense of the flag.

At the stations the soldiers were serenaded by brass bands, presented with silk flags, and inundated with speeches and prayers. At the principal stops along the way they were met by the local militia or other volunteer companies, resplendent with color and brass, and paraded through the streets. Again they would listen to speeches by the mayors, the prominent citizens, by everybody who had oratorical aspirations and sufficient influence to secure an opportunity to air his eloquence. Sometimes they were feasted to such an extent that the recollections lingered for scores of years and seemingly suffered nothing in vividness from the lingering. "Tables were set along the sidewalk in the shade of magnificent trees, and these tables were literally loaded with all the good things that could tempt an epicure. There were, besides, fair ladies without number to welcome us, and wait upon our needs."[406]

With them the recruits carried all the little tokens and articles of comfort, necessary or otherwise, that sentiment could conceive of or fancy design: "patent estopples for our canteens; patent pocket filters; patent knapsacks; . . . havelocks, pincushions, bandages, and lint . . . small parcels of pepper and salt, writing materials, tiny Testaments, and large pieces of soap" all the product of Yankee inventiveness or feminine consideration or manufacture. And along with this they carried a mental store of "advice and suggestions from explorers, old campaigners, doctors, and fools [which] appeared from day to day in the newspapers." [407]

The short railroad lines and varying gauges of tracks of the period made changes from one train to another frequent, the stops long, the accommodations varied but never good. The roughness of the tracks made the speed seem faster than it really was, for the coaches seemed sometimes to run on only one side of their trucks at a time and to jump alternately back and forth first on one rail and then on the other. Men, provisions, and fuel were likely to be packed into the same car, but if, in the roughness of the travel, men, bacon, and cordwood became mixed up in the same pile it was merely

[406] Hinkley, *Third Wisconsin Infantry*, p. 7. See also Chetlain, *Recollections of Seventy Years*, pp. 72-73. One of the most complete accounts of the daily life is J. D. Billings, *Hardtack and Coffee* (Boston, c. 1887).

[407] E. R. Jones, *Army of the Potomac*, pp. 43-44.

another source of merriment for the rest. The constant cheering from men, women, and "niggers" sustained the good spirits and prevented them from forgetting the importance of their mission.[408]

Of such situations the telegraph promptly apprized the people at home, and they at once began to attribute a premature heroism to the soldiers and to magnify their hardships. The public demanded excitement and it was going to get it if it had to help in the creation of it. The following is a fair example of the news received at home: "The gallant Seventh [New York] has already had quite a taste of the hardships of campaign life. Not a wink of sleep have its members enjoyed since they left New York. From 2 A. M. to 3 P. M., they waited in the Baltimore depot for orders from Washington. A wearisome task it was, but they bore up under it like true soldiers. A merrier and more determined crowd was never seen. They all longed for a brush with the Baltimore 'Plug Uglies'." [409]

Sometimes, especially in the West, railroads were far distant and the men had to be hauled in wagons, or to march forty or fifty miles to the nearest depot,[410] but in one way or another they arrived at their destination and the duties of camp life succeeded the festivities and sleepless nights that had preceded. Of course it must be understood that these scenes were not reënacted with each company that left in the later periods of the war. Each community, as its first soldiers left, had its spell of celebration but, as contingent followed contingent and the war dragged on into months and years, the enthusiasm simmered down to individual leave-

---

[408] Wilkie, *The Iowa First*, p. 47.
[409] *New York Tribune*, April 22, 1861.
[410] Byers, *With Fire and Sword*, p. 13.

takings, and whatever zeal was left was expended in trying, by fair means or foul, to fill the quotas and avoid the stigma of a draft.

Having arrived at their destination the troops often found that no provision had been made to quarter them, and so they had to take possession of any means of shelter that the situation afforded. For instance the first regiments arriving at Keokuk, Iowa, were housed in empty halls, store buildings, and elsewhere and one company was located in the court-house, where the troops, bedded down on clean straw, were much more comfortable than in their later camps.[411]

Even more elegantly situated were some of the regiments at Washington which were sheltered temporarily in the United States Capitol, the Patent Office, and the Georgetown College buildings. Of the Rhode Island troops "bunking" in the Patent Office it was asserted that "never since American inventive genius was first aroused did the Patent Office contain such remarkable models of American manufacture as those which now sleep three deep in 'bunks' spread along the edge of the cabinets. . . ."

It was an Irish regiment that was accommodated by the Georgetown College halls [412] while some Massachusetts and New York regiments had marble-trimmed barracks in the Capitol. The Massachusetts Eighth was placed under the dome, which, open at the top, reminded them of a large Sibley tent. The Massachusetts Sixth, famed for its skirmish with the Baltimore mob, occupied the Senate Chamber, while the New York Seventh was consigned to the chamber of the House of

---

[411] Upham, "Arms and Equipment," in *Iowa Journal*, vol. 16, p. 45.

[412] *Harper's Weekly*, vol. 5 (June 1, 1861), p. 347.

Representatives. Here they thronged and tramped around at will, writing or sitting on the desks in the daytime and sleeping under them at night. "We joked, we shouted, we sang," said a New York militiaman. "We mounted the Speaker's desk and made speeches,– always to the point; for if any but a wit ventured to give tongue, he was coughed down without ceremony. Let the M. C.'s [*sic*] adopt this plan and silence their dunces." [413]

The stores and accessories of these amateur legislators were heaped about as promiscuously as the men. The galleries under the Senate Chamber were converted into granaries and larders, huge ovens capable of baking 16,000 loaves a day were installed in other parts of the basement, and the courtyard of the Treasury building was reserved for cooking and eating arrangements. [414]

Meanwhile the government was rushing to supply tents and soon gave them out in profusion. There were at first two principal kinds of these; for officers, wall tents ten feet square and with three-foot walls on the sloping sides; for non-commissioned officers and privates, wedge tents six feet square and named for their shape. In the Army of the Potomac each regiment was supplied with two tents each for the colonel, lieutenant-colonel, major, and adjutant, two for two surgeons, one for each captain, one for the two lieutenants of each company all of the wall variety, besides 250 wedge tents for the men and two hospital tents, each fourteen by fifteen feet in floor area. [415]

---

[413] Theodore Winthrop, "Washington as a Camp," in *Atlantic Monthly*. vol. 8 (July, 1861), pp. 105-108; *New York Tribune*, May 7, 1861.

[414] *Harper's Weekly*, vol. 5 (May 25, 1861), pp. 326, 331.

[415] Trobriand, *Army of Potomac*, p. 79.

But the tent most favored in the early days, used by some regiments, and adopted for the regulars was the Sibley tent, named for its inventor. It was a cone sixteen feet in diameter at the base, supported by a center pole with an iron tripod foot. The top of the pole supported an iron ring one foot in diameter over which was draped a conical cape which was raised for ventilation and to let out the smoke. Sixteen men occupied each of these tents and slept as radii of the circle with their feet toward the center, where a fire could be built when necessary. With this arrangement the purpose of the ventilation appliance is apparent. While favorites in camp, these tents were too unwieldy to be carried about and consequently were not used during campaigns.[416] The government supplied 240,000 of these larger tents for the first winter's encampments, all of which, except a minimum for the officers, were left behind when the armies took to the field. But these were not all wasted since they were used by new recruits coming into the old camps.[417]

The tent that soon replaced all others for the privates for field use was the shelter tent, usually irreverently referred to as "dog tent" or "pup tent." This has been the service tent of the army ever since. It was a piece of stout cotton cloth, somewhat lighter than duck, four feet wide and six feet long. Each man could have one, and two men would fasten their halves together, stretch them over a ridge pole three feet from the ground, and thus be fairly well protected from dews and light rains.

---

[416] *Ibid.*, Winthrop. "Washington as a Camp," *loc. cit.*, p. 111; Upham, *loc. cit.*, pp. 42-43. For photograph of a camp, showing Sibley and wall tents, see *Harper's Weekly*, vol. 5 (May 25, 1861), p. 332; *cf.* also *Official Records, Atlas*, plate 174.

[417] Count of Paris, *Civil War*, vol. 1, p. 293; Barney, *Twentieth Iowa Infantry*, p. 36.

But even toughened veterans could not keep comfortable in them.

Many men threw away their shelter tents, declaring it an outrage to issue so worthless an article and then compel them to carry it on the march. Others bought lumber with their own money and utilized the tents, along with the lumber, in constructing small huts in which they could get warm. After a time the general aversion began to wear off and those who discarded them became very solicitous to have others issued to them.[418] Even the turbulent Wilson Zouaves, on duty off the coast of Florida, became a more contented lot after receiving a fresh supply, so much better they found them than nothing.[419]

Over 300,000 shelter tents were issued during the first year of the war. These were soon improved by the use of rubber cloth and, by degrees, were supplemented by the waterproof poncho. That useful article, then as now, was a square piece of cloth with a hole in the center for the head. It was worn as a rain cape, as needed, in the daytime and at night formed the floor of the shelter tent. Forty thousand of these were used in 1861 and 1,500,000 in 1864.[420]

To men accustomed to the soft beds of civilization, and living in an era when night air was thought to be unhealthful, such accommodations as these were for a time a severe trial. Especially was this true where the accommodations were insufficient for the number of men. In a western regiment, for example, there were only thirteen tents for the rank and file of each com-

[418] Scott, *Story of a Cavalry Regiment*, p. 371; Count of Paris, *op. cit.*, vol. 1, p. 293; Barney, *op. cit.*, pp. 169-170.

[419] *Harper's Weekly*, vol. 5 (October 26, 1861), p. 687.

[420] Count of Paris, *op. cit.*, vol. 1, p. 293.

pany. Consequently the wedge tents, made to cover four men apiece, were forced to do service for six or seven. In these, before the days of the poncho, they spread their blankets on the ground, a box, or a board and slept. The more prominent bones ached severely under this treatment until they became calloused to such usage and then the possessors came to be oblivious of the hardness of their beds. Even in the officers' tents cots were few and most of them slept like the men, rolled up in a blanket on a board or on the ground.[421]

There was an art in the pitching of these tents and those who failed to observe the rules had to suffer the consequences. If one pitched his tent in a low place and failed to dig a trench around it, he was likely to awaken in a pool of water during a sudden shower and perhaps with the tent collapsing upon his prostrate form, due to insecure fastening of the tent pins. But even such as this came to be looked upon in later days as a part of the routine of life. Of course they preferred dry blankets but, if they had to use them, wet ones would do.[422]

At the other extreme of comfort in tents was the fire-place tent, some two thousand of which were sent to the Western Department and some of which were ordered for the Massachusetts soldiers. It was an umbrella shaped tent, eighteen feet in diameter, with side draperies. The center pole was a three-inch gas pipe which served also as a stove pipe for a small air-tight stove which accompanied the tent. The combined weight was 120 pounds and the price was $55.00.[423] This tent was never widely used; its weight and cost put it

---

[421] Wilkie, *op. cit.*, pp. 41-42.
[422] Hinkley, *op. cit.*, p. 9.
[423] *New York Tribune*, November 8, 1861.

more in the class of barracks than of tents, and it was found more satisfactory to build regular barracks than to bother with the hybrid.

The favorite quarters for training and concentration camps were large wooden barracks and, for winter quarters in the field, log cabins. The barracks were of varying shapes and sizes and of two general patterns. The more primitive type was wedge shaped, built of rough boards standing on end and leaning against a ridge pole, to which they were nailed. The ends were closed by gables containing doors, which, in addition to unintentional interstices, were the sole source of ventilation and light. The whole bore a striking resemblance to an elongated hog-house or a detached clapboarded roof of a "shot-gun" dwelling house.[424] Elevate such a shed as this upon four walls and you have the other type.

These barracks were often built by the first troops to occupy them, otherwise they might have done without. The government furnished the lumber, usually rough, and the men did the work, also rough. Some of the barracks were of pine lumber, others were of logs and mud; some were shingled, some were not; some were heated, most were not. Ordinarily they were about twenty by fifty feet in area, though sometimes twenty by eighty, and housed one company each. Frequently they were double and held two companies. Some had no floors, windows, or chimneys while others had rough board floors and a window in the middle of each side. Generally the later barracks were better built in every way than the first.

The sleeping arrangements were simple – very sim-

---

[424] See picture in *Harper's Weekly*, vol. 5 (August 24, 1861), p. 535.

ple. Two platforms, one above the other and each about twelve feet in width, extended the full length of the building, leaving a four-foot aisle on each side. On these platforms the men were corded, fifty men to each platform, twenty-five on each side, with their heads together in the middle and the feet of the taller ones hanging over the edges. But such barracks had their virtues. They could be built at an average cost of two dollars a man,[425] in a day when lumber at ten dollars a thousand feet was considered exorbitant in price and a fit subject for governmental investigation.[426]

A camp for one regiment would present a spectacle of ten to twelve such buildings placed in a row and about twenty feet apart, with perhaps a smaller building inserted in the middle of the row for the regimental band, in the days before such bands were dispensed with (July 27, 1862) in favor of "fifers" and drummers. Behind each building was a cook shack and, in cavalry regiments, farther in the rear were the stables: long low sheds closed on one side; one for each company and one for the field and staff officers. In front of the barracks would be the parade grounds some fifty yards in width, and flanking this or in front would be the officers' barracks, smaller, but more convenient than those of the men.[427] Such camps, located conveniently near to some good spring or other source of water supply, were dotted all over the country and most of them contained not more than four regiments each.

The concentration camps, fewer in number and better located for quick and easy transportation, were merely hypertrophied regimental camps. Troops poured into

---

[425] Scott, *op. cit.*, pp. 4-5; Upham, *loc. cit.*, pp. 45-46.

[426] *New York Tribune*, January 13, 1862.

[427] Scott, *op. cit.*, pp. 4-5, 9.

Army quarters at Chattanooga, 1864

them at intervals and poured out at others but usually in the first year they were full to overflowing. Benton Barracks at St. Louis, housed something like 40,000 men.[428] Cairo, Illinois, at that time merely a monstrous mud hole over which were superimposed houses and sidewalks built on ten-foot stilts, was nevertheless, on account of its strategic position, a concentration camp capable of accommodating as high as 50,000 troops.[429] Camp Dennison, near Cincinnati, contained 12,000 men in June, 1861, and Camp Curtin, near Harrisburg, contained 20,000 a year later.[430]

The log cabins of the winter camps in the field were of less formal style than the ordinary barracks but were often more comfortable. They were improvised by the soldiers and varied accordingly, but agreed in the particulars that they were built either of round or split logs, plastered with mud, and with roofs made of tents, tent flies, and waterproof blankets, and doors of boards or rubber blankets. Some of them were lofty and roomy and divided into several different compartments, while others were only about six feet square, with walls three or four feet high and in this space containing two beds, a table, a rack for arms, a cache for clothing, and a fire place.

These fire places were both the joy and the bane of existence in winter camp. They were of the "California" type and consisted of a hole in the ground covered with stones, the smoke being carried out through a narrow channel under the wall opposite the

---

[428] *Downing's Diary*, p. 19.

[429] *Ibid.*, pp. 183-184; Chetlain, *op. cit.*, p. 80; *Harper's Weekly*, vol. 5 (June 1, 1861), p. 350.

[430] *Harper's Weekly*, vol. 5 (June 22, 1861), pp. 390, 394; vol. 6 (September 13, 1862), p. 587.

entrance and there received by a chimney. The chimneys were the source of most of the trouble. They were built of brickbats, stones, or sticks and mud, and often were most erratic in their performances.[431] "One of the 'vexed questions' of our war," said a veteran, "was the smoky chimney. Many were the tears shed, and 'tall' the swearing, in consequence of the builder's lack of skill in this intricate branch of his handicraft." Lighting a fire for the first time was a critical, anxious moment. A numerous company of friends would gather to see the effects, "watching the cloud of smoke as it hovered and trembled in doubt, whether to go up or down." Usually it came down and so did the chimney – often several times before a partial success was effected. The man who made good chimneys was a popular person and was able to trade well upon his rare accomplishment.[432]

Of food the soldier in camp usually got all he wanted though not always just what he wanted; in the field he took his chances at full rations, half rations, or no rations, forage or hunger. The army ration was generous though somewhat monotonous. One pound of biscuit – otherwise known as hardtack, pilot bread, or crackers – or twenty-two ounces of bread or flour, one and one-quarter pounds of fresh or salt beef or three-quarters of a pound of bacon constituted the bulk of the ration. To this was added for each one hundred men, eight gallons of beans, ten pounds of rice or hominy, ten pounds of coffee, fifteen pounds of sugar, four gallons of vinegar, two pounds of salt, one and one-quarter pounds of candles, and four pounds of soap. Such rations seemed sinfully extravagant to European obser-

---

[431] Trobriand, *op. cit.*, pp. 125-126; Jones, *op. cit.*, p. 149; Sperry, *Thirty-third Iowa Infantry*, p. 51.

[432] Jones, *op. cit.*, p. 149.

vers. How, even with their large appetites and wasteful methods of cooking, the soldiers could consume such a ration was beyond their comprehension.[433]

Among the American soldiers this fare had, as usual, its defenders and its defamers. The devourers of "salt horse" and pickled pork were likely to tire of the diet and liken it to prison fare,[434] and, as already shown, their complaints were frequently just, because of the evils resulting from the contract system. The remark was frequently made that the fare was not what they were used to at home, but, on the other hand, it was confessed that it was true that "we did not have the variety, such food as buckwheat cakes and honey, spiced cakes and peach preserves . . . but we had a good solid substantial food, such as a soldier must have to fit him for marching and fighting." [435]

Perhaps the attitude toward the diet was colored very largely by individual conditions. Yet even a soldier who had made a twenty-one-mile tramp through the hot sun with only one slice of pork and a cracker to eat found it possible to be cheerful about it.[436] The men could find something funny in the situation of visitors commiserating with them over the fact that they had to drink their coffee without cream,[437] or could affectionately christen their camp "Camp Mush" because of their long continued diet on that kind of gruel.[438] They could live on part rations or by foraging

---

[433] Count of Paris, *op. cit.*, vol. 1, p. 297.

[434] Haven, "Camp Life at the Relay," in *Harper's Magazine*, vol. 24 (April, 1862), p. 631.

[435] S. D. Musser, "The Quartermaster's Story," in *The 148th Pennsylvania Volunteers*, p. 283.

[436] *New York Tribune*, May 7, 1861.

[437] Wilkie, *op. cit.*, p. 42.

[438] Barney, *op. cit.*, p. 53.

for long periods and, while they grumbled at the time, could construct fond memories out of the situation later. Who cannot remember the stories old soldiers used to tell, of how they had to wait till after dark to eat their bacon, hardtack, or cheese so they could not see the other things they ate with them?

On the other hand the soldiers frequently lived in the lap of luxury. For instance the New York Seventh was for a time located on an estate near Washington, of which a journalist said, "The cellars of the villa overflow with edibles, and in the greenhouses is a most appetizing array of barrels, boxes, cans, and bottles, shipped here that our Sybarites might not sigh for the fleshpots of home." [439] Supplies of fresh food were constantly available to most of the northern camps and the troops were by no means dependent solely upon the office at Washington for their food. Cattle were driven to the camps and killed and eaten on the spot. The Army of the Potomac was so well supplied in this way that much of the meat was wasted.[440]

First regiments especially were frequently so showered with delicacies, furnished by the neighborhood in which their camps were located, that they could scarcely take care of them all. When the first troops were encamped in Keokuk, Iowa, a feast was prepared for the whole two regiments, and the tables were so loaded down with food that, as a newspaper correspondent expressed it, "after fifteen hundred soldiers had filled their not insignificant capacities almost to bursting, and a like number of citizens had likewise partaken, there were more fragments remaining than in the famous supper given to the Five Thousand."[441] Though such hospitality wore itself out, many a soldier after a couple of years in active service looked back upon those early days in camp and wondered what he ever could have found to grumble about.[442]

Perhaps the soldiers suffered as much from the way in which they prepared their food as the majority of them ever did from the quality. The cooking, especially in the western camps was usually done by details of men, five or six in number or as many as were deemed necessary, who served for varying periods of time before relieved by others. These cooks procured the rations from the quartermasters and, after the meals were prepared, the companies marched up to the kitchens where each soldier received his allowance, and then marched off to his quarters to eat it.[443] Elsewhere the rationing and cooking was more individual, and especially was this true after the contingents took to the field, but in either case the quality did not vary greatly.

A very essential part of the meal, however or whenever prepared, was the coffee. The chief requirement was that it be hot and strong. No strict culinary principles were followed in its preparation. An incredibly large quantity was dumped into a big kettle or tin can and boiled till all the strength was gone. "The liquid," said a victim, "looks very much like the water of the Rio Grande, or the Missouri 'on a bender,' but its taste is good, and its effects plainly perceptible." Whether tired, wet, cold, or just plain hungry, such coffee was looked upon as a necessity for existence by the soldiers –

---

441 Wilkie, *op. cit.*, p. 27.
442 Sperry, *op. cit.*, pp. 2-3.
443 Wilkie, *op. cit.*, pp. 41-42; *Downing's Diary*, p. 19.

as necessary as tobacco was to many, yet the users of both, it was asserted, would have retained coffee if either had to be given up.[444]

In spite of its embalming propensities this coffee must have been less deleterious in its general effects than a certain concoction called "slapjacks." These seem to have been the homesick soldiers' nearest approach to the griddle cakes they had left behind them. They were made, it is averred, by "mixing flour and cold water together and frying the dough in grease. After becoming cold this bread might well be manufactured into mallets, as it possesses the two qualities requisite – hardness and toughness – and produced much sickness." [445] The table ware for these repasts was simple and imposed no intricacies of etiquette upon the users. A knife, a fork, a tin plate, and a tincup was the sum total until November, 1863, when, by general order, a tin spoon was added to the list.[446] But on the march, or in the field this minimum was enough.

The officers generally, and the men sometimes, organized their mess on a more communal style. The rank and file of the company, fifty to seventy-five or eighty men, would form a mess enabling them to get along without drawing their full allotment of rations from the commissary. The difference was paid in money and generally formed a common fund for the company, and was controlled by it without the interposition of their superior officers. Some times a regiment would try similar economy on flour. A number of regiments encamped around Washington built earthen ovens and made their own bread. The amounts saved in this way

---

[444] Sperry, *op. cit.*, pp. 61-62.
[445] Barney, *op. cit.*, p. 42.
[446] *Official Records*, series iii, vol. 3, p. 1030.

were not enormous, but the advantage derived, especially from fresh bread, must have been very comforting.[447]

One correspondent who complained loudly of the official fare wished the government to commute all rations in money, at the rate of thirty cents a day. For less than this sum, he said, a number of men had utterly refused the government provender and supported themselves from the venders around the camp. Others boarded themselves in a homelike and decent manner within that allowance. Then he became more generous. Let the government allow three dollars a week to each man, and let the regiments procure a caterer and live like men,[448] he declaimed. Doubtless they could do so, for the government was trying to keep the cost of a week's rations between ninety-eight cents and a dollar and forty cents. Without doubt, with this difference, the men could have fed themselves in princely style according to the plan projected.

The soldiers found it difficult to be as cheerful about their clothing as they were about the army food, the reason being that, by means well known, they were able to provide themselves with other and supplementary food and, however obtained, its spurious source was not easily ascertained after consumption. But the source of supply of uniforms was more distant and could not be supplemented, without detection, by levies upon the community. Such supplement could not even be obtained by purchase in any great quantities. The choice lay, then, between the early shoddy with its rags and tatters, and nothing. Of course there was only one

---

[447] Count of Paris, *op. cit.*, vol. 1, p. 297; Trobriand, *op. cit.*, p. 126; *Official Records*, series iii, vol. 1, p. 739.

[448] Haven, *loc. cit.*, p. 631.

choice to be made, and it was made with as much grace as could be expected under the circumstances. Whenever the clothing collapsed, as it generally did in the first outfits, makeshifts had to be resorted to, or if the damage were not too extensive, it might be repaired by the amateur efforts of the wearer.

Shoddy and "loose construction" were unforgivable faults, and were so considered, but the mere matter of bad fit could be viewed lightly except in the case of shoes. In the indiscriminate manner of distribution so frequently followed, men were quite likely to be apportioned raiment far out of proportion to their build, a difficulty that could be remedied to some extent by trading. But where one standard size was sent for all, or when manufacturers had erratic notions about human anatomy and its proper draping, some ludicrous situations resulted. Such an occasion occurred when the women of Dubuque, Iowa, made uniforms for a company of soldiers from their town, who were on their way to subdue the insurrection in Missouri. When shorn of its hyperbolic language, the following account by a newspaper man who accompanied them, is illustrative of the attitude of the soldiers toward the misfits they received:

"They are admirable fits, all of them, except eighty or a hundred. . . . A majority of the boys are able to get their pantaloons from the floor by buttoning the waistbands around their necks – others accomplish this desirable result by bringing the waistbands tight up under the arms and rolling them up six or eight inches at the bottom. To be sure this is a little inconvenient in some respects – a fellow has to take off his belts, then his coat, and then ascend one story before he can reach his pockets, and after reaching them they are so deep that one has to take his pants off entirely before he can reach the bottom. Each pocket will hold a shirt, a blanket and even the wearer himself if at any time he finds such a retreat necessary.

"And the coats fit beautifully – almost in fact as well as the pants. To be sure half of them are two feet too large around the waist, and almost as much too small around the chest – but then these two drawbacks admirably offset each other. In the cases of fifteen or twenty of them the top of the collar is but a trifle above the small of the wearer's back, and in the cases of about as many more the same article is a few inches above the head of their owners. The same collar also in some cases terminates beneath each ear, and in many others it sweeps away around in a magnificent curve, forming a vast basin whose rim is yards distant from the neck of its possessor. And the sleeves, too, have here and there a fault – some are so tight under the arms that they lift one up as if he were swinging upon a couple of ropes that pass underneath his armpits – others strike boldly out and do not terminate their voluminous course till at a distance of several inches beyond the tips of his fingers, while others conclude their journey after marching an inch or so below the elbows." [449]

As a concession to the angered women of Dubuque the correspondent shortly afterward explained that the bad fit was not due to their error but to that of the cutters who had supplied them and as a further palliative he warmly commended their patriotism. But he stuck to the essence of his criticism regardless of the fact that he would soon be returning home to face them. [450]

[449] Wilkie, op. cit., pp. 21-22.
[450] Ibid., p. 26.

In remedying such errors in construction some of the men soon became very adept. They learned to trim and repair, alter waistbands and splice and insert as necessary. Extending this adaptability to the point of thrift they could even double the life of a trouser leg by cutting it off, when the knee wore through, and turning the back to the front.[451] Often, as related in a previous chapter, the soldiers were in the last extremity for the want of enough and proper clothing. Though their own improvidence may have been partly responsible for this condition in the later years of the war, yet the condition, as such, frequently did exist and must be considered as a vital phase of the life of the soldier.

The daily routine of camp life was about as monotonous as the government rations. At sunrise, sometimes four-thirty or five A. M., came the morning gun or reveille, the signal for the sleepy soldiers to arise and arrange their toilet. This was a simple task, since they slept in their clothes and frequently wore their hair short and their beard long; but at least they were supposed to have all the straws and cockle burrs out of their hair and whiskers and have their shoes on.

Then came the roll call and next, a couple of hours after rising, the call to breakfast. Sometimes between the roll call and breakfast a short drill was inserted and performed "with great drowsiness of the flesh and profaneness of the spirit." If at breakfast no grace was said, according to the standard of the time, at least the necessary words were mumbled by a goodly number though in sadly disarranged order. Whatever of savor the food lacked was more than atoned for by the spicy comments and execrations of its partakers.

---

[451] S. C. Jones, *Reminiscences of 22d Iowa Volunteer Infantry* (Iowa City, 1907), pp. 8-9.

Following breakfast came about three hours of regimental drill, then dinner at noon. In the afternoon was a period of rest for some and target practice for a few. Once in a while a camp would be found where time was taken for daily tent inspection. Then at about four in the afternoon would come drill again: marches, practice in the use of arms, bayonet exercise, complicated maneuvers, and any of the various evolutions and movements prescribed by the manuals.

Sometimes this evening drill was watched by the women of the neighborhood, when, if they were young and pretty, considerable difficulty was encountered in centering the attention of the soldiers on their duties. If they were the reverse, it was surprising the amount of alacrity they displayed in their drill. Late in the evening came supper, and then the fun began for those who were not doing picket duty.

The frolic continued till ten o'clock when tattoo was sounded, sometimes by the rattling of drums and sometimes, early in the war, by band music. This was a signal to prepare for bed but, since this preparation usually consisted merely of removing the shoes, providing the weather was not too cold, the noise did not cease till the taps were sounded. This came at ten-thirty and if thereafter the lights were not out and noise stopped a visit from a sentry was likely to be the result.

After a day spent in this way, the sleep was usually sound and uninterrupted except when a nervous sentinel took a shot at a stump or a cow through error. After a few hours of oblivion, reveille again would interrupt the slumbers and scarcely a man could be found to complain that the hour of rising was too late.[452]

---

[452] Practically all regimental histories, diaries, and reminiscences contain

In his hours of rest, more numerous in winter quarters than elsewhere, the soldier found means of recreation in all the various ways that will suggest themselves to the minds of men far from home and not knowing when if ever they will return. Song, debate, rough horseplay, tricks on the officers, long letters, and poetry were all indulged in. When these failed to satisfy they sometimes resorted to gambling, drinking, and turbulent outbursts in general.

In the evenings the revelling usually became noisiest. Singing and instrumental music alternately gave way to fierce discussions about anything or nothing, which when started usually lasted till taps. Sometimes these local gatherings gave way to formal entertainments and debates where the weighty questions of the day were ably and eloquently discussed according to strict parliamentary rules. Such subjects as "The Right of Secession," "The Qualifications of Citizenship," and "The Relative Incentive Influence of Love and Fear" were favorites. Glee club recitals, musical entertainments, and recitations including the new poem "Barbara Frietchie" also were frequent.[453]

Of daytime sports wrestling, sparring, baseball, horse racing, and shooting were commonest, and, when these failed to entertain, straight poker could generally arouse an interest.[454] Craps seem not yet to have invaded the North. Of less formal nature but more exciting while they lasted were the escapades involving breach of dis-

---

references to the daily routine. Frequent accounts are also found in newspaper and magazine articles. Those especially consulted were: Scott, *op. cit.*, pp. 371-409; Wilkie, *op. cit.*, pp. 36-39; Winthrop, "Washington as a Camp," *loc. cit.*, pp. 111-113; Haven, *loc. cit.*, pp. 630-632.

[453] E. R. Jones, *op. cit.*, p. 150; Haven, *loc. cit.*, pp. 631-632.

[454] E. R. Jones, *op. cit.*, pp. 151-152.

cipline or discomfiture of the officers. If a man's horse
lay down with him while crossing a ford, it was an occasion of spontaneous hilarity, but if a major of portly
and dignified mien got immersed in a swamp, it was
enough to put the regiment in good spirits for the rest
of the day.[455]

Milking the cows and catching the stray pigs and
chickens that wandered into the camp was a profitable
as well as amusing pastime as long as the pursuers were
not discovered. But rushing the guards and giving them
chase until either escape was effected or the runaways
were caught was a more exciting recreation until the
guards were supplied with ammunition. Thereafter
this delightful pastime was utterly spoiled.[456]

There does not seem to have been any alarming
amount of drunkenness in the camps, yet as a diversion
and solace, large quantities of beer and even whiskey
were consumed at many of the barracks.

At camp Ellsworth in Keokuk, not only did the local
dealers minister to the demands of German-Americans
for beer, but donations in the form of kegs of whiskey,
bottles of brandy, and barrels of beer kept pouring in
so steadily that an appeal had to be sent out for the
home folks to send pipes, tobacco, and books, lest the
men be totally incapacitated for the coming campaign
in Missouri.[457] In some companies it was customary to
have "from two to a dozen barrels of lager beer on tap.
We were not notorious beer drinkers," explains a soldier, "but some of the officers started the practice and it
was considered the correct thing to have a glass of beer

---

[455] Sperry, *op. cit.*, p. 74.

[456] Wilkie, *op. cit.*, pp. 33-35.

[457] *Ibid.*, pp. 39-40, 48 ; Barney, *op. cit.*, p. 22.

to offer your friends when they came to see you. We took pride in the hospitality of the camp." [458]

In strong prohibition centers this practice was sternly discountenanced and great efforts were made to suppress it. For instance at Mt. Pleasant, Iowa, where a cavalry regiment was stationed, liquor selling was considered "as nothing less than the work of the devil himself." Being afraid that the morals of the soldiers were in danger of corruption, but having no suitable law at hand for its suppression, "parties composed of citizens and volunteers, whose ambition it was to make others as good as themselves, entered several houses occupied by the children of sin, and spilled their liquors in the street." [459]

Prohibitions against the sale of liquor to soldiers naturally were not always successful. Artful ways of smuggling whiskey into camp were tried by ingenious venders, and in those days "boot legger" was not a mere figure of speech. A typical ruse was one employed at Governor's Island, New York, shortly after the draft riots. A regiment of soldiers, arriving too late to help in suppressing the riots, were stationed there pending developments. Being cut off from the mainland, many were parching under the liquor restrictions. Then a benefactress came to them in the shape of an old woman selling sausages. To men who had been living on salt and smoked meat for so long a time, the very idea of sausage was repellent. Consequently sales seemed likely to be very small until a whispered communication brightened up the faces of the men and the sausages were sold in a hurry. The skins were filled with bourbon

---

[458] E. R. Jones, *op. cit.*, p. 46.
[459] Scott, *op. cit.*, p. 18.

whiskey. This trick was soon discovered and stopped, but immediately others were resorted to.[460]

Homesickness, so frequent in the army, resulted in another form of recreation. Army life changed the morals of many men, its worst effects being exercised upon those who had lived under too close restraint at home, while many other turbulent spirits were considerably improved by the experience. But in either or any class there was constant anxiety about family, friends, or neighbors, and a corresponding eagerness to receive letters and packages from them. The packages often contained articles practically useless to soldiers on a campaign or even in camp, but the effect was the same, to gladden the spirit of the recipient and make him the object of envy of his less favored brethren. In return men, but little experienced in writing, spent hours of labor in spelling out replies.

Delayed supply trains caused mental as well as physical anguish, for a delayed train meant a delayed mail and often, when such trains arrived, the mail was even more heartily received than other things. It was nothing short of a calamity for a heavy mail to be captured by the enemy. But revenge was sweet when the enemy's mail fell into the hands of Union soldiers and many a period of hilarity was enjoyed while reading the love letters intended for the Confederate soldiers.[461]

Newspapers were read until worn out and even became articles of exchange when trading on enemy soil. Anticipating this need the *New York Tribune* company at the beginning of the war made a standing offer of a dozen free copies of the daily and of the weekly *Tri-*

---

[460] E. R. Jones, *op. cit.*, p. 119.
[461] Sperry, *op. cit.*, p. 82.

bune to the colonel of each regiment, throughout the
period of the war, if they would only keep the publish-
ing company informed of their forwarding address.[462]
This would have been a pretty big contract to fill if it
had been generally taken advantage of. One is almost
inclined to wonder whether the results of this generosity
had anything to do with Horace Greeley's later anxiety
to bring the war to a hasty close. Oftentimes the soldiers printed their own newspapers, taking advantage
of any presses that might be captured in Confederate
territory. Such papers usually were of transient existence and were often used to voice discontent and criticism of the officers. The publication of these newspapers was merely another medium whereby the soldiers utilized their surplus energies and vented their
pent-up feelings.[463]

Another side of their contact with home was the
letters written by the soldiers and their efforts to relieve the physical wants of their families. Some soldiers were able to save a considerable proportion from
their salaries to send home to their parents or to their
wives and children, and it was a very common thing for
single men to lend money to married men for the same
purpose.[464] There were even instances related where the
home connections were not immediately broken : where,
in the early days, when discipline was but a by-word,
wives, even with small children, sometimes accompanied their husbands, and followed the army over five
hundred miles before returning – the return then being
only because they had run out of clothing.[465]

---

[462] *New York Tribune*, May 9, 1861.

[463] A. M. Schlesinger, "The Khaki Journalists, 1917-1919," in *The Mississippi Valley Historical Review*, vol. 6 (December, 1919), pp. 350-359.

[464] *Downing's Diary*, p. 134.

[465] Barney, *op. cit.*, p. 35.

The letters home conveyed not only accounts of the trials and experiences of the men but sometimes they aspired to literary elegance and, if the recipient were a sweetheart, even to poetry. The less said about most of the poems the better. Any man who has passed his twenties can look back and realize from his own experience just what such poetry consisted of and how it must have weighted the mail with its honeyed phrases. Some verses, not intended for such serious purposes, really approached cleverness, but it is a boon to posterity that not much of it has been preserved.[466]

That homesickness was a very potent cause of desertion is unquestioned. The laxity of discipline here also was a contributing factor. The combination resulted in plights like in a story told by Mark Twain which was supposed to be an actual occurrence. While relating to the Confederate army, the situation was so nearly parallel to conditions in the North as to apply equally well there. "A private appeared at the door, and, without salute or other circumlocution, said to the colonel:

" 'Say, Jim, I'm a-goin' home for a few days.'

" 'What for?'

" 'Well, I han't b'en there for a right smart while and I'd like to see how things is comin' on.'

" 'How long are you going to be gone?'

" ' 'Bout two weeks.'

" 'Well, don't be gone longer than that; and get back sooner if you can'." [467]

---

[466] Copious samples of poetry both from soldiers and civilians are to be found in Moore, *Rebellion Record*, vols. 1-9 *passim*. A more compact work by the same editor is, Frank Moore, *Civil War in Song and Story* (1889), *passim*.

[467] S. L. Clemens, "The Private History of a Campaign that Failed," in *The Writings of Mark Twain* (New York, c. 1899), vol. 21, p. 273. For like conditions in the North, see Barney, *op. cit.*, p. 17.

Homesickness was not always so difficult to allay. Men here and there could be found who were maudlin in their letters to their wives on one day, and then would spend the next day commenting in artistic style about all the pretty ankles that the wind revealed.[468]

Constant companionship of men with each other made the arrival of women in the camp an object of special interest. If a soldier's wife paid him a visit, he was at once the envy of the rest of the camp. Men longed for the sight of anything suggesting femininity. "We want a *Fille du Regiment*," was an expression of this desire, "a dark or blue eyed houri of seventeen or older – one for whom all could entertain Platonic affection, and upon whom could be expended that surplus love which is now bottled up or expended upon stars, whiskey punches, or moonlight." [469]

Of the unromantic side of camp life much could be said and volumes have been written, but to little purpose. The unromantic side of warfare is the side of which the soldier sees the most, of which he complains in his generation, and which his children promptly forget. Sheridan's Ride, Marching through Georgia, the heroic defense of Fort Sumter, Pickett's Charge, Maryland My Maryland, and Barbara Frietchie, are echoed in legend and song by succeeding generations, and buckets of gushing sentiment are spilled over the sentinel sleeping at his post. All of these were grimly prosaic things when really experienced. It is a significant fact that great wars are not produced by the veterans of the last preceding great war. These veterans remember too well the drudgery and the disgusting ac-

---

[468] Wilkie, *op. cit.*, p. 35.
[469] *Ibid.*, p. 26.

tualities of the conflict to wish to see the scenes repeated, though at the same time they may be helping to disseminate the stories of romance and adventure. Even the open-air life of the soldier was not sufficient to counteract the influences unfavorable to his health. Of the 359,528 deaths in the Union army, as compiled in 1885, 249,468 were from other causes than the enemies' bullets, and nearly all of them were from disease. Five men died of disease for every two who died of wounds received in battle.[470] The daily exposure combined with crowded and ill-ventilated barracks caused sickness and the easy spread of epidemics. Most camps had hospitals but these were frequently inadequate, and medical service was likely to be poor. Sometimes all the physicians in the town nearest the camp would be called upon and the combined strength would be inadequate.[471] An eastern army surgeon discovered that much sickness in the camps around New York was caused by bad food and by the bad whiskey to which the men resorted as an alternative.[472] The United States Sanitary Commission, organized by civilians, did much to correct unsanitary conditions in camp and to relieve sickness and suffering, but the government failed to cooperate with it properly and, as often as not, placed actual hindrances in the way of its operation. As a result it never came to be as effective as it might have become under more favorable circumstances.[473]

Some officers were thoroughly incompetent of the

[470] *Official Records*, series iii, vol. 5, pp. 664-665.

[471] Scott, *op. cit.*, p. 19.

[472] T. T. Ellis, *Leaves from Diary of an Army Surgeon* (New York, 1863), pp. 23, 25.

[473] The most complete work on Sanitary Commission is C. J. Stillé, *History of United States Sanitary Commission* (Philadelphia, 1866).

task of enforcing or of even understanding the sanitary regulations. "I have ridden through a regimental camp," said an old officer, "whose utterly filthy condition seemed enough to send malaria through a whole military department, and have been asked by the colonel, almost with tears in his eyes, to explain to him why his men were dying at the rate of one a day."[474]

Guard-houses were even more unsanitary than camps and sometimes were so filthy as to be all but uninhabitable.[475] To serve out a long sentence in such a guardhouse must have been sufficient penalty for anything less than a capital crime. Fortunately for the soldiers in such camps not all offenses were punishable by guardhouse confinement. In other camps, where prisoners were better kept, the situation would be reversed. To be bucked and gagged must have been anything but pleasant; to be tied up by the thumbs till only the toes and balls of the feet rested on the ground soon became a torture; yet these and many other forms of corporal punishment, short of actual flogging, were in use.

Some gamblers in a New York regiment, for instance, were given a table, some dice, a tincup, and some beans and compelled to play all day long for beans. Perhaps this might not have been considered a hardship, nor the wearing of placards labeled "Gambler" on their backs, if the further theory had not been put into practice that gamblers have no time for meals. According to current opinion, however, it was useless to punish the men for gambling while it was "so prevalent a vice with the officers." [476]

[474] Higginson, "Regular and Volunteer Officers," in *Atlantic Monthly,* vol. 14, p. 355.

[475] Ellis, *op. cit.,* p. 24.

[476] *Harper's Weekly,* vol. 7 (November 7, 1863), p. 711.

Cowards were sometimes drummed out of the army. One mode of doing this was to march them out between two files of officers, their heads cropped, placarded with large signs bearing the epithet "Coward," while the band played the "Rogue's March." Similar though less severe penalties were meted out for such offenses as drunkenness. To make the punishment symbolical, the culprit would be clothed in a barrel with only his head, legs, and arms sticking out while bearing some such label as "Too fond of whiskey. Forged an order on the surgeon."[477]

Beyond such minor punishments were those meted out by regular court-martial, such sentences extending even to the death penalty. Considering the number of desertions throughout the war in comparison to the very small number who were ever executed for the offense, it can easily be ascertained how little effect capital punishment had, as it was administered.

While many soldiers thus disported themselves, leading as carefree an existence as the discipline would allow, there was the usual minority who devoted at least a part of their leisure time to religious exercises. Perhaps their number was proportionally smaller than in civil life due to the fact that conscientious scruples kept many religious people from volunteering. At any rate their number was very small in comparison with that of the men who preferred to seek consolation in something more cheerful than mid-nineteenth-century devotional exercises.

In some camps local preachers would hold prayer meetings with rather disappointing results, especially where the meetings were held every night.[478] On Sun-

477 *Idem*, vol. 6 (June 28, 1862), pp. 411-412.
478 *New York Tribune*, May 6, 1861.

days there was usually more of rest, quiet, cleanliness, and care in dressing than on week days. Around Washington the camps and men would receive a regular Sunday cleansing, followed by inspection; then in the afternoon religious services would be held. Two regiments would be included for each service and there most of the soldiers would be found, some listening, some smoking, some sleeping, all being less noisy than on ordinary occasions.[479]

One instance is related where Bible reading was imposed as a sort of punishment. A company had adopted the rule for itself that every man who indulged in profanity should read aloud a chapter from the Bible for each offense. The book thereafter, while the rule was in force, was in constant use. One person in a week was said to have read all of Genesis and Exodus, and started Leviticus, and had a fine prospect of finishing the Old Testament before his three-months enlistment expired.[480]

The United States Christian Commission, organized by the Y. M. C. A. on the same plan as the Sanitary Commission, endeavored to minister to the spiritual needs of the soldiers, but the general impression derived from the reports,[481] as compared with other sources is that the results were rather disappointing. The government naturally took no positive steps to regulate religious activities, except to give certain preach-

---

[479] Haven, *loc. cit.*, p. 632-633.

[480] Wilkie, *op. cit.*, p. 34.

[481] The most complete source is United States Christian Commission for the Army and Navy, *Annual Reports* (Philadelphia, 1863-1866). These *Reports* cover period from 1862 to 1865, inclusive. *Cf.* also, E. P. Smith, *Incidents of United States Christian Commission* (Philadelphia, 1869), an excessively fervent account by a clergyman who was Field-secretary of the Commission.

ers the title of chaplain on the understanding that they otherwise stood on the same footing as privates. As long as the Christian Commission attended to its own business and did not obstruct, the government did not interfere with it. Indeed in one instance an almost benevolent attitude was shown by Secretary Cameron.

General McClellan, in the spring of 1861, while in charge of the western department sent the following message to the War Department: "Will you please authorize me to use boards to put up places for worship at Camp Dennison. Parties furnish nails and labor." The reply was terse and to the point: "The Lord's will be done. Simon Cameron." [482]

It was a thrilling experience to the novices in war whenever the news finally came that their regiment was to be transferred to the front. Usually they were carried either by railroad or boat or both. In the state of the railroads of that period it was a fortunate regiment that could, like the militia from Indianapolis, go straight through for a journey of about eight hundred miles to Philadelphia without changing cars. It was the Pennsylvania railroad that made this feat possible. Yet, having reached Philadelphia, it was deemed better to ship them the remaining distance by boat.[483] But it was probably the danger from Baltimore "plug uglies" rather than the lack of rail facilities that determined this route.

Railroad transportation was oftentimes by cattle cars and sometimes the regiments filled the cars so nicely that a soldier was led to conclude that the calculation must have been made after they had buried two of their

---

[482] *Official Records*, series i, vol. 51, part i, p. 388.
[483] *New York Tribune*, April 22, 1861.

comrades, "for there would have been no room for them had they been yet with us." The wisdom of the use of cattle cars instead of coaches became very apparent after a short travel, "for had there been such things as windows or doors we certainly should have been sifted through before we reached our destination." [484]

In the frontier states the difficulties of transportation were naturally greater than elsewhere. Some railroads even offered to carry all volunteer companies free of charge. But, since such transportation would probably not have exceeded a hundred miles, except in rare instances, it was of no overwhelming benefit. Hence these intermittent trips were supplemented by marches or by stage-coach. From Des Moines to Council Bluffs the price for each soldier by stage-coach was four dollars.[485] With soldiers clad in the scanty and flimsy clothing provided during the first year of the war, these journeys were often attended with much suffering.

In the western section as many troops as possible were taken down the Mississippi river in steamboats and barges, and the way they were stowed on board was both uncomfortable and perilous. If possible a whole regiment was loaded into one boat with their equipment and baggage. The consequence was that every available bit of space was occupied by standing men. Those near the rail were in danger of being pushed overboard and those in the middle of being suffocated or trampled upon. The negroes on the slave ships of the preceding century could scarcely have been more uncomfortably stowed away than these men who were unwittingly destined to help right the earlier wrong.

---

[484] Barney, *op. cit.*, p. 31.
[485] Upham, *loc. cit.*, pp. 43-44. Thence by steamboats.

Yet, in spite of this close packing, the men often suffered severely from cold, when wind and snow swept over the open barges in which they were corded.

An almost contemporary account of the loading of a transport is given thus by one of the victims: "The company were marched to the hurricane roof – as near the stern as they could be got – and placed directly across the boat; each successive company as it arrived were [sic] placed parallel to the first, until the top of the boat was filled; the remainder were then allowed to occupy the forecastle, the space between the cabin and the guards and, if room was still wanting . . . some of the companies were under the necessity of sharing quarters with the mules and horses on the lower deck – sleeping on the coal pile and in close proximity to the engine and boilers." They were "huddled together like hogs in a pen – jostled and jammed from side to side – compelled to eat and sleep on the filthy decks – without exercise during the day, and trampled upon at night while endeavoring to sleep – with rations of half cooked meat and tasteless pilot-bread, and constantly inhaling the impure atmosphere engendered by the dense crowd on board, and arising from mules and horses on the lower deck." What made the situation even more intolerable was that the officers ate at the cabin table and had good fare, and slept in state rooms with guards stationed to keep the privates out. It was no consolation to the soldiers to know that they had paid for this service. It seemed to them that it was merely another instance of special privilege.[486]

At least one commander, more humane than the rest, refused to accept such transportation and marched his

486 Barney, *op. cit.*, pp. 172-175.

men back to camp until better arrangements could be made.[487]

On starting out upon his first campaign, the soldier usually had a very exaggerated opinion of the articles necessary for him to carry along, for his personal comfort and convenience. Furthermore there was no strict regulation from above on this subject. The consequence was that he was frequently laden to the breaking point with a lot of material that may as well be classed as junk. In the earliest regiments, tents and mess equipments were of such voluminous size as to necessitate immense trains of baggage to follow each regiment, but shortly the individual shelter tent and eating utensils were loaded upon the shoulders of the individual soldier, thus complicating his already vexed problem of portage.[488]

The burden was all the heavier because of the thoughtfulness of home folks. With a knapsack filled with all the things "that kind friends at home had thought necessary for a soldier's comfort, a haversack containing two-days rations, a musket with accoutrements and forty rounds of ammunition" the load could seldom be less than fifty pounds.[489] One soldier, sweating under the remembrance of his burden, declared it would have been a respectable load for a mule.[490] But it seems that even mules would have balked at carrying such loads as some cavalrymen chose to impose upon their mounts. The following account presents the problem as it appeared to the soldier.

"Fully equipped for the field, the green cavalryman

[487] Upham, *loc. cit.*, p. 44.

[488] *Ibid.*, p. 42.

[489] Hinkley, *op. cit.*, p. 9.

[490] Byers, *op. cit.*, p. 28.

was a fearful and wonderful object. Mounted upon his charger, in the midst of all the paraphernalia and adornments of war, a moving arsenal and military depot, he must have struck surprise, if not terror, into the minds of his enemies." Upon his own body "he carried a big sabre and metal scabbard four feet long, an Austrian rifle or a heavy revolver, a box of cartridges, a box of percussion caps, a tin canteen for water, a haversack containing rations, a tin coffe-cup, and such other devices and traps as were recommended to his fancy as useful or beautiful." The combined weight of all this in addition to heavy clothing, including an overcoat, was something like fifty pounds.

This excess of baggage resulted in great personal discomfort to the soldier. "When he was on foot he moved with a great clapping and clanking of his arms and accoutrements, and [was] so constrained by the many bands crossing his body that any rapid motion was absurdly impossible."

When mounted the appearance was even worse. The cavalryman's horse carried "fastened to the saddle, a pair of thick leather holsters with pistols, a pair of saddle-bags filled with the rider's extra clothing, toilet articles, and small belongings, a nose-bag, perhaps filled with corn, a heavy leather halter, an iron picket pin with a long lariat or rope for tethering the horse, usually two horse-shoes with extra nails, a curry-comb and horse-brush, a set of gun-tools and materials for the care of arms, a rubber blanket or poncho, a pair of woolen blankets, a blouse, a cap or hat, and such other utensils and articles of clothing or decoration as the owner was pleased to keep." All this entailed an additional burden of about seventy pounds upon the horse.

The combined effect was to produce a very spectacular appearance. "When the rider was in the saddle, begirt with all his magazine, it was easy to imagine him protected from any ordinary assault. His properties rose before and behind him like fortifications, and those strung over his shoulders covered well his flanks. To the uninitiated it was a mystery how the rider got into the saddle; how he could rise to a sufficient height and how then descend upon the seat was the problem. The irreverent infantry said that it was done with the aid of a derrick, or by first climbing to the top of a high fence or the fork of a tree."

Besides all this regulation load some carried an armored vest weighing an additional eight or ten pounds. But it was not long before the size of this load began to diminish. Both horses and men suffered from the weight, and soldiers soon learned what was actually necessary for existence and what was not. Accordingly the armored vests, lariats, picket-pins, and nose-bags were conveniently lost. Clothing was reduced to an absolute minimum. A pair of blankets gave way to a single one, and two men wrapped up together in their combined pair to supply the deficiency. "It became a fine art how to lessen the burden of the horse; and the best soldiers were those whose horses were packed so lightly that the carbine was the biggest part of the load. If it was a wonder in the first campaign how a cavalryman could get onto or move his horse when equipped for the field, the wonder afterward came to be, how a man could live with so meagre an equipment." [491]

This "losing" of the soldier's equipment suggests the

---

[491] Scott, *op. cit.*, pp. 26-29.

matter of wastefulness in the army. To European observers, from countries where the population always had to exercise strict economy and minute efficiency in order to keep themselves supplied with the necessities of life, the American soldiers seemed lavishly wasteful: they cooked too much, they ate too much, and they threw away too much of what they cooked. The Count of Paris considered the ration enormous but it never seemed so to the American soldiers. The United States was still, at that time, a country with an expanding frontier and the people had never learned the necessity of frugal economy. Wastefulness may therefore be considered as a national trait, but only so because conditions of life had never made economy seem necessary.

But the wastefulness, attributed to soldiers, which did the most damage was the neglectful treatment of the supplies entrusted to them by the government. For one reason or another the men were overloaded and judicious "losing" of the surplus was the result. Even necessary articles of winter clothing were thrown away in the spring if the quartermaster was tardy about making arrangements to store them. Feeling that the government would be sure to supply their needs anew when the chilly months approached, the soldiers refused to sweat themselves limp carrying this extra baggage. One instance is cited of an old negro, with mercenary as well as collective instincts, who, in the neighborhood of Vicksburg, picked up and stored away over a thousand overcoats and blankets in the spring of 1863. He was shrewd enough to suspect that many of the soldiers would be anxious to pay him a possible "six bits" apiece for these coats when the first cold spell came on and the quartermaster had not yet supplied their deficiencies.[492]

Again, the appetites and the bartering instincts of soldiers led them to dispose of really necessary clothing and equipment. Whiskey is given as one of the chief products received by this exchange.[493] So extensive did the loss of property become through such means that congress soon felt obliged to take action and forbid (March 3, 1863) that any clothing, equipage, and the like be "sold, bartered, exchanged, pledged, loaned, or given away" by the soldiers. Such materials were to be seized wherever found not in the possession of their rightful owners and the fact of possession was to be considered *prima facie* evidence of its having been acquired by one of the prohibited methods.[494] The thrifty Mississippi negro was at the time of his salvaging expedition liable to confiscation of his stores under this act.

Aside from these deliberate methods of disposing of encumbrances, much material was lost in time of battle. At such times, the quartermaster-general reported, "knapsacks are piled, blankets, overcoats, and other clothing thrown off, and, whether victorious or defeated, the regiments seem seldom to recover the property thus laid aside." [495]

In the field there was generally so much uncertainty about the arrival of supplies that foraging came to be a recognized mode of subsistence. In the Vicksburg campaign and Sherman's campaign in Georgia and the Carolinas, the armies were so far from their bases of supplies that for long periods at a time practically no

---

[492] *Downing's Diary*, p. 113.

[493] Upham, *loc. cit.*, p. 40.

[494] *U. S. Statutes at Large*, vol. 12, p. 735.

[495] *Official Records*, series iii, vol. 2, p. 805, report of November 18, 1862.

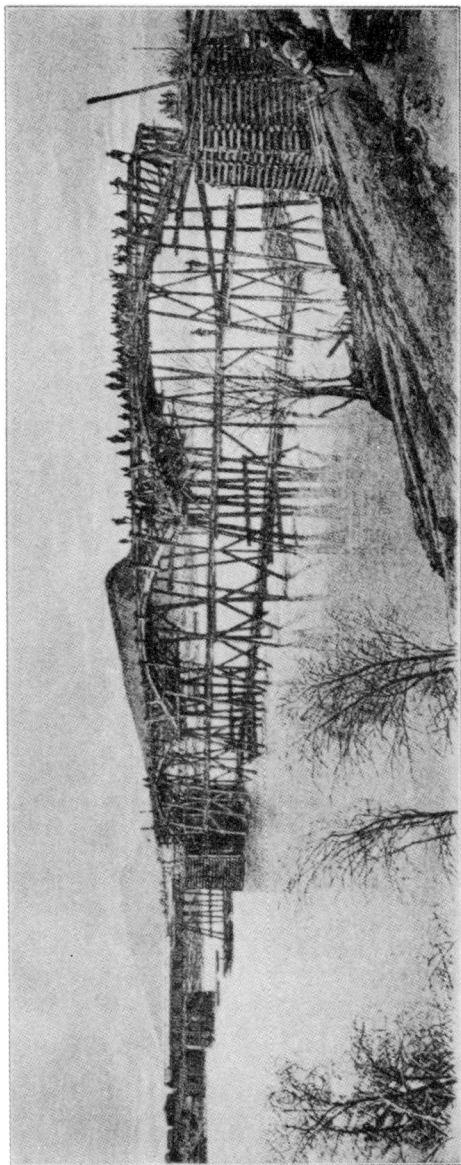

MILITARY BRIDGE OVER TENNESSEE RIVER AT CHATTANOOGA, 1864

other means of subsistence was possible. When, as after the capture of Corinth, new rail connections were made with the base of supplies, soldiers received regular rations [496] and had little real need of foraging. But when such communications were cut off and "two hardtacks, a little salt pork, a little salt, and some coffee to each man" was supposed to enable him to carry a load of fifty pounds on an all day's march,[497] it was little wonder that men foraged.

Often the only regular supplies for an army of a hundred thousand men had to be transported many miles over almost impassable roads. Swamps were sometimes encountered where wagons would sink to the box and the mules would mire down till they fell. Teamsters then would hold their heads above the slime while a footing was made of boughs and other teams were employed to pull them out.[498] Under such conditions it was difficult enough to keep army trains up with the troops and to carry up supplementary ammunition; no efforts could be spared to supply food. That must come from the citizens of the neighborhood.

In such cases the goods were presumably purchased. That is, the quartermaster issued requisitions on the Secretary of War for all material taken and then, if the owner could prove his loyalty to the country, he would get his money; if not, he would be considered a rebel and would get nothing. Though the transaction thus presumably assumed the aspect of legal purchase, the officers in reality took whatever they wanted and paid whatever they thought it to be worth.[499]

---

[496] *Downing's Diary*, p. 77.

[497] Sperry, *op. cit.*, p. 62.

[498] Musser, *loc. cit.*, pp. 284-285.

[499] *Downing's Diary*, pp. 57, 71-72; *Official Records*, series iii, vol. 3, p. 868.

All foraging except such as was officially authorized was theoretically discountenanced. Actually it was often overlooked. In any region where it was especially desired to placate the people, repressive measures were adopted to prevent unauthorized foraging. Frequent rolls were called, and individuals who did not answer to their names were presumed to be guilty. On their return to the ranks they were liable to a guard-house sentence or to extra duty.[500]

Elsewhere and on other occasions foraging was but little restricted. Sometimes the officers were actually in collusion with the men. Of this type was a captain in the campaign in southern Missouri who (in 1861), with his men, longed for a mess of fresh vegetables. Accordingly a raid on a turnip patch was planned. To prevent further investigation, if the colonel caught them, the captain warned the men that they should take no offense if he swore pretty hard at them, but by all means be sure to get the turnips.[501] On another occasion it was related that in the campaign around Vicksburg a general caught some men cutting up a hog shortly after an order against the killing of live stock. On inquiring into the reason for this infraction of rules he was told that a drove of wild hogs had attacked the men and that they had fired in self defense and killed one of them; whereupon the wise general rode on.[502] That some such rules against the killing of animals were necessary at that time is evidenced by the testimony of another soldier in the same campaign that, on the Arkansas side of the river, the men were so careless of

[500] *Downing's Diary*, p. 81.
[501] Barney, *op. cit.*, p. 73.
[502] *Downing's Diary*, pp. 138-139.

rebel property that they sometimes would kill cows just for their livers.[503]

Sherman's army on its march through Georgia and South Carolina deservedly gained the greatest notoriety for foraging as well as for wanton destruction. On leaving Atlanta they were ordered to take forty rations with them of hardtack, coffee, sugar, salt, pepper, candles, and soap but to forage for meat along the way. The success that they met with is commemorated in history, legend, and song.[504] The methods have been described by many participants, the following description being representative:

"Starting out early in advance of the command, they would do their pillaging, return to the main road to await the arrival of the command, and along in the afternoon we would find them, often loaded down with good things for their comrades to eat. They sometimes came upon rich plantations where the owners had about everything they wanted, including a well filled larder. When there was no wagon at hand, they would look the premises over and, finding the family carriage and horse, they would load it [sic] down and start for the main line of march. I have often seen them with a fine family carriage filled with smoked meat, and on the outside were tied chickens, turkeys, and geese or ducks. Then, to cap the climax, one fellow would be seated in the carriage dressed in the planter's swallow tail coat, white vest and plug hat, while another one would be astride a mule and dressed in similar fashion." [505]

It cannot be questioned that this system was attended

503 Sperry, *op. cit.*, p. 13.
504 *Downing's Diary*, p. 229.
505 *Ibid.*, p. 241, note.

not only with enormous waste but wanton and sometimes malicious destruction as well. Even in Tennessee
and as early as 1862, a soldier recorded in his diary
how he and his comrades set fire to the fences along the
road heedless of the consequences and that, when the
owner of a plantation was away with the Confederate
army, there usually was not much left of his property
when they got through.[506]

This tendency was greatly increased in Sherman's
march to the sea and, when the troops reached South
Carolina, they threw restraint to the winds and pillaged
at their will. "Every man seemed to think that he had
a free hand to burn any kind of property he could put
the torch to. South Carolina paid the dearest penalty
of any state in the Confederacy, considering the short
time the Union army was in the state. . . ." [507] The
number of fires of incendiary origin increased day by
day until ten to twenty red clouds could be seen from
the place of encampment every night.[508]

Sometimes a sudden revenge would be meted upon
the foragers or "bummers," or they would meet with
unexpected resistance: a bucket of scalding water from
the hands of an irate female guarding her chicken
roost, or bullets from a "sniper" in the bushes.[509] Once
in awhile a man would be found hanged and placarded
with a warning against foraging, or shot dead and likewise decorated. On one occasion twenty-one infantry-
men were reported found lying dead in a ravine with
their throats cut but with no such notices attached.[510]

---

[506] *Ibid.*, pp. 80, 87.
[507] *Ibid.*, p. 259, note.
[508] *Ibid.*, p. 252.
[509] *Ibid.*, pp. 104, 168.
[510] *Ibid.*, p. 256.

Evidently the officers in command made but little effort to suppress wanton pillage in South Carolina, the seat of the rebellion. But, on entering North Carolina, strict orders were issued that burning of property should cease and that any soldier caught in the act of starting an incendiary fire should be shot on the spot. This order seems to have had a salutary effect, for the destruction rapidly diminished and practically ceased after the surrender of Joseph E. Johnston.[511]

One problem involved in sustaining an army in the field, not so generally thought of as the question of food but quite as important, was the matter of water supply. For an army on the march it was not always possible to select a camping place at a site convenient to a good and sufficient source of water supply. No mere well, or two or three of them, would suffice for any length of time for an army of a hundred thousand or more thirsty and dirty men and their equally thirsty horses.

Around Petersburg, while Grant's army was conducting its interminable siege, the men solved this difficulty by digging numerous wells, lining some of them with barrels placed one on top of the other. Where barrels could not be had, large excavations were made, extending backward into a flight of stairsteps down which the men climbed to dip up the water.[512]

In the rear of Vicksburg the problem of water supply was complicated by the fact that the Confederates had polluted the streams with their dead horses. Consequently whenever wells or cisterns were found unpolluted soldiers sometimes had to stand in line for more than an hour waiting their turn to fill their canteens.[513]

---

[511] *Ibid.*, p. 272.
[512] *Harper's Weekly*, vol. 8 (August 6, 1864), p. 502.
[513] *Downing's Diary*, p. 128.

Troops were fortunate when, as at Corinth, they could drill deep wells where a constant supply of pure water could be secured.[514] How fortunate they were was only revealed when a few months later some of these same men had to take their choice between a consuming thirst and the green, stagnant water of Mississippi bayous. Some could withstand the temptation for a time but eventually they gave in, threw themselves down, "brushed aside the green scum and drank that hot, sickly water. . . ." These men knew nothing of the germ theory of disease, but they soon suffered the effects of their indulgence. A diary of one of the men shows that a week later some of the men were suffering with chills and fever. Still two days later he reports that a large number were sick and unable to walk. On the tenth day occurs the entry: "Over half the boys in our regiment are sick with the fever and ague, all because of the very poor water we had to drink while on the march." They were dosed with blue-mass pills, some of the worst cases were sent away to a more healthful climate, many died, and many others, the author declares in a note, "never fully recovered from the diseases contracted while passing through that malarious region. . . ."[515]

From two or three to a half dozen times a year there came a day to each regiment when all were anxious to be present at roll call and were in a more than ordinarily cheerful mood – this was pay day. The process of mustering for pay was so tedious and prolonged that plenty of good spirits were necessary to keep the interest from flagging. First came an inspection of the companies in detail, following which the mustering

---

[514] *Ibid.*, p. 77.
[515] *Ibid.*, pp. 136-137, 139, 141 and note, 142-143.

officer, usually a staff officer of the brigade, called the roll. During this process the men stood in open ranks with the officers at their posts, the non-commissioned officers and privates carrying their guns at support. As each name was called the person signified brought his gun to "order arms" and "arms at ease" at the same time answering to his name. Return was then made on the rolls of all men absent for any reason, with the reason stated, the mustering officer himself checking those named as on guard or in the hospital. The rolls were then signed and certified to by the captains and sent to the mustering officer who annotated them as to the condition of the men, their discipline and the like. The rolls were then copied in quadruplicate, one copy being sent to the adjutant-general at Washington, two to the paymaster-general, and the fourth kept in the regiment. The paymaster then calculated the sum due each man and, whenever he received the necessary funds, he proceeded to the camp to make the payment and then to leave for duties elsewhere.[516]

This system was almost incomprehensible to foreign observers and was naturally exasperating to the men. Furthermore, the long periods during which he had to wait between pay days often left the soldier in dire want and, if a man of family responsibilities, in extreme anxiety as to the needs of those at home. Payday was supposed to occur every two months but in the field the soldiers were fortunate if they got their pay at four month intervals and authentic instances are recorded where they went six and eight months.[517]

The amount of the pay was large or small according

---

[516] Trobriand, *op. cit.*, p. 112.
[517] *Ibid.*, p. 114; *Downing's Diary*, pp. 227, 284; Sperry, *op. cit.*, p. 168; Scott, *op. cit.*, p. 386, note.

as it was viewed by foreigners or by the soldiers themselves. Men like General Regis de Trobriand, the
Prince de Joinville, and the Count of Paris considered
the pay enormous as compared with the sums paid in
Europe, while privates in the army, comparing their
pay with the amount they were accustomed to, viewed
it as a mere pittance. Measured in dollars the pay of
privates was $11 at the beginning of the war, which sum
was raised to $13 by Act of August 6, 1861.[518]

Actually the pay of the soldiers steadily diminished
throughout the war through the depreciation in the
value of the greenbacks with which, after February,
1862, they were paid. In order to cover this loss to the
soldiers their pay was increased from $13.00 to $16.00
by act of June 20, 1864,[519] but this slight increase did
little to remedy the situation at a time when greenbacks
were worth only from forty to fifty cents on the dollar.
Moreover the soldiers themselves realized the depre-
ciating value of their pay and one of them made the
fairly accurate estimate that at one time they were
fighting for $6.00 a month and that after 1862 they
never had as much as $8.00 a month.[520]

Yet when the pay had been delayed for a period of
half a year or more and unused clothing allowances
were due, in addition to a possible $75.00 or $100.00 of
federal bounty money, the soldier might find himself
possessed all of a sudden with a seemingly princely sum
of money, often in excess of $200.00.[521] Frequently this
regular source was further supplemented by trading

---

[518] *U. S. Statutes at Large*, vol. 12, p. 326.

[519] *Idem*, vol. 13, p. 144. The reason for this increase was realized at the
time; *e.g.*, see Trobriand, *op. cit.*, p. 114.

[520] Scott, *op. cit.*, p. 386.

[521] *Downing's Diary*, p. 284.

with the natives, selling them coffee (sometimes already once boiled), or again even trading on their hostility to the federal stamp on money.

In the border states, and Missouri especially, there was among the secessionist element so deadly a hostility to the federal government that, at least in 1862, they were willing to trade any federal or "Lincoln money," dollar for dollar for Confederate money. This gave certain soldiers a splendid opportunity. Fac-simile Confederate Treasury notes could be bought at that time at four dollars a thousand in New York,[522] and these were disposed of by trading with the gullible zealots of Missouri. A woman was said to have refused "Lincoln money" for some meals served to soldiers but gladly accepted a $5.00 fac-simile Confederate bill in payment. It was even averred that a patent-medicine label was passed upon a secessionist by explaining to him that it was a new style Confederate bill. This, however, seems a pretty strong statement to stand the test of the traditional Missouri incredulity.

With the regular supply of money, and sometimes an irregular supply in addition, the suddenly rich soldier found himself tempted to spend it freely, especially if he had no family or dependents to help. Knowing that life was an uncertainty at best, he was inclined to make the most of his wealth; to squander, to gamble, to buy whiskey, or to desert.[523]

For a soldier in this frame of mind it was not at all difficult to gratify his wishes. In fact the only safe disposal of the money was to send it home for safekeeping, and even this was not always possible or feasible.

---

[522] *Harper's Weekly*, vol. 6 (October 11, 1862), p. 656, advertisement.
[523] Barney, *op. cit.*, pp. 54, 64.

Grafters, pay-discount sharks, gamblers, and sutlers were ever ready to relieve the soldier of any inconvenient burden of money. The soldier hard pressed for money was easy prey to the professional money lenders. The early militia regiments, instead of being paid like the regular army, received monthly warrants upon the treasury, which it took sometimes two or three months to cash. Taking advantage of the dire necessity of soldiers and their families, "a shoal of land sharks, some of them well known to public fame," formed combinations to buy up the warrants at six or seven dollars for eleven,[524] thus realizing fifty per cent. or better on an investment without risk, for a term of sixty to ninety days. These men must have been the forerunners of the later bounty brokers. Fortunately when the volunteer army was organized and the regular pay system introduced into it, this system of graft could not continue.

Without hypothecating his wages in any such manner, the soldier had to exercise care to prevent spending it before the next pay day in the purchasing of conveniences or luxuries. Sometimes a negro woman would be found who would do a soldier's dirty washing for a small sum. Thereby relief from drudgery was purchased by many at the rate of about twenty-five cents a week.[525] Even this small sum amounted to more than two days pay a month and could little be afforded by many. In the winter of 1862-1863 stoves in Arkansas were said to have sold at $120.00 to $150.00 apiece, yet the soldiers managed to club together and buy a few though they were not an absolute necessity.[526] Photog-

[524] *New York Tribune*, May 30, 1861.
[525] *Downing's Diary*, pp. 141, 157.
[526] Sperry, *op. cit.*, p. 51.

raphers were always to be found among the camp followers, and they carried on a lucrative business in tintypes for the men to send back home.[527] The newspapers and magazines were replete with advertisements of conveniences for soldiers, such as stoves, tent warmers, and solid gold pen points – iridosmine tipped, guaranteed to outwear a gross of steel points. All of these got their share of customers but frequently the soldiers failed ever to get the articles they sent their money for.[528]

One article very extensively bought by soldiers in 1861, but advertised for a good two years thereafter, was the steel-plated vest, guaranteed bullet-proof under certain conditions. These vests were made of blue cloth "cut in military style, with two plates of steel, formed to fit the body and fastened between the cloth and the lining, so as to cover the front of the wearer from the neck to the waist. Samples of the plates were exhibited in the camps, with deep marks upon them where bullets had failed to penetrate, a spectacle which, with the glib tongues of the dealers, induced a few of the officers and men to buy. . . ."[529]

According to the advertisements these breastplates were thoroughly tested with pistol bullets at ten paces and with rifle bullets at forty rods, presumably had saved the lives of officers of all ranks, and were worn by the bravest and best men in the army. They came in three sizes and ranged in price from $5.00 to $7.00 for privates and from $7.00 to $9.00 for officers.[530] The ad-

---

[527] *Downing's Diary*, p. 99, note. By use of notes Downing separates his reminiscences from the body of the diary.

[528] *Ibid.*, p. 211 and note.

[529] Scott, *op. cit.*, pp. 27-28.

[530] See *New York Tribune*, April 15, 1862; *Harper's Weekly*, vol. 6 (March 8, 1862), p. 160; *idem*, vol. 7 (March 14, 1863), p. 176 for typical advertisements.

vertisements guaranteed them to be simple and light, but the soldiers found them to be cumbersome and heavy, weighing from eight to ten pounds each, and accordingly they customarily went the way of all encumbrances.[531] General Sheridan is quoted as saying that officers who wore steel vests were "driven out of decent society by general contempt." [532]

Gambling has already been mentioned as a frequent pastime in the army: it was also a very fruitful means of quick transfer of money. After a pay day the gamblers in the regiment were always especially busy,[533] and very frequently a soldier, after having gone half a year between pay days, found himself destitute in a few hours. The game of "chuck luck" seems to have been a favorite form of gambling. Twelve to twenty soldiers would assemble at each "bank," get down on their knees and lay their money on certain numbers. The "banker" then threw the dice and always made a balance regardless of whoever won or lost.[534]

The temptation to risk money on such games of chance seems to have been almost irresistible at times. One of the war diarists, who most frequently laments gambling in the army, also shows a very strict accounting of all money spent, a notable feature being that on each pay day most of the money was sent to the writer's father for safe keeping. This writer enters for the date November 7, 1864, that he drew $148.00 in pay and $100.00 of bounty money. The usual reference to sending home most of this amount, say two hundred dollars, does not appear. But three days later there appears the

---

[531] Scott, *op. cit.*, p. 28.
[532] *Autobiography of A. D. White* (New York, 1905), vol. 1, p. 220.
[533] *Harper's Weekly*, vol. 7 (November 7, 1863), p. 711.
[534] *Downing's Diary*, pp. 153-154.

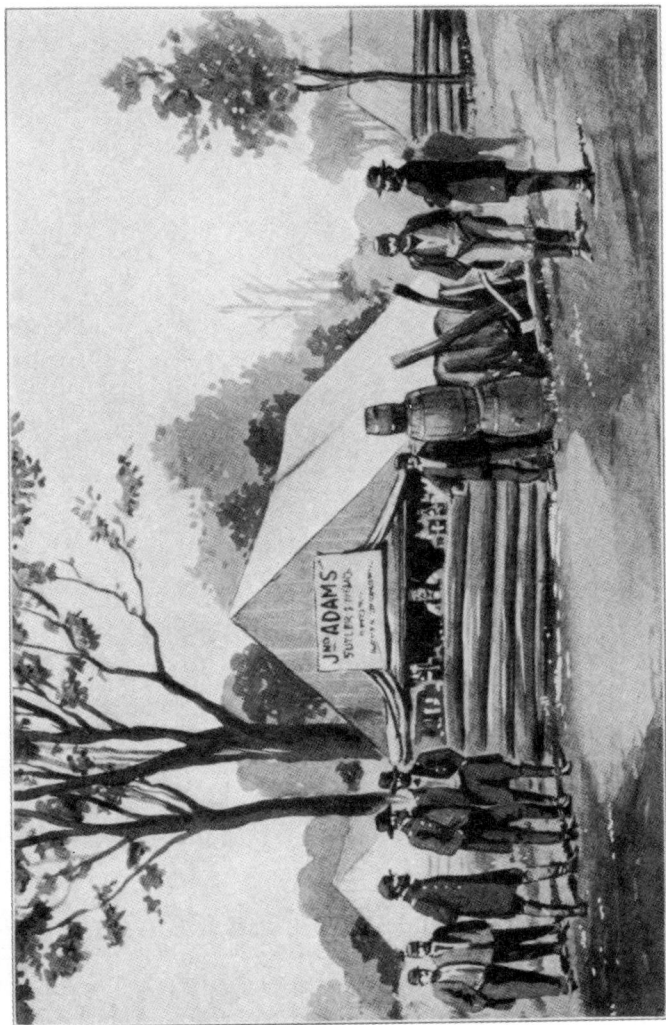

The Semi-official Profiteer

item, "I borrowed $25.00 from William Barrett until next pay day." Only inference can be drawn from these memoranda of an ordinarily methodical diarist. The only record of expense between these two entries was that of $18.50 for a watch.[535]

Gamblers came and gamblers went, their trade was a seasonal one, but sutlers were an ever-present evil. One might win from the gamblers occasionally but the sutlers always won. To make matters worse they were protected in their trade by the government and could usually charge all the traffic would bear. Consequently they were the most incessant source of drain upon the soldiers' pay. Sutlers had a sort of semi-official connection with the regiments. They usually secured the concession through political influence in their states,[536] and held a sort of commission for the job giving them sole power to deal in certain commodities with the soldiers in the camps. Their stocks were usually limited, but monotony of army fare and the many small needs which the government did not supply made them a sort of necessary evil in the regiments.

The remarkable thing is that, considering the prices charged, there was not more general dissatisfaction with them than actually existed. Among prices charged at City Point, Virginia, in 1864, were $1.00 to $1.25 for a can of fruit; sweet potatoes, fifteen cents a pound; cheese, sixty cents; onions, fifteen cents; butter, eighty-five cents; and other things in proportion.[537] The situation in the West was equally bad, a $4.00 barrel of potatoes bringing $12.00 in 1863, and this was Union

---

[535] *Ibid.*, pp. 227-228.
[536] Joinville, *Army of Potomac*, p. 14.
[537] *Harper's Weekly*, vol. 8 (December 10, 1864), p. 787.

money, not Confederate.[538] Furthermore both these prices are the value and cost in the same medium of exchange – greenbacks. In silver the potatoes would probably have been worth $2.00.

Sometimes the sutler's game was spoiled by foraging parties, and, in Sherman's army, after they reached Atlanta, the sutler was almost a useless encumbrance in the regiment. Before the fall of Atlanta they had been getting a dollar a plug for tobacco and fifteen cents each for cigars, but the day after, plug tobacco sold for five cents and cigars for twenty-five cents a hundred. Tobacco was dug up everywhere and the soldiers for once were able to indulge themselves to the limit, at almost no expense.[539]

The whole matter of the supervision of the sutlers' business came up during the regular session of congress in the autumn of 1861. Thereupon these merchants fought valiantly to prevent the enactment of regulations limiting their control over the soldiers' purses. It was said that the sutlers levied a per capita contribution upon each member to defeat the measure but, as was said at the time, "to men who charge five cents a piece for postage stamps, and two cents a piece for the commonest envelopes, this sum is a mere bagatelle." [540]

The bill as it finally passed was somewhat of a compromise. By the act of December 24, 1861, previous legislation allowing sutlers a lien on the pay of the soldier was repealed,[541] but by the act of March 19, 1862, the lien was restored to the extent of one-sixth of the soldier's monthly pay each month. This act also

---

[538] *Downing's Diary*, pp. 98, 132, 154.
[539] Hinkley, *op. cit.*, p. 142.
[540] *New York Tribune*, December 9, 1861.
[541] *U. S. Statutes at Large*, vol. 12, p. 331.

enumerated the articles to be sold, intoxicants being for-
bidden, and provided for a board of officers in each
regiment to fix the prices each month. No sutler could
sell to any soldier on credit to the extent of more than
a quarter of his month's pay each month and his legal
claim was to be only one-sixth.[542]

The weakness of this act was that the fixing of
prices was left to a board of officers of each regiment,
thus allowing as much diversity in prices as there were
regiments, and also, in many cases, leaving the fixing
either in the hands of persons incompetent to judge or
willing to split profits with the sutler. The consequence
was that sutlers ordinarily did about as they pleased
with the limitation only that, if their prices became too
exorbitant, the soldiers would either do without or procure the stores elsewhere.

[542] *Ibid.*, pp. 371-373.

The Collapse of State Recruiting

The Collapse of State Recruiting

BY LATE summer of 1861 the fervor of recruiting, which had been so marked in the spring, had largely subsided. The quotas under the calls for that year were oversubscribed in the aggregate but the distribution was grossly unequal. New Hampshire, Massachusetts, Connecticut, and New Jersey in addition to the slave states of Delaware, Maryland, and Missouri failed to meet their assigned quotas for volunteers under the call of May 3 and the acts of July, 1861. But Missouri, when her militia regiments are counted, more than overcomes her shortage, thus leaving a clear record of greatly oversubscribed quotas in the West as opposed to a bare compliance or actual failure in the East.[543]

In general this success, where it was a success, was due to the salutary shock received from the battle of Bull Run. The failure of the government to accept in April as many men as wished to volunteer for the war tended to dampen the ardor of potential volunteers. The panic attendant upon the collapse of the militia stirred the government out of its lethargy, without evoking in it any real conception of the problems with which it was faced, but the revived recruiting spirit which followed did much to undo the bad effects of the earlier governmental torpor.

A number of circumstances made the problem much

---

543 *Official Records*, series iii, vol. 4, p. 1264.

more difficult than it would have been if the conditions of April could have been restored. The surplus labor supply of the early spring had been absorbed both by the army and by the increased demands of farm and shop, thus leading each prospective volunteer to weigh his earning capacity in civil life against the relatively meager pay of the army. Then too the unwholesome publicity attendant upon the abuses in connection with the clothing and subsistence of the recruits acted as a restraint upon the lukewarm. The prophecy of the *New York Tribune* that "the Government will find that volunteers will not respond with much alacrity to future calls," [544] was rapidly materializing, especially in the East. The crowds no longer thronged to the recruiting stations without some additional enticement. Already the mercenary element was beginning to appear.[545]

As autumn approached the agricultural region of the West again had its seasonal labor surplus at the very time when the East was suffering from depleted labor ranks due to the rise of war industries. Thus the West was able to overbalance the shortage of the East in response to the calls for troops, but nevertheless the fact was made apparent that the peak of volunteering zeal had been passed. The spring of 1862 with its new demands for agricultural labor and its still increasing demands for factory labor would require some different method of recruiting.

A slight effort at systematization of recruiting was of some help in tiding over the winter of 1861-1862 and in completing the recruiting of the first volunteer army.

---

[544] *New York Tribune,* July 20, 1861.
[545] Trobriand, *Army of Potomac,* p. 72.

Until September the War Department had been in the habit of accepting regiments not only from the governors but from individuals as well. This resulted in a combination of federal and state acceptances more annoying in its effects than pure state control. Independent recruiting officers would start to raise a regiment and then, having difficulty in completing the task, would resort to decidedly underhanded methods to complete the work. Disgraceful rivalries arose which "led would-be colonels to bribe subordinate officers to transfer themselves with their men from one regiment to another." [546] On one occasion, at least, a shooting affray grew out of such practices and two men were killed and several wounded.

These practices were checked first in New York, then in Pennsylvania and Ohio, and finally in all the loyal states and territories by orders that, "all persons having received authority from the War Department to raise volunteer regiments, batteries, or companies in the loyal States. . . ." should report at once to the governors of their respective states and thereafter conform to their supervision. [547] In the following February this policy was made complete by the declaration that thereafter no independent organizations would be recognized; the state governors were to be the only legal authorities for raising volunteer troops and commissioning their officers. [548] What the earlier provision initiated the later made permanent.

The popular judgment concerning this change was quick and favorable. Being in line with the stricter state-rights doctrine it coincided with the wishes of a vast

---

[546] *New York Tribune*, September 11, 1861.
[547] *Official Records*, series iii, vol. 1, pp. 483-484, 489, 495-496, 518.
[548] *Ibid.*, p. 898.

majority of the people. As a movement toward uniformity it could not be objected to by military men. The only class injured by the change were the officers of the independent regiments and they were of no preponderating influence. The effect upon them was that they had either to hurry up and fill their regiments or else have the remnants consolidated and themselves deprived of their offices by action of the governors.[549] As for the soldiers in these independent organizations, the change to state control was decidedly beneficial. Hitherto the authorized officers had been placed too much upon their own resources and consequently the subsistence and care of the men was often very uncertain. Under the new ruling the men were sent to camp as soon as they were accepted, with the consequence that it became easier to find men to complete those organizations.

The feeling that recruiting in general was benefitted by the change [550] would be difficult to confirm. The majority of the regiments were unaffected, and recruits had always had the choice of entering either a state or an independent organization. The temporary revival of recruiting in the autumn of 1861 seems, even in New York, due rather to the seasonal slackness of labor in the agricultural regions, than to this change of governmental policy.

Though the move, on the face of it, seems like a further surrender to the state-rights principle, yet nothing was surrendered which, under the existing system, could not well be dispensed with. The independent organizations in no respect resembled actual direct recruiting efforts on the part of the federal government.

---

[549] *New York Tribune*, September 11, 1861.
[550] *Ibid.*, September 28, 1861.

They were merely isolated and spontaneous growths accepted by the War Department in the same way that state organizations were accepted. The officers were practically irresponsible until the regiments were completed and mustered. Therefore in terminating independent acceptances the federal government merely completed state control without giving up more than a semblance of national authority.

The tardiness of recruiting was already becoming acute before these regulations were issued. By early September it was found necessary to issue special appeals, extraordinary inducements, often of a pecuniary nature, and even covert threats of possible future drafts in order to stir up the laggards. Numerous reasons were given as to why prompt enlistment was as desirable as necessary: it was a noble cause; the pay was the highest in the world; the rations were the largest and best of any army anywhere; the reign of shoddy was over; good camp and hospital equipage was universal; weapons of the most desirable and effective patterns were being supplied; the Treasury of the United States was ample and its credit good; bad officers were being replaced by good; weather conditions in the field were ideal, the winter months south of the Potomac being only a long genial autumn; the rush season of work was over and a slack period coming on; the odds of numbers would now be with the Union instead of against it, because of the withdrawl of Confederate troops for harbor defense.[551] Thus the arguments ran the gamut from sound truth to sheer exaggeration and balderdash.

Even in the frontier states of the West with their surplus of male population, their rural structure, and the

[551] *Ibid.*, September 2, 1861, editorial.

possibilities of Indian uprising as additional incentive to alertness, similar arguments had to be used. "Shall it be said," asked the governor of Iowa of his constituents, "that you were unworthy the great deeds which were done in your behalf by that regiment of heroes [the Iowa First], that you were laggards in the great work which they so well began[?] Shall the fair fame of the State, which they have raised to the highest point of greatness, lose its luster through your backwardness to the call of your country, made in the holiest cause which ever engaged the efforts of a people? With you rests the responsibility. Men alone are wanted. Arms, equipments, liberal pay, the applause and gratitude of a nation, await the volunteer."[552] Such an appeal was not a mere display of rhetoric; it represented a real need growing out of actual conditions. The increasing knowledge of the magnitude of the rebellion was making men very cautious as to how they pledged themselves for three years or the war. Encouragement of enlistments by special appeals to particular classes had already been tried and had failed. Regiments filled but slowly and as early as August 31 permission had been given to muster men in squads.[553]

This situation seems to have made but little impression upon the War Department. Its action indicated the belief that the structure of the army was complete and that nothing more was necessary but to keep the army up to the limits established by the proclamations of 1861 and wait for the Confederacy to collapse. Perhaps with proper armament and training this attitude would have been justifiable, but under the existing circum-

---

[552] Shambaugh, *Messages and Proclamations*, vol. 2, pp. 485-486, September 10, 1861.

[553] Briggs, "Enlistment of Iowa Troops," in *Iowa Journal*, vol. 15, p. 349.

stances the conduct of the War Department from December to April can be reckoned as nothing short of sheer folly.

Yet the first step in this procedure bore, on the surface, the marks of statesmanship. An order of December 3, 1861, emanating from General McClellan, decreed a complete reorganization of the recruiting service. After the units then in process of organization in the various states were completed, no more troops were to be raised except upon special requisition by the War Department. General superintendents of recruiting were to be appointed to take charge, at the first of the year, of the central depots in each state. There volunteers would be concentrated, clothed, and instructed in the arts of war. The training was to be in the hands of experienced soldiers detailed as drill masters. To keep the ranks of the regiments in the field filled up, two commissioned officers and four other men from each regiment were to form recruiting squads to tour the country, and send volunteers in squads to the general rendezvous.[554]

This would seem to be a serious effort to recover national prestige by centering all initiative in recruiting in the War Department. As applied it was no such a thing. It was, in effect, a declaration that the governors had finished their work and done it well, and that now, since no more new organizations were needed, the federal government felt able to maintain the army at that standard. The governors were not peremptorily deprived of their prerogatives: they were simply given an honorable discharge in recognition of a faithful work well done.

---

[554] *Official Records*, series iii, vol. i, pp. 722-723.

The machinery thus established might well have been made the basis of a national system of recruiting or even of a *levee en masse* had not a burst of overconfidence on the part of Secretary Stanton led him to commit one of the colossal blunders of the war. Just when the new machinery was installed, adjusted, lubricated, and beginning to run smoothly, he issued, on April 3, 1862, an order discontinuing the recruiting service for volunteers in every state from that date. The order was thorough-going in every respect: the officers and men detached on volunteer recruiting service were ordered to return to their regiments; the recruiting offices were to be closed; and the public property belonging to the volunteer recruiting service was to be "sold to the best advantage possible, and the proceeds credited to the fund for collecting, drilling, and organizing volunteers." [555]

No sufficient justification of this action has ever appeared. Stanton's eulogistic biographer [556] ignores the question, and his chief defender against the attack of McClellan [557] (in the latter's autobiography) prefers to dwell upon the sins of the general rather than to find fault with the secretary. Stanton's own apology is disingenuous. In a dispatch to General Halleck, May 1, 1862, he said: "The order stopping recruiting was for the purpose of compelling returns from the respective governors. They have now been received." [558]

Why it was necessary to wreck the whole organiza-

---

[555] *Idem,* vol. 2, pp. 2-3.

[556] G. C. Gorham, *Life and Public Service of E. M. Stanton* (Boston, 1899), 2 volumes. No adequate life of Stanton has yet been written.

[557] W. D. Kelley, *Lincoln and Stanton* (New York, 1885). This work is confessedly partisan and is written in the characteristic political style of the then famous "Pig-Iron" Kelley.

[558] *Official Records,* series iii, vol. 2, p. 29.

tion in order to attain so small an object is not explained; perhaps it is best for his reputation that no attempt was made. The only plausible answer is contained in the words of the contemporary historian, Henry C. Lea: "We have sedulously deceived ourselves as to the magnitude and duration of the struggle in which we are engaged. . . . Deluded with the idea that the rebellion was constantly near its end, we have habitually resorted to temporary expedients, when a permanent system was indispensable. . . . Our rulers announce that no more men are wanted, and close all the recruiting offices. Six months later, the nation wakes up to find that its magnificent battalions have melted away." This corresponds with James B. Fry's statement that the act was in response to the popular demand for economy.[559]

Stanton's explanation, even if true and justifiable, would not warrant palliation of the policy adopted toward recruiting in the seven months following the general orders of December 3, 1861. During all that time no single step was taken to provide for a further increase of the army beyond the limits set during the preceding summer. The attitude early in 1862 was one of roseate confidence. Before the abolition of recruiting the armies both west and east were in motion; Forts Henry and Donelson had fallen, and McClellan had arrived upon the Peninsula bound for Richmond. Then, when every effort should have been made to bring the war to a speedy conclusion, this remarkable order came and so overconfident was the whole North that scarcely a ripple of interest was created by its issuance.

[559] Henry Charles Lea, "Volunteering and Conscription," in *United States*

Even a month later it was the avowed purpose of the Secretary of War merely "to keep the force up to its present standard." [560] In order to fill up the depleted regiments, commanders of armies in the field were authorized to requisition the War Department for more troops, whereupon the governors would be authorized to recruit the necessary contingents. [561] This was not a restoration of the abandoned system of recruiting but merely a slight reversion to the state-rights principle as a temporary expedient to keep depleted organizations from falling to pieces before the rebellion should be crushed.

Meanwhile another lesson of the war was being taught and tardily learned. Little comfort could be derived from Shiloh and Pittsburg Landing. Nor did the tardy occupation of Corinth and the dilatory tactics of McClellan on the Peninsula presage a brief life for the Confederacy. The armies were being wasted away by death, desertion, and sickness more rapidly than they could be recruited by the indirect method employed. Consequently by order of June 6, 1862, the recruiting system, abolished in April, was reëstablished. [562] But it was still another month, after the Seven Days' Battles had wrecked the hope of capturing Richmond and ending the war, before any active steps were taken actually to enlarge the army. It took a disaster in 1861 to cause the creation of the first army of half a million; it took a calamity in 1862 to jar the War Department loose from its attitude of complacency with

Service Magazine, vol. 1 (March, 1864), pp. 239-240; "Fry's Report" (see note 12), part i, p. 9.

[560] *Official Records*, series iii, vol. 2, p. 29.
[561] *Ibid.*, p. 28.
[562] *Ibid.*, p. 109.

that first half million. The precedent was rapidly being established that no progressive measure should be adopted until adversity compelled it.

While the United States Congress and Administration were thus leisurely presuming to hold their own, the Confederacy was exerting every effort to marshal her whole military force to bring about a dictated peace based on permanent separation. At the very time that Stanton issued his order abolishing the recruiting system, the Confederate Congress was debating the conscription act which it passed less than a fortnight later:[563] an act more perfect in many respects than any similar act passed by the United States Congress throughout the war. It is significant that, in the year during which the South was raising troops under this act and before the United States adopted a similar practice, the Confederacy was winning that remarkable series of victories from Gaines's Mill to Chancellorsville.

When the real gravity of the situation on the Peninsula began to dawn upon the administration, frantic efforts were made to compensate for the past errors and brace the army to meet the new demands. Lincoln, Stanton, and William H. Seward, were about equally alarmed, but all were desirous of keeping the fear from spreading to the people generally. It was recognized that a proclamation calling for more volunteers would look to the people like an acknowledgment of defeat. Therefore a subterfuge was resorted to, more remarkable for its ingenuity than for its results. Seward, as-

---

[563] "Journal of Congress of the Confederate States," in *Senate Documents,* 58 Cong., 2 sess., vol. 2, pp. 114 *et seq.*; Confederate States of America, *Statutes at Large from the Institution of the Government to February 17, 1864* (Richmond, 1862-1864), vol. 2, First Congress, pp. 29-32.

suming the initiative, hastened to New York, after having secured a letter from Lincoln expressing a wish for more men. After consultation with some of the more influential politicians there, he discovered that recruiting was practically at a standstill, that the order of June 6 had not counteracted the effect of that of April 3, and that if any more men were to be secured it must be through a special appeal.

Here the ingenious part of the scheme appeared. He drew up a draft of an appeal to the President asking him to call out more men, and telegraphed to the governors asking permission to use their names as signatory to the petition. At once there came replies from seventeen of the governors and acting heads of state governments expressing approval in one way or another of the proposed scheme, though not all were agreed that they would be successful in raising more men. Nevertheless their names were attached to the petition which was then antedated from June 30 to June 28 and presented to the President. The tone of the missive was optimistic. The recent victories (real or fancied) were mentioned, and the men were asked for, not to retrieve disaster but to hasten to a speedy conclusion a victory already in immediate prospect. In other words the appeal which should have been made immediately after Donelson was made after Gaines's Mill, assuming that the situations were parallel.

In the meantime the President was prepared for the overture and a form for his reply had been placed in his hands. The only question was as to the number of men to be called for. Seward at first proposed 150,000, Stanton felt that 300,000 would be better, while Lincoln was at first disposed to call for 200,000. Some were asking for half a million or even a million men, but finally the suggestion of Stanton was adopted. The President then dispatched to the various governors the form letter presented him by Seward, and the following day (July 2, 1862) formal orders were issued from the War Department for the raising of the 300,000 volunteers.[564] Just what was accomplished by this roundabout procedure is difficult to say but this much is certain, that it was a further concession to the state-rights prejudices of the people.

This reversion to the state-rights principle was made complete a few days later. As soon as the call for the 300,000 volunteers had been issued, Seward next telegraphed the governors of the northwestern states and the military head of Kentucky to meet with him at Cleveland, Ohio. As a result of the consultation held there, it was determined to leave the recruiting and management of the new contingents, so far as possible, in the hands of the governors until the troops were mustered into the service. This, it was hoped, would provide a uniform and efficient system.[565]

Now that additional troops had finally been called for, they were wanted in a hurry. Since the call was made without any legal sanction anyway, it might as well have been antedated by four or five months, when troops in the slack season of the year would have been more plentiful. A tacit recognition of this fact is concealed in a message from Lincoln to sixteen of the northern governors a day after the assignment of quotas.

---

[564] F. W. Seward, *Seward at Washington as Senator and Secretary of State* (New York, 1891), pp. 100-112; *Official Records*, series iii, vol. 2, pp. 180-188.

[565] Seward, *op. cit.*, p. 110; *Official Records*, series iii, vol. 2, pp. 198-200, 203, 205.

"I should not want the half of 300,000 new troops,"
he said, "if I could have them now. If I had 50,000
additional troops here now I believe I could substan-
tially close the War in two weeks. But time is everything, and if I get 50,000 new men in a month I shall
have lost 20,000 old ones during the same month, having gained only 30,000, with the difference between old
and new troops still against me. The quicker you send
the fewer you will have to send. Time is everything.
Please act in view of this." [566]

The replies to this message presaged the difficulties
recruiting was to encounter. Governor Israel Washburn
of Maine said, "Recruiting for three years is terribly
hard. Shall be obliged to resort to drafting, unless I
can be authorized to take volunteers for three or six
months." Governor Samuel Kirkwood of Iowa reported
that harvesting prevented rapid recruiting, but mentioned that a regiment of three-months men could easily
be raised. Governor Andrew G. Curtin of Pennsylvania
suggested that "if the enlistments were made for a
shorter time, say six months, it would greatly increase . . ." the numbers raised and hasten the formation of regiments. Adjutant-general John W. Finnell
of Kentucky asked that his state be allowed to raise a
portion of the new call with twelve-months men, saying
that he could get "better men and more expeditious"
in that way. Governor Oliver P. Morton of Indiana
said, "I am now raising five regiments, but the work
[is] tardy. I think I can raise fifteen sooner on a new
system." Governor John A. Andrew of Massachusetts
answered, "If you wish militia for three months, Mass-

---

[566] *Official Records*, series iii, vol. 2, pp. 200-201.

achusetts can furnish several thousand within the period named by you." [567]

These fears were substantiated by the results. Class appeal, emotional messages and speeches, even the offer of special pecuniary rewards failed in most cases to recruit the ranks as rapidly as was desired.[568] It was futile longer to talk of a short decisive conflict, even though the President professed to believe an additional fifty thousand at once would be sufficient. Accordingly the appeals for men took on more the tone of patriotic urging to self sacrifice, than the bombastic tone of a year earlier. "Our old men and our boys, unfit for war, if need be, our women must help to gather harvests," said Governor Kirkwood, "while those able to bear arms go forth to aid their brave brethren in the field. . . . The time has come when men must make, as many have already made, sacrifices of ease, comfort, and business for the cause of the country." [569]

When these ordinary methods failed, two alternatives remained, either to draft or to increase the bounties to such an extent as to tempt the men away from other forms of employment. Both were used. The question of state draft had been raised at least a year before it was applied. As early as August 24, 1861, Governor Hamilton R. Gamble of Missouri, when calling out the militia to suppress insurrection in that state, declared that if the desired number of men did not respond it might become necessary to resort to a draft.[570] Less than three

[567] *Ibid.*, pp. 201-206.

[568] N. M. McAllister, "The Citizen's Story," in *History of the 148th Pennsylvania Volunteers*, pp. 31-33; Briggs, *loc. cit.*, pp. 356-357. For bounties see later chapter on The Mercenary Factor.

[569] Shambaugh, *op. cit.*, vol. 2, p. 497.

[570] *Harper's Weekly*, vol. 5 (September 7, 1861), p. 563.

weeks later the governor of Iowa was using the same
sort of threat to secure an additional four regiments.[571]
Only a short time later Secretary Cameron felt called
upon to forbid the carrying of the latter threat into
execution, his excuse being that the patriotism of the
people could be relied on to carry the states through
the war.[572] In the East also the threat was unofficially
used at about the same time.[573] But no serious attempt
at drafting was made during that period nor until well
into the second year of the war.

In the meantime the Confederacy had stolen a march
upon the Union by the passage of its conscription act.
The full significance of this act coming to the cog-
nizance of the North at about the same time that news
was arriving of the victories of Lee over McClellan,
caused it to be received with emotions ranging from
admiration to anger and disgust. By some specious type
of reasoning the editor of the *New York Tribune* considered that a dirty and ignoble trick had been played
upon the North. In a curiously inaccurate and ill-rea-
soned statement he explained the causes why it was
necessary to call more men in the North. "It [the federal government] *had* men enough three months ago,
as things then were, to have broken the back of the
Rebellion. But the traitor chiefs, realizing their extremity, took the last desperate step that usurpation and
tyranny could devise. They ordered a levy *en masse* of
all the Whites and Mulattoes in the South between 18
and 55 years of age, and sent their myrmidons into every

---

[571] Shambaugh, *op. cit.*, vol. 2, p. 486.

[572] *Harper's Weekly*, vol. 5 (October 12, 1862), p. 643; *New York Tribune*, September 26, 1861.

[573] *New York Tribune*, September 2, 1861.

county and neighborhood to enforce the decree." [574] A philippic of invective accompanied this accusation, in which the chief tyranny of the South was described as the forcing of men of Union sympathies into the Confederate army. It was the same editor and many others like him who, a year later, were condemning as copperheads men in the North who objected to northern conscription on the same principle.

The knowledge of the Confederate conscription measure must have had something to do with the militia legislation initiated shortly after the call of July 2. A Washington item of July 8, 1862, announced to the reading public that Senator Henry Wilson had introduced "a bill which is virtually a conscription act." [575] In reality the bill was merely a revision of the old militia act of 1795, the principal change in it being that, instead of a three-months term, the President of the United States should specify the period for which the militia could be called out. [576] Neither draft nor any other form of conscription was mentioned in the bill. The manner of raising the men, as in previous militia acts, was left to the discretion of the governors.

Even so mild a bill as this was shortly superseded by one even less objectionable to the opponents of a strong central government, in that it set the maximum term of service at nine months. This bill had an easy course in congress. There was no debate on its military features, the focal point of controversy being the extraneous question of freedom for slaves (of rebels) – and their mothers, wives, and children – who were employed in

---

[574] *Ibid.*, July 4, 1862.
[575] *Ibid.*, July 9, 1862.
[576] *Congressional Globe*, 37 Cong., 2 sess., p. 3197.

the Union army. In the House of Representatives the bill passed a few minutes after its being called up, and became a law July 17, 1862.[577]

In its final form the act authorized the President to call out the militia for a period not to exceed nine months and to apportion quotas for the same among the various states. The militia was defined as all able-bodied male citizens between the ages of eighteen and forty-five, and the quotas were to be apportioned among the states according to their representative population. The degree of authority granted to the President in the enforcement of this bill was dependent upon the states themselves. Where adequate provisions were made by the state legislatures and enforced by the executives, for the calling out of the militia, the President would merely issue the call, apportion the quotas, and receive the men when raised. Elsewhere, where no state regulations existed or where regulations were inactive, the President himself was given the authority to provide regulations for the enrollment and raising of the militia.

Again no reference was made to drafting or any other form of conscription. Obviously states might draft if they chose but there was no obligation to do so. The real strength of the law lay in the clause that "If by reason of defects in existing laws, or in the execution of them, in the several States, or any of them, it shall be found necessary to provide for enrolling the militia and otherwise putting this act into execution, the President is authorized in such cases to make all necessary rules and regulations. . . ."[578]

---

[577] *Ibid.*, pp. 3289, 3320-3321, 3337 *et seq.*, 3397-3398; *U. S. Statutes at Large*, vol. 12, pp. 597-600.

[578] *U. S. Statutes at Large*, vol. 12, p. 597.

The phrase *all necessary rules and regulations* was broad enough to admit of various interpretations. If the President chose to consider that this gave him authority to draft, he might draft, but this possibility would not make of the militia act a draft act. Any state could avoid even this presumptive possibility of a draft by making and enforcing its own regulations. At the very most, this act was merely a mild persuasive act to stimulate the activities of the states rather than an act granting any considerable centralized authority to the federal government.

The draft of 1862 was, therefore, based upon executive interpretation rather than direct legislative sanction. As the full realization of the situation in Virginia became apparent to the administration, the desire for a rapidly increased army became more urgent. The 300,000 volunteers called for on July 2 seemed inadequate to the needs, even if they could be secured. But there was serious doubt as to the possibility of raising even that many men in time for them to be of any service against the emboldened Lee, who was already planning his campaign against Pope. Accordingly the first step was taken by the executive department toward federal control of recruiting. Under authority of the Militia Act of July 17, 1862, as well as of the act of 1795, an order was issued by the War Department on August 4, and communicated to the governors on the following day, calling for a draft of 300,000 men, to serve nine months, unless sooner discharged. This number was to be in addition to the quotas of July 2, the provision being made that if any state should not by August 15th "furnish its quota of the additional 300,-000 volunteers authorized by law, the deficiency of volunteers in that State" would also be made up by a special draft from the militia.[579]

This placed a definite responsibility upon the several governors to raise double their original quotas or else submit to a draft. By no stretch of the imagination could the militia act be construed to give authority to draft men for more than nine months. Therefore militia might be substituted for volunteers in tardy states. The legality of this proposed supplementary draft is very questionable, since it would not fall proportionally according to representation upon all states. Yet the illegality was one merely of form since it could be avoided simply by apportioning the new quotas upon the basis of 600,000 men and crediting upon these quotas the number of volunteers received from the states in question.

That this more legal method was not adopted was due probably to the desire to avoid the question of counting each three-year man raised as the equivalent of four nine-months men. To have done so would have been to halve rather than to double the original quotas. Since most people thought that the war would not exceed another nine months anyway and that the sacrifice of a three-year volunteer would, therefore, be no greater than that of a nine-months militiaman, the slight irregularity was scarcely noted. But in apportionment of credits for later quotas this difference of length of service had to be considered.

Regulations for the enrollment and drafting of the militia followed closely upon the new call. The gov-

[579] *Official Records*, series iii, vol. 2, pp. 291-292, 295-296. On p. 296 the date "18th of August" appears instead of "15th of August." By comparison with the order (p. 291) and later references to it – *e.g.*, p. 333 – it is apparent that the earlier date is the correct one.

ernors of all the states were requested to designate the
rendezvous of the drafted militia, appoint the comman-
dants of the same, and cause the enrollment of all able-
bodied male citizens between the ages of eighteen and
forty-five to be taken in each of the counties, or towns
and cities, by the assessors or other officers; the enrollment of each such citizen to contain his name, age, occupation, remarks showing whether or not he was in the
service of the United States and if so in what capacity,
and any other facts which might determine his exemption from military duty.

For those states lacking in adequate militia laws the
regulations stipulated further how the draft itself was
to be conducted. The lists of the enrolled persons were
to be filed in the offices of the sheriffs of the respective
counties. A commissioner for each county (appointed
by the governor at a salary of four dollars a day) was
to hear and decide upon all claims of exemption. The
commissioner was to give notice of the time and place
at which the claims would be received, and fix the time
at which the draft should be made. Persons claiming
exemption were required to give proof of their claims
before the commissioner previous to the day of the
draft, and if exempted their names were to be crossed
out.

A list of those to be automatically exempted was
made to include all persons then "in the military service
of the United States; all telegraph operators and con-
structors actually engaged on the 5th day of August,
1862; all engineers of locomotives on railroads; all ar-
tificers and workmen employed in any public arsenal
or armory; the Vice-President of the United States;
the members of both houses of congress and their re-

spective officers; all custom house officers and their clerks; all post officers and stage drivers . . . employed in the care and conveyance of the mail of the Post Office of the United States; all ferrymen . . . employed at any ferry on the post road; all pilots; all mariners actually employed in the sea service of any citizen or merchant within the United States; all engineers and pilots of registered or licensed steam-boats and steam-ships, and all persons exempted by the laws of the respective States from military duty. . . ." No exemptions were to be made for disability unless it were of such permanent character as to render the person unfit for service for a period of more than thirty days, and then only by certificate of a surgeon appointed by the governor in the county for that purpose.

The draft was to be made by placing the names of all the persons remaining on the enrollment lists, not striken off as provided, on separate folded ballots, these ballots then to be placed in a wheel or box, by the sheriff, and a number equal to the quota of the county or municipality drawn out by a blind-folded person appointed by the commissioner. The persons whose names were thus drawn were then to be notified and any person so drafted was to be given the privilege of furnishing an able-bodied substitute if he were of draft age.

These drafted men or their substitutes were then to assemble at their respective county seats within five days after the time of drafting, there to receive transportation to the place of rendezvous. In each of the states, provost-marshals, appointed by the War Department on nomination of the governor, were to enforce the attendance of such drafted persons at their designated rendezvous.[580]

---

[580] *Ibid.*, pp. 333-335, a general order dated August 9, 1862.

These legal provisions and executive regulations have been enumerated at some length for a twofold purpose: first, to show how far the central executive department had progressed in its reaction against the purely state-controlled recruiting of the preceding year; and, second, to show how far this proposed scheme fell short of actual federal supremacy. Under the calls for troops prior to August, 1862, quotas had been assigned at least roughly proportional to the population, but there was absolutely no coercive force other than that of public opinion or patriotic fervor to compel the raising of the assigned quotas. The states were supreme. They could raise the men or not just as they chose, and the federal government had only the choice of accepting those which were raised or of doing without.

It has been noted that upon the first call for militia six governors returned defiant answers, while two more (from Delaware and Maryland) evaded favorable replies. Four of the defiant governors were supported by their states in secession from the Union. The victory of the Union elements in Missouri and Kentucky and the consequent overthrow of Claiborne F. Jackson and the shelving of Beriah Magoffin constituted no assertion of federal authority, but merely the declaration of the controlling factions in those states that they would cast their lot with the Union rather than with the Confederacy. The same results were obtained in Delaware and Maryland through the graceful conformity of the governors to the popular will. But in each state the result was in harmony with the same principle: the majority or controlling faction should determine whether or not the requisitions from the federal government were to be honored. The same principle prevailed in the more northern states the only distinction being that

in the latter the element favoring a military chastise-
ment of the South was in the larger majority.

In contrast to this pronounced state-rights supremacy
of the spring of 1861, the detailed orders and regulations of August, 1862, have the appearance of a decided
reaction in favor of federal supremacy. But a closer
view shows that this supremacy was not a thing of authority but merely a self-assured executive leadership,
accepted by the state governors because of the glaring
need of closer coöperation between the federal and state
branches of the government in prosecuting the common
cause. The detailed provisions for the draft were without any direct legal sanction and could scarcely have
been enforced in any unwilling state without military
force – and there was no surplus force to perform such
duty even if the President had been willing to use it.

Finally, as before stated, all these regulations were
merely for those states which had no adequate militia
laws of their own, and formed a model for the states
in general rather than a uniform federal mechanism.
In this connection the concession to state control, even
in the drafting regulations, should be noted. County
officers and special commissioners were to attend to
every detail of exemption and drafting until the time
that the men were ready to be transported to their rendezvous. Even then the provost-marshals who were to
enforce the service of the drafted men were to be appointed only on nomination by the governors. There
was not a detail in the whole scheme which did not rest
ultimately upon the sufferance of the state governments
and their subsidiary parts.

If there was any accretion to the national authority
emanating from the draft of 1862 it was certainly not

due to any increase in the power of congress nor to any inherent prestige to the executive proceeding from its self-appointed leadership. If such nationalizing effects are to be discerned at all, they are due to the growing desire of the people in general to subordinate petty differences to the common good, in order to win the war. This desire found expression in the acceptance by the governors of the leadership of the federal executive. Only the operation of the draft could show the degree to which such national interests succeeded in overcoming state interests.

It became quickly apparent that the draft was not intended as the primary source of man power. Rather it was merely a whip to encourage volunteering. But, in order that it might reap its full effect, the draft was made three fold in its aims: first, to raise an army of 300,000 militiamen; second, to round out the quotas of the 300,000 men called for on July 2; third, to fill the depleted ranks of the regiments already in the field. The first purpose was to be accomplished directly by the draft; the second by a special draft if the recruiting were not completed by August 15; the third was provided for in an order of August 14, calling for a special draft to replenish the old regiments if they were not filled by volunteers before September 1.[581]

Previous legislation, as well as executive clemency, allowed adjustments to such a degree that several states escaped the draft on all of these counts. The militia act, upon which the draft was based, authorized the enlistment of volunteers to fill up the depleted regiments, in unlimited numbers for a term of one year and, as a special inducement to such volunteering, offered a bounty

---

[581] *Ibid.*, pp. 380-381.

of fifty dollars for each such enlistment. The same law allowed a bounty of $25 to each of 100,000 volunteers for nine months,[582] and previous legislation had been granting for the past year and continued to confer a bounty of $100 each upon three-year volunteers.[583] These federal, in addition to state and local bounties, as will be shown in a later chapter, had much to do in securing the required number of volunteers without draft.

The leeway for avoiding the major militia draft was opened up shortly after the draft itself was ordered. In response to a request from Governor Edwin D. Morgan of New York requesting that surplus three-year volunteers should be counted in lieu of an equal number of militia the Secretary of War replied as follows:

"The subject of your telegram received today has been under careful examination for some days. If the whole 300,000 called for by the draft could be promptly obtained by volunteers, and as quickly as by draft, it might be unnecessary to make the draft. The quota of volunteers called for and now filled up in several of the States comprehends only the allotment to new regiments, leaving the old regiments unfilled. It is designed to receive volunteers to fill up the old regiments, and any excess after they are filled will be credited to the State as so much on the draft; and if enough volunteer to fill up the old regiments, that perhaps might dispense with the draft. The Department will receive volunteers for old regiments to the time the draft is made." [584]

There were equally generous provisions for relieving individuals from the draft. The exempted classes,

[582] *U. S. Statutes at Large*, vol. 12, p. 598.
[583] *Ibid.*, pp. 269-270.
[584] *Official Records*, series iii, vol. 2, p. 354, dated August 11, 1862.

enumerated in the regulations for the draft, were deemed sufficient to relieve all the most important civil officers as well as essential industrial workers from liability to service. This list was added to from time to time as officials in powder mills or railroad owners began to request exemption of certain employees, and, where such exemptions were not granted, it was sometimes arranged that the drafted employees should be discharged after draft.[585] State officers when not provided for by state laws, physicians, surgeons, and even clergymen, were later exempted by special orders.[586]

Some states went to greater extremes than this. For instance New York exempted preachers, Shakers, Quakers, professors, teachers and students in all colleges and public academies (as distinguished from private schools), teachers of common schools, idiots, lunatics, infamous criminals, habitual drunkards, and paupers, in addition to those regularly exempted by federal decree.[587]

Another concession to state pride was made in the matter of the substitution and volunteering of drafted men. The draft seemed to most citizens as a sort of disgrace though many were willing to run the risk of being drafted rather than to volunteer. Therefore the draft had to be resorted to in those states where ordinary efforts had proved insufficient to procure the full quotas of men. Many men after being thus drafted, wishing to avoid the stigma of being conscripts and no doubt wishing also to avail themselves of the bounty which had hitherto failed to tempt them, asked to be allowed to volunteer. Taking advantage of this opportunity to

---

[585] *Ibid.*, pp. 336, 337, 348, 358, 398.
[586] *Ibid.*, pp. 392, 458-459, 512.
[587] *Ibid.*, pp. 668-669.

secure three-year men instead of ordinary militia for nine months, the Secretary of War granted the desired boon.[588] Drafted men who were able to hire substitutes were ultimately given a space of ten days after their muster in which to procure such substitutes provided no extra expense was incurred thereby by the government.[589]

As a further concession to liberality in the administration of the draft, the governor of Ohio exempted members of religious denominations whose creed forbade the taking up of arms, but, unlike New York, required a payment of $200 from each person so exempted in commutation of his services and for use in hiring a substitute for him. From this source the state received in the month of October something like $50,-000.[590] This item is of special interest since it is in a small way a forecast of the later national policy of commutations.

In spite of multifarious concessions, the process of enrollment and draft progressed but slowly. Indian outbreaks in Minnesota retarded the work there.[591] Organized resistance, particularly among the foreign element in parts of Wisconsin and Pennsylvania, and in Maryland, made the work of the itinerant county officers, who made the house to house canvass for enrollment, very uncomfortable.[592] So many persons attempted to leave the country or to evade enrollment by

---

[588] *Ibid.*, pp. 650, 670.

[589] *Ibid.*, p. 881.

[590] *Ibid.*, pp. 650, 662, 693, 704.

[591] *Message of Governor Ramsey to Legislature of Minnesota, delivered September 9, 1862* (a pamphlet in the Iowa State Historical Library, Saint Paul, 1862), p. 24.

[592] This subject is discussed more fully and authorities are cited in chapter on The Slacker Problem.

moving from one locality to another that for a time it was necessary to restrict migration. It was decreed that any person liable to draft who should culpably absent himself from his state or county should be arrested and placed in the army. The cost of arrest, transportation, and a five-dollar fee for the arresting officer was to be deducted from the pay of the soldier. For such cases the privilege of writ of habeas corpus was suspended.[593]

Before the draft was completed the President took this matter more thoroughly in hand by ordering that rebels, rebel sympathizers, and all other persons discouraging enlistments, or resisting drafts, should be subject to martial law and court-martial. The writ of habeas corpus was suspended in their cases also. This decree, countersigned by Seward,[594] constituted one of the usurpations of authority so bitterly denounced by the opposition in congress during the next two years. In general such threats as these were of little practical value, since they were unenforceable except at the will of the governors. They produced more harm through the discord engendered than could be offset by any possible advantages.

The ineffectiveness of drafting through state agencies was further shown by the tardiness of the returns. Speed was the prime essential in the project from the start. Therefore the date set for the beginning of the draft was September 3, the drawings to take place from 9 A. M. to 5 P. M. and each succeeding day at the same hours until the entire quotas had been exhausted. But this date was not strictly adhered to. As the time of the draft approached and the frantic efforts to fill the quotas with

---

[593] August 13, 1862, *Official Records*, series iii, vol. 2, pp. 329, 345, 349, 370, 525-526.

[594] Dated September 24, 1862, *ibid.*, pp. 587-588.

volunteers had not entirely succeeded, the governors began to pour in requests asking for postponement. Each such petitioner was certain that, if he were given just a few days longer, he would be able to dispense with a draft altogether and thus secure results more promptly than the draft itself would.[595] Under the circumstances there was no other alternative than to assent, since there was no legal method of coercing the governors into prompt compliance. To refuse their requests and have them disregard the decree would be the abdication of leadership.

The only escape from this dilemma was to cast the responsibility for postponement upon the states. Accordingly, a week before the day designated for the draft, seventeen of the governors were requested to begin operations as soon after September 3 as possible, they themselves taking the responsibility for the extention – the order from the War Department could not be changed.[596] It is doubtful whether this subterfuge did much credit to the national government. It was merely another way of confessing that a draft of the state militia by presidential decree was an impossibility under the existing conditions, and that it devolved upon the states to complete the thing in any way that they saw fit.

Having secured this postponement the governors drafted whenever they saw fit. On September 15, Governor David Tod of Ohio announced that he had post-

---

[595] *Ibid.*, pp. 430, 436, 442, 446, 450-451, 453, 462, 465-467, 470-471, 474, 493, 497, 547, 548, 640-643.

[596] *Ibid.*, pp. 465-468, 470-471. Iowa, Missouri, Kentucky, Kansas, West Virginia, and the District of Columbia had already raised their quotas, while for apparent reasons no quotas had been assigned to California, Oregon, and the phantom Union state of Virginia.

poned the draft a second time, setting the date at October 1. On the same day Governor Andrew of Massachusetts requested a similar postponement. Later, on his own initiative, he announced another delay, setting the date at October 15. This was followed by still further procrastination until December.[597] Even then he had not raised his quota and was compelled to draft in order to secure as much as ninety per cent. of it.[598] So slow were the returns from the various states that as late as November 24, nearly three months after the draft was supposed to have been made, the War Department was impelled to ask fourteen of the governors to report by telegraph immediately, first the number of volunteers for three years secured since July 2, and second, the number of men drafted for military service or volunteers for nine months.[599]

In answer the governor of Maryland reported that all of the counties had not yet drafted. Massachusetts reported that her draft would be executed on December 8. The governor of Wisconsin stated, "We drafted 4,500. How many will come in and not be exempted it is impossible to tell." Later reports show the number to have been 958. Other states reported in vague terms while, on the other hand, Pennsylvania stated that her draft would no doubt produce at least thirty regiments, a supposition which was borne out by the later reports, which show that she raised 32,215 men by the draft — over one-third of all raised in the United States.[600]

As a direct means of raising men, the draft of 1862

[597] *Ibid.*, pp. 547, 548, 642, 866.
[598] *Ibid.*, p. 291.
[599] *Ibid.*, p. 865.
[600] For the replies see, *ibid.*, pp. 866-867. The total numbers raised by the various states are on p. 291 of the same volume.

was a failure. The highest number of men attributed to the draft is 87,588 out of quotas of 334,835.[601] But not all of the men thus recorded were drafted. Only 65,305 are counted by the War Department as militia, while 18,-884 were nine-month volunteers,[602] as allowed by the act of July 17. A discrepancy still exists between this latter total and the former, the difference very likely representing the number of twelve-months men accepted.

A proper valuation of the work of the draft can only be reached, however, by showing its influence on recruiting during the time that it remained as a threat. In July the western states had expressed grave doubts as to their ability to raise their quotas of the 300,000, but in the end Wisconsin and Indiana, alone of the western states, were compelled to draft, returning a total of only 958 and 337 men each, though doubtless in Indiana, as certainly in the case of Wisconsin, the number should have been somewhat larger. The other ten states which could not escape the draft were confined without exception to New England and the Atlantic seaboard, Maryland alone being excluded.[603] When the total quotas for the calls of July 2 and August 4 are compared with the credits for troops received, a better estimate can be made. Of quotas the total was 669,670 while the total number of men raised was 509,-053.[604] While this shows a deficiency of about twenty-five per cent. the record is considerably brightened by the fact that there was an excess of about 87,000 three-

---

[601] *Idem*, vol. 4, p. 1265.

[602] *Ibid.*, p. 216.

[603] See list of quotas and credits, *idem*, vol. 2, p. 291; vol. 4, p. 1265. Maryland returned no troops from her draft.

[604] *Idem*, vol. 4, p. 1265.

year volunteers above the quota of the first call. This number equalled in service 348,000 militia, thus evening the score in the matter of time credits.

It would be a mistake to attribute even this degree of success to the draft alone. The one-hundred-dollar federal bounty, in addition to the numerous state and local bounties, was at least equally potent in influence. The number of the three-year volunteers who received the bounty, in comparison with the scant number of nine-month *volunteers* who did not receive it is in itself a sufficient comment on the potency of the bounty as compared with the draft alone. Men wishing to volunteer to escape the draft would inevitably have chosen nine-months volunteer service to three-years service if the bounty had not been offered for the longer term.

The coercive power of the draft was more moral than statutory and seems to have exerted its direct influence more upon the state and local governments and patriotic organizations than upon the people direct. It was the efforts of these intermediaries that secured for the western states immunity from the draft. Patriotic appeals and bounties could be more effective there than in the Atlantic seaboard states, hence the sectional division between the states which drafted and those which did not.

There was no sharp cleavage in degree of patriotism between east and west, but there was a sharp distinction in economic activities; hence in 1862, as in 1861, it was the West which was most prompt in recruiting. The very states whose governors had in July reported that they could by no means reach their quotas emerged a few months later untouched by conscription. But, in the meantime, conditions had changed. The rush season in the agricultural region had passed and there was, as usual, a surplus labor population seeking steady employment till the following spring. The perennial optimism that the war would be of short duration made them just as willing to enlist for three years or the war as to enlist for nine months, especially since a more liberal bounty could be secured in that way. There were still few who realized that they would serve until well into their third year.

On the other hand, in the East the war industries had so absorbed the labor market that the bounties, as then offered, were insufficient to lure men from their jobs. Hence the East had to draft.

While the draft produced but few men directly, it drove home the conviction that, if the war should continue into the third year a more efficient method than anything yet devised would have to be invented in order to raise the necessary men. The long time consumed and the perpetual postponements of the governors practically nullified the draft decree. In the West the result would likely have been in no wise different if no draft had been threatened. Furthermore the process of draft to procure men for a mere nine-months service was too much like the mountain laboring and bringing forth a mouse.

Although most of the lessons of 1862 were to be lost upon the makers of the draft law of 1863, at least these two were learned – that the draft should be conducted solely by federal officers, and that the term of service should be the regular three years. This much of development of national authority may safely be attributed to the executive militia draft.

The Enrollment Act: A Threat of
National Force

The Enrollment Act: A Threat of National Force

THE relief obtained through the recruiting efforts of 1862 was of but short duration. After the call for the draft had been issued and before the final returns were all in, a series of disasters and doubtful victories had done much to neutralize the efforts at recruiting. Bull Run, Antietam, Perryville, Fredericksburg, Stone's River, and lesser engagements had cost the Union army about 75,000 in killed, deserters, and wounded – as listed in ascending numerical order.[605]

The Confederate loss over the same period was about equal to that of the Union, but her rigorous system of conscription, scouring the countryside, mountains, and cities for men, kept her armies recruited more promptly than those of the North. Furthermore the process was a continuous one, not a cal l, a draft, and a period of inactivity but a constant and steady filling up of depleted ranks as rapidly as they were thinned. Thus, while fewer in numbers, the Confederate armies could be kept at a higher point of efficiency by keeping the regiments rounded out and full while the Union was struggling along with a combination of depleted old organizations and thoroughly untrained new ones. Neither old nor new regiments could be as efficient as those of the Confederacy because of this difference.

But the military reverses of the latter months of 1862

---

[605] Livermore, *Numbers and Losses in the Civil War*, pp. 87-97.

had a worse effect than the mere depletion of the Union army. They made it definitely certain that no early termination of the war could be expected. The draft of 1862 was hardly over before it began to become evident that recruiting efforts would have to be redoubled, and it presently became apparent that the efforts of the future must dwarf everything that had been done in the past. But the drain of another half year's exhaustive campaigning was to elapse before the slow machinery could be got into motion. Chancellorsville, Vicksburg, Gettysburg, and minor skirmishes were to diminish the effective force by another fifty thousand,[606] and the terms of the nine-months men were to expire in the meantime.

The summer of 1862 had taught the futility of depending upon unassisted volunteering to check this drain. The succeeding draft had illustrated the folly of depending upon the state governors to comply promptly with federal requisitions. To call the militia without a draft was worse than useless, as a belated effort was to show. In June, 1863, when not only the states of Maryland and Pennsylvania, but West Virginia and Ohio as well, seemed in danger of invasion, the President called upon those four states to furnish 100,000 six-months militia for their own defense. Seven weeks later, when the danger was past and the call rescinded, barely 12,000 had responded, and of these Indiana, which was not included in the call, furnished the largest number and nearly one-third of the total.[607]

There was no anxiety to renew the expedient of mili-

---

[606] *Ibid.*, pp. 98-104.

[607] *Official Records*, series iii, vol. 3, pp. 360-361, 611; vol. 4, pp. 1264-1265. The totals here cited in the *Records* include 3284 furnished by Missouri in November, 1864. The 12,000 mentioned from the other five states were in addition to what Missouri furnished at the later emergency.

tia drafting with the lessons of 1862 still so vividly in mind. The indiscriminate methods of administration, the tardiness of returns, and the short terms of the men were all undesirable adjuncts of that method. But there was the further objection, namely, that militia would have to be organized into new regiments, whereas the crying need was not for more regiments but to replenish the old ones.

In addition to the above considerations there were a number of abuses, growing out of the first two years of recruiting, that were badly in need of correction. The question of credits was a vexatious one and constantly getting worse. Quotas had been assigned for the calls of April 15 and May 3, 1861, but not many persons felt that they were equitably distributed. Then followed a period of thirteen months during which "no formal assignment of quotas to states was made, and there was no fixed system of calling out troops. As circumstances demanded, requisitions were made upon the governors. In many cases troops were tendered by the governors and accepted by the United States without calls being made. Authorizations to individuals and independent acceptances were given, and many troops were brought into service in this way without said authorization passing through the state authorities. As a result of this want of a general system in calling out troops . . . it was found necessary, before fixing the quotas under calls of 1862, to determine the quotas of the respective states for 1861. This was done by considering the number of men the state had in the field, as shown by the records of the Adjutant General of the army." [608]

But this was a totally inadequate arrangement, since

---

[608] "Fry's Report" (see note 12), part i, p. 160.

many men enlisting in the navy were not counted and sufficient attention was not given to the length of service of the various classes of troops. The effect of draft and of bounties in causing men to enlist elsewhere than in their home communities was an unsolvable problem, and the continued use of three-months, six-months, nine-months, twelve-months, and two-year men was adding daily to the perplexities of the War Department. The question of quotas and credits was one necessary to be settled before another general call for troops. Furthermore this was the question which caused more bickering between governors and the War Department than any other matter during the remainder of the war.

Other ills which were equally in need of cure but concerning which there was no general agitation arose in connection with the means of evasion of military service. There were too many ways, under the previous draft regulations, wherby a person could be exempted from service, and it was possible for any well-to-do person, if he did not escape through exemption, to avoid service after draft by procuring a substitute to serve for him.

The third session of the thirty-seventh Congress was called upon to consider the matter of military legislation in the last month of its career. Some step in advance of militia drafting had to be taken or else it would be time for congress and the War Department to turn the settlement of the war over to the diplomats. Congress must decide just how far the nation should go in systematizing the recruiting service and in compelling service. It was the state-rights leanings of the leaders of the majority party in congress that determined that the legislation, as passed, should hold national control of recruiting merely as a threat to secure state action. Quite different theories lay behind their plan to make this threatened draft a conscription only of poor men and, at most, a trivial tax upon the rich. Conscription was not a new idea in the United States. It had had its advocates long before the matter was considered in congress, but no clearly defined idea seemed to be extant as to the meaning of the term. For that reason some of the earlier expressions upon the subject are open to various interpretations. One of the most celebrated of these declarations was that of John Hughes, the Roman Catholic Archbishop of New York. In a sermon of August 17, 1862, he was reported as stating that "The people should insist on being drafted and so bring this unnatural strife to a close . . ." by strength of might alone.[609] This utterance was destined to return and plague him. During the draft riots of July, 1863, he was repeatedly reminded of his early advocacy of a plan that was having so ill an effect upon his Irish followers in New York City. He endeavored to show that he had meant something far different from the literal content of his words but the argument does not carry conviction.[610]

During 1862 and 1863 many people were undergoing a change of opinion on the question of conscription. Horace Greeley, who had, in the spring of 1862, been so bitter in his diatribe against the Confederacy because of her treachery in passing a conscription act, could reason in August of the same year that since the South had started conscription it was perfectly honorable for the United States to draft and thus give

---

[609] *Harper's Weekly*, vol. 6 (August 30, 1862), p. 547.
[610] *New York Tribune*, July 14, 16, 1863; *Harper's Weekly*, vol. 7 (April 25, 1863), p. 258.

southern sympathizers "a bowl of the same soup." [611]
By the summer of 1863 he was an ardent supporter of
every essential portion of the enrollment act.

While the enrollment act was under discussion in
congress, it was possible for various and sundry persons to discover that they had favored conscription from
the start. Conscription should have been enacted in the
special session of July, 1861, declared Representative
Aaron A. Sargent, and Senator James A. McDougall
declared he had wanted conscription from the first. [612]
Both these men were from California, where it was
easier to favor conscription because of the fact that the
state on account of its location was not being called on
for troops for use outside the state.

As for the main body of congressmen, their attitude
on conscription was of two chief types. The first was
that of the republicans and war democrats, who were
opposed to anything resembling unqualified conscription. They were willing to allow the federal government direct supervision of the draft, and to make the
term of service of drafted men equal to that of the volunteers, yet they were unwilling to resort to draft in
any case until all efforts at state recruiting had failed.
These persons favored high bounties for volunteers,
trembled with horror at the suggestion that all men
should be equally liable to draft, were willing to ex-
empt all who were rich enough to buy substitutes, and
could view with tolerance the sins of the substitute (and
bounty) brokers. These men heartily favored the war
and its vigorous prosecution but were, for the most
part, honestly convinced that the states should be the

---

[611] *New York Tribune*, August 9, 1862.
[612] *Congressional Globe*, 37 Cong., 3 sess., pp. 1220, 997.

units and agents of recruiting. The federal government should intervene only as a final resort and then should mitigate its interference to the utmost by lessening the burden of draft upon all who were able to pay for the privilege.

The other type of opinion was that held by the anti-administration democrats, most of whom felt that the war had been uselessly provoked. Some of these believed that the best thing the country could do was to retire as gracefully as possible from the conflict and let the seceding states experiment with their theories to suit themselves. In this attitude they took the same ground as Phillips Brooks and other leading abolitionists, including at one time Horace Greeley himself. Clement L. Vallandigham, Representative from Ohio, was the classic type of this faction.

Others of this so called copperhead group merely accepted the war as an existing fact, regretted the entry of the United States into it, but were in favor of maintaining the honor of the states which they represented until a peace could be arranged. They insisted that the federal government should leave the recruiting of troops solely to the states. The outstanding example of this type of thought in the United States was Governor Horatio Seymour of New York. Most of the anti-administration democrats in congress adhered to the same doctrines. Perhaps not half a dozen members in both branches of congress were actually disloyal to the Union.

But these two types of men, abolitionist and copperhead, so widely differing on one side of a sphere of thought that they met on the other side, did not represent the determining factions in congress. There the issue was between republicans and pro-administration democrats on the one side and the more moderate anti-administration democrats and constitutional union men on the other. Their chief divergence of opinion on conscription was between a modified and a strict interpretation of state rights; between a threat of proletarian conscription on the one side and opposition to any federal conscription on the other. Yet differences of opinion were so highly accentuated between these two so slightly different groups that the word *traitor* became the favorite epithet of the day.

The enrollment act was not of spontaneous origin but was the outgrowth of an attempt to modify the various militia acts so as to avoid in the future some of the embarrassments of 1862. The first form of the bill saw the light of day on January 28, 1863, when Senator Henry Wilson, chairman of the Committee on Military Affairs, introduced a bill "for the encouragement of reenlistments, and for enrolling and drafting the militia, and for other purposes." [613] Senator Wilson of Massachusetts, who until twenty-one years of age had been Jeremiah Jones Colbaith of New Hampshire, had been one of the organizers of the republican party in Massachusetts. He had been in the Senate since 1855, a member of the Committee on Military Affairs since 1857, and its chairman since March, 1861. From his experience as well as from his long and consistent stand as abolitionist, free soiler, and pioneer republican he was a capable man for handling military legislation such as this. His training equipped him to understand the problem, and his connections placed him in an ex-

[613] *Ibid.*, p. 558.

cellent position for forcing his bill past the obstacles within his own party.

The enrollment bill, good or bad, was more the work of Henry Wilson than of any other person. There were men in the Senate who favored much more vigorous and effective legislation than Wilson was willing to champion, but his organization was always as capable in suppressing improvements as in condemning the opposition of the minority; hence he must bear the chief responsibility for the emasculated measure that became the act of March 3, 1863. This contention is borne out by his attitude toward the bill from the start to the finish.

The first bill, as it was called up for consideration on February 4, was simply a measure to permit the President to call out the militia for a period as long as two years, and to give to the War Department more discretion in the administration of draft measures. To enforce obedience from drafted men (a matter much neglected in 1862) it provided that men as soon as drafted should be considered in the service and subject to martial law unless or until released by exemption or other means.[614] The strong points of the bill therefore were that the service of the militia would be lengthened, the execution of the draft more centralized, and the attendance of drafted men at the rendezvous rendered more certain. The weak points, yet points boasted of by Wilson, were that the President could not appoint the drafting officials and that the states would continue to train the militia. As though this were not enough, he at once proposed to weaken the bill still further by amending

---

[614] *Ibid.*, pp. 711, 705.

it so as to allow drafted men to furnish substitutes.[615]
On this proposal, be it said in favor of his colleagues,
he had been balked in committee, but at once he proceeded to carry the fight to the floor of the Senate chamber. Without question the rights of the well-to-do- must
be protected.

As opposed to this feeble stand of the administration
leaders, the tenor of the opposition is displayed in the
immediate attack upon the measure by Senator John
L. Carlile of Virginia who declared the bill despotic
and inclined toward conscription.[616] These were the two
typical bases for the stand of the opposite parties upon
the discussion of the bill from the first to the last. The
warfare was on between the forces for modified state
recruiting and pure state recruiting.

The bill which precipitated this discussion was soon
recommitted [617] and thereafter never reappeared. In
place of it a bill "for enrolling and calling out the National forces, and for other purposes" was presented on
February 9 and brought up for discussion just a week
later.[618]

As a basis for understanding the attitude of its proponents and opponents, and the arguments and en-
mities engendered by it, the substance of the act as it
was finally amended and passed will be given first.[619]

The justification for the act was the necessity of such
a measure and the praiseworthiness and honorableness
of service "for the maintenance of the Constitution and
Union, and the consequent preservation of free government."

---

[615] *Ibid.*, pp. 705, 711.

[616] *Ibid.*, p. 708.

[617] *Ibid.*, pp. 737-739.

[618] *Ibid.*, pp. 816, 976.

[619] *U. S. Statutes at Large*, vol. 12, pp. 731-737.

The national forces were declared to consist of all able-bodied male citizens of the United States, and all aliens who had declared on oath their intention of becoming citizens, between the ages of twenty and forty-five. These persons were liable to military duty upon call of the President, who was given full power to call them forth and draft them as needed.

Persons exempted from the operations of the draft were of three classes. The first of these included only such persons as were physically or mentally unfit for service and persons who had been convicted of a felony. The second class included a restricted number of officials: the Vice President of the United States, the judges of the various federal courts, the members of the Cabinet and the governors of the various states. Lastly it was arranged that the sole supporter of aged or infirm parents or of orphaned children should be exempted.

Those not exempted were divided into two classes, the first of which included all men, married or single, between twenty and thirty-five years of age and all unmarried men from thirty-five to forty-five. The second class included only the married men from thirty-five to forty-five years of age. The latter class was not to be called out until the first was exhausted.

The administration of the law was delegated to a provost-marshal-general, who was made the head of a separate bureau of the War Department, and a corps of provost-marshals, all appointed by the President. For purposes of enrollment and draft the whole country was divided into enrollment districts, which, as far as possible, corresponded to congressional districts, and a provost-marshal was placed in charge of each.

The provost-marshal-general was given the duty of

making rules and regulations for the governance of his subordinates, and had direct supervision over the arresting of deserters and the enrolling and drafting of the national forces. The actual work of arrest, enrollment and the like was to be attended to by the provost-marshals.

An enrollment board, made up of the provost-marshal, a physician, and one other person, was provided for each district, and their duties as to enrollment and examination of the various classes and individuals were carefully defined.

Care was taken to arrange as accurately as possible for an equitable distribution of the burden of the draft. Previous credits were to be considered in assigning future quotas. Drafted men were to receive the same pay and federal bounty as the volunteers. Furthermore notifications were to be served upon all drafted men within ten days so that no question should exist as to who was drafted and who was not.

Section 13 was a concession to the man of means. Anyone who could afford it was given the privilege of either furnishing a substitute or paying $300 commutation in lieu of such substitute. Persons who tried to evade service by any other than this stipulated method were to be deemed deserters and subject to trial by court-martial.

Presumably adequate regulations were drafted for the governance of medical inspection. Surgeons on the boards were subject to martial law if apprehended for making incorrect reports.

To aid further in the enforcement of the draft, definite precautions were taken to prevent resistance either on the part of conscripts or others. Any person guilty of resisting a draft of men, counseling or aiding any person to resist any draft, assaulting or obstructing any officer in making a draft, counseling any person to assault or obstruct any such officer, counseling any drafted man not to appear at the place of rendezvous, or willfully dissuading any person from the performance of military duty was to be arrested by the provost-marshal and, upon conviction, to be fined not to exceed five hundred dollars or imprisoned not to exceed two years, or both. Further regulations for the prevention of desertion and to authorize the use of drafted men in any organization as needed completed the essential parts of the act.

This was an act combining statesmanship, contradictions, and absurdities. As a reaction against unrestricted state control of the army it substituted enrollment and draft, directed by the President and executed by his appointees, and the soldiers thus raised were to be used where needed and not as new organizations. Ample coercive measures to compel obedience were provided, and the equalization of quotas arranged for. Exemptions were few, and a beginning of medical examination was authorized and ordered. Thus far the law seemingly displayed a high degree of reaction against state rights in war making.

But the method of enrollment was cumbersome, the drafting process was too localized, and provisions for medical examination were totally inadequate. A ridiculous distinction was made between married men below and above thirty-five years of age for purposes of classification, there were no provisions for industrial exemptions, and the organization of the Provost-marshalgeneral's bureau was left incomplete. Yet these were faults easily amended and could easily be attributed to the inexperience of Americans in dealing with conscription. Even with these defects the law could have been used with enormous benefit to the army and economy to the country if it had not been consciously nullified by other provisions.

Very clearly the law was never intended as a direct procurer of men but merely as a whip in the hands of the federal government to stimulate state activities. Even the name of conscription was avoided by its friends who always spoke of it as the "enrollment bill." Only its enemies called it a "conscription bill," which term was considered by the administration men as an unfair epithet. But they knew whereof they spoke for, as they shaped it, the bill was not a conscription bill in any general sense; it was merely a piece of class legislation designed, even in the last resort, merely to stimulate mercenary enlistments and to match the rich man's dollars with the poor man's life. None would have been more horrified than Henry Wilson at the suggestion that every able-bodied man drafted should be compelled to serve in the army unless his services would be of more benefit to the military strength of the country in some other capacity.

Wilson was never a real friend of conscription. In his defense of the bill he declared that its prime object was to raise men [620] but this statement is belied by his whole conduct in connection with the act and its enforcement. As chairman of the Committee on Military Affairs, he was consistently friendly to state as opposed to national control of recruiting. He was the prime instigator of the plan for the exemption of the well-to-do and he

[620] *Congressional Globe,* 37 Cong., 3 sess.. p. 981.

maintained to the last a hearty contempt for the general government as a recruiter of soldiers.

On the floor of the Senate, in April, 1864, he said: "The Federal Government has enlisted during this war but very few men. . . . The Federal Government does not know much about enlisting men. It has done but very little of it during this war and that at enormous expense." [621] Again in June of the same year, while debating the revision of the enrollment bill, he said: "The Federal Government is a very poor agent to enlist men. . . . Although we have our provost marshals up and down the country, nineteen twentieths of the men enlisted are really enlisted through the influence of the people of the localities of the men . . . and not by the positive toil and labor of the national Government officers." [622] Yet earlier in the month he had said, "The enrollment act, as it now stands, is almost perfect in its framework, being the result of a great deal of experience." [623] These statements are not contradictory but actually supplement each other in Wilson's ideas of recruiting: the enrollment act was "almost perfect" because it was merely an incentive to local recruiting and not because it laid any pretense to federal primacy in that work.

For a consideration of the legislative history of the act these weaknesses and inequities need not be considered. They were not contested by the opposition, since any loophole in the legislation would weaken its effect and might perhaps even give a later opportunity for the discrediting of the responsible persons and

[621] *Idem*, 38 Cong., 1 sess., pp. 1404-1405.
[622] *Ibid.*, p. 3383.
[623] *Ibid.*, p. 2804.

party. The opposition centered its efforts upon the strong points of the bill where, from the beginning, they had but little chance of success, leaving the provisions of substitution, commutation, and bounty largely to the discretion of the republican caucus. Their course in regard to these subjects will be considered in later chapters.

The enrollment bill, unique in itself, had a singular career in congress. Rushed through the Senate in one day, without the verbosity and dilatory tactics which usually attend the *deliberations* of that body, the bill was carefully guarded from all contact with the opposition in the House of Representatives. True, ample time was given for debate: for two days a war of words waged. Constitutionality versus necessity were prominent themes but subordinated always to party recriminations. The democrats were early made to feel that they could accomplish little but to vent their spleen and reveal the most objectionable features.

It was intended from the start that no amendments whatever should be offered, but toward the last a slight concession was made: one hour would be left open for amendments without debate. At no time during the three days in which the bill was before the House did its managers let it get out of their control. The only comfort that the democrats could derive was some slight modification made by the republicans themselves to correct certain obvious injustices, points not vital to the bill itself. Then, when in its amended form the bill went back to the Senate for concurrence, a strange thing happened. The bill had been passed in the first instance with almost no debate, but now, when it was too late to change it materially except in an improbable conference, a torrent of oratory broke forth and consumed what must have been a wearisome day – at least it is a wearisome day's work to read the twenty-eight pages of solid fine type which this debate occupies in the *Congressional Globe.*[624]

The chief arguments advanced by the proponents of the bill were the necessity for such a measure, its constitutionality, and its equitable distribution of the burdens of war. All of this would have formed valid argument for an out-and-out conscription bill, and the last point at least did not apply to the bill in question.

Senator Wilson ably presented the argument of necessity when, on February 16, the bill finally emerged from the committee. "To fill the thinned ranks of our battalions," he said, "we must again call upon the people. The immense numbers already summoned to the field, the scarcity and high rewards of labor, press upon all of us the conviction that the ranks of our wasted regiments cannot be filled again by the old system of volunteering. If volunteers will not respond to the call of the country, then we must resort to the involuntary system. If we summon the militia, we must have new regiments and new officers – raw soldiers and untrained officers – enormous expenses and impotent forces. The nation needs not new regiments nor more officers; it needs new bayonets in the war-wasted ranks of the veteran regiments. In the ranks of these battle-scarred regiments one new recruit is worth more than three in new regiments under untried officers; and the chances of comfort, health, and life are far greater in the old than in new regiments.

---

[624] *Idem*, 37 Cong., 3 sess., pp. 976-1002 for career in Senate, 1213-1293 *passim* for career in the House, 1363-1391 for reconsideration in Senate.

"Volunteers we cannot obtain, and everything forbids that we should resort to the temporary expedient of calling out the militia. Such a call would waste the resources and absorb the energies and increase but little the military forces of the country. The needs of the nation demand that we should rely not upon volunteering, nor upon calling forth the militia, but that we should fill the regiments now in the field, worn and wasted by disease and death, by enrolling and drafting the population of the country under the constitutional authority 'to raise and support armies'."

So felicitous an introduction was worthy of a much abler bill than the one which it accompanied, especially since he went on to say that "The enactment of this bill will give confidence to the Government, strength to the country, and joy to the worn and weary soldiers of the Republic around their campfires in the land of the rebellion." [625] How different were these sentiments from his later slighting remarks as to the ability of the federal government and his current endeavors to make the bill bear more heavily upon one portion of the people than upon the rest.

The almost indecent haste with which the bill was hurried through the Senate scarcely gave the opposition time to rally their forces before the vote was taken. Yet a glimpse of the store of opposition argument was shown when Senator Henry M. Rice of Minnesota cited the hesitating policy of recruiting as practiced in the past, the refusal to take men when they were eager to enlist, and the mismanagement of those accepted. "We have had men enough in the field," he said, "to set the world at defiance. One third of the number,

---

[625] *Ibid.*, pp. 976-977.

under proper management and proper direction would have crushed out the rebellion long ago." [626]

On the floor of the House the burden of the defense fell to Abraham B. Olin of New York. He at once took up the cudgels in defense of the constitutionality of the measure which had already been contested in the Senate. "This 'power to raise and support armies,' expressly given by the Constitution to Congress, should," he contended, "be exercised by Congress, and not petitioned for as a boon from the State governments. This idea of calling upon the Governors of the States to furnish troops has its origin in that accursed doctrine of States rights, State sovereignty, which has been chiefly instrumental in bringing upon the Republic our present calamity." Some additional light was cast upon the origin of the drafting provisions when he observed that "Some of the best and most enlightened intellects of the army have been brought to the preparation of this measure." [627]

This argument was all the more effectual because of the fact that nobody in the House took a sufficiently advanced national view as to show that the bill itself belied the category into which it was placed. If the champions of the bill were unconsciously state rights in sympathy, the opponents were openly so and it did not behoove either side to point out the weaker points in the measure, though some of both parties did eventually support the complete excision of section 13, with its provisions for substitution and commutation.

The chief arguments of the opposition were that the bill was unconstitutional, that white men should not be

---

[626] *Ibid.*, p. 998.
[627] *Ibid.*, p. 1214.

conscripted in order to free negroes, and that the power
granted to provost-marshals to arrest spies and persons
suspected of treasonable practices amounted to nothing
less than despotic military interference in the private
affairs of citizens. This opposition began by a temperate
attack upon the clause in article 7 whereby the provost-
marshals were empowered "to inquire into and report
to the Provost Marshal General all treasonable practices," and upon the provision in section 25 providing
for indefinite military imprisonment of draft resisters.[628]

But the moderate tone of the debate was changed by
a violent speech of James H. Campbell of Pennsylvania who by implication called all opponents of the
bill, traitors, and then, waxing bolder, declared "The
error of the Government has been *leniency*. If it had
given to traitors a drumhead court-martial and hempen
cord, it would better have pleased the loyal men in the
United States." [629]

This outburst was all the more inexcusable since
Campbell held the floor at the time purely through the
courtesy of Clement L. Vallandigham of Ohio and was
directing the attack against him. When Vallandigham
protested against being treated like a blackguard,
Campbell emphatically told him that he *was* a blackguard, whereupon a disturbance was created, particularly in the galleries, calling forth a reluctant protest
from the Speaker.[630]

Considering the nature of the attack made upon him,
one can only remark at the comparative mildness of
Vallandigham's reply. Very largely ignoring the attack,

---

[628] *Ibid.*, pp. 1215, 1217, 1219, speeches of C. J. Biddle of Pennsylvania
and H. B. Wright of Pennsylvania.

[629] *Ibid.*, p. 1218.

[630] *Idem*, appendix, p. 172.

he turned his chief attention to the proposed power of the provost-marshals over civilians, to the intolerance of the administration as well as its failures, and to the sad state of the Constitution. Speaking of the provost-marshals he observed, "And every congressional district in the United States is to be governed – yes, governed – by this petty satrap – this military eunuch – this Baba – and he even may be black – who is to do the bidding of your Sultan, or his Grand Visier. Sir, you have but one step further to go – give him the symbols of his office – the Turkish bow-string and the sack." The necessity for a draft he could attribute only to opposition of the people to the war, engendered by loss of confidence as a result of abuse of power.

The action of members defeated for re-election in forcing through such legislation received its share of his attention. "You, an accidental, temporary majority, condemned and repudiated by the people, are exhausting the few remaining hours of your political life in attempting to defeat the popular will, and to compel, by the most desperate and despotic of expedients ever resorted to, the submission of the majority of the people, at home, to the minority, their servants here." Such experiments hitherto, he warned, had always resulted in "expulsion or death to the conspirators and tyrants." Yet, he said, "I shall do nothing to stir up an already excited people . . . because I desire to see no violence or revolution in the North or West."

The "treasonable practices" clause was to him a relic of the despotism of Edward III, and a fitting conjugate to military arrests and suspension of habeas corpus. This would round out the policy of despotism. No person would be safe.

The right of the minority to register its objections he defended with forceful analogy. The Earl of Chatham, Edmund Burke, Charles James Fox, and Isaac Barré had denounced the war on America and they were praised for it. The Federalists had denounced the War of 1812 and were considered patriotic. Lincoln himself had denounced the Mexican war without being considered treasonable yet when one American condemned a fratricidal war within the country, no such leniency was shown him and he must, perforce, be considered a traitor or a criminal.

The position of the anti-war democrats he defined as follows: "We seek no revolution – except through the ballot box. The conflict to which we challenge you, is not of arms but of argument." And finally, "I have spoken as though the Constitution survived, and was still the supreme law of the land. But if, indeed, there be no Constitution any longer, limiting and restraining the men in power, then there is none binding upon the States or the people. God forbid. We have a Constitution yet, and laws yet. To them I appeal." [631]

However mistaken this line of argument may have been, the venom in it was nothing to compare with that of the opponents who preceded and followed his speech. Whereas Vallandigham appealed to arguments and ballots Campbell had bandied the words "traitor" and "blackguard" and had spoken of "drumhead court-martial and hempen cord," and a successor, John A. Bingham of Ohio even descended to advocacy of lynch law, while replying to Vallandigham's speech. The reference was to a supposed Ohio democrat – though name, date, and place were suppressed – who, when re-

---

[631] *Ibid.*, pp. 172-177, quotations on pp. 173, 177.

cruiting was at its height, was reported to have said
" 'stop, brother Democrats, stay at home and vote; and
let the army of the Union perish'."

"I now submit to the country," said Bingham, "that
if there were any such utterance made, the author of it
should not only be arrested and imprisoned, but that the
man who, in such an hour of peril, would attempt to
keep back citizens from the defense of their homes and
the relief of their brothers in arms, should not only be
imprisoned, but should be hung by the neck, without
judge or jury, till he be dead." [632] The nature, time, and
circumstances of the speech left nothing in doubt as to
the personal application of the remarks.

As a refreshing anti-climax to such bloodthirsty mur-
murings Daniel W. Voorhees, "The Tall Sycamore of
the Wabash," entertained the House, with sarcastic remarks upon the attitude of the majority. He satirized
Olin's homily as to how the democratic members
should comport themselves in debate, ridiculed the
rage of Campbell and the eccentricities of Bingham,
praised what he considered the masterly effort of Vallandigham, and then began to take the defeated members of the republican party to task for presuming to
lecture their reëlected democratic colleagues. "In common decency you ought to keep silent, as mere cum-
berers of the ground whose days are numbered. Popular majorities have been piled up against you by thousands and tens of thousands. Loyal people have spoken
your knell; the funeral bell has been tolled over your
political graves by patriotic hands; the grass is growing green on the sod which covers you. And yet you
dare come here to lecture living men!"

---

[632] *Idem*, body of the work, p. 1229.

Then, adverting to the subject in question, he outlined the causes of democratic opposition to the bill in particular and the war in general. A righteous war he would support wholeheartedly but not a war to free negroes. The Emancipation Proclamation was the cause of the slacking up of recruiting. Then, resorting to the most horror-provoking argument of the "copperheads," he said, "If the American people, deceived, betrayed, and outraged are unwilling to support the war policy of this Administration any further unless coerced to do so by such legislation as this conscription bill, then let us stop fighting at once, and try what virtue there may be in peaceful remedies." [633]

During the last two days of the debate, telling speeches in opposition to the bill were delivered by George H. Pendleton of Ohio, Charles A. Wickliffe of Kentucky, Elijah H. Norton of Missouri, and John B. Steele of New York. [634] The stock arguments were repeated time and again and such points as the superior recruiting ability of the governors, and the danger of entrusting too much power to the President were brought out in addition. But the most pessimistic prophecy of them all was uttered by Chilton A. White of Ohio. There was scarcely a constitutional guarantee that he did not see trodden down by the despotic measures embodied in the bill. One clause, relating to treasonable practices, he considered merely as a measure under which to persecute the democrats. He objected to the arrest of persons who dissuaded others from performing military duty. Who was to define of what dissuasion consisted? Even his speech, he conjectured, might be so construed, as indeed it was. The democrats,

[633] *Ibid.*, pp. 1230-1234, quotations on pp. 1230, 1234.
[634] *Ibid.*, pp. 1256-1257, 1258-1259, 1273-1274, 1263-1265 respectively.

it was his conviction, would resort only to freedom of speech in assailing the conscription policy, but, if the republicans intended to retaliate by the use of military force, then, he warned them, "an eye for an eye and tooth for tooth will be the law." [635] It was such talk as this that gave the republicans all the more opportunity to declare that the democratic members were plotting the destruction of the Union.

Most of these fears of the democrats were as groundless as they were ineffective. Time that they might have spent in condemning the undemocratic features of the bill and thereby creating a public sentiment in favor of a more equitable arrangement, was wasted in picturing a centralized military machine as objectionable to Wilson and Olin as to themselves. None realized better than did Vallandigham, the futility of their opposition, yet he and his group elected to take their stand against the centralizing features of the bill — its only claim to merit — instead of exerting themselves against its evils. Consequently they lost their sole chance to revive their waning political fortunes. If the war had turned out to be a failure, they would have been hailed as political prophets and their reputations would have been secure. But they guessed wrong and consequently they dug their political graves by the speeches which at the time were hailed as statesmanlike and patriotic by a very large portion of the citizens of the loyal states.

The passage of the bill was prearranged by its managers in the committee on military affairs. Olin, when he presented the bill, did so with a motion that it be recommitted, [636] thus allowing debate upon the motion but preventing any proposal of amendments upon the

---

[635] *Ibid.*, pp. 1224-1226.
[636] *Ibid.*, pp. 1213-1214.

bill itself, since the motion and not the bill was before the House. The intention was to withdraw the motion when the debate was finished. The democrats could raise sufficient force neither to pass nor defeat the motion and it would have been useless to attempt it anyway since there were plenty more parliamentary tricks available to keep the opposition in suppression. When it was felt that sufficient time had been given to the democrats to wear off their exuberance of spirit, Thaddeus Stevens secured the passage of a motion to set the time of closing the debate, to allow thereafter one hour for the offering of amendments without debate, and then take the vote. To this arrangement Vallandigham and others agreed, since it was the only concession to be obtained.[637]

This machine-like procedure of lawmaking made labored replies by the republicans rather unnecessary. Yet from time to time response was made. Mr. Olin said of the alleged unconstitutionality, "This is the oft-repeated, feeble device of still more feeble minds, to assert that some proposed measure is unconstitutional when their ingenuity can suggest no other objection to the measure."[638] Mr. W. McKee Dunn of Indiana, interspersed his speech with letters from democratic officers and men in the Union army who demanded that more vigorous legislation be passed.[639] Benjamin F. Thomas of Massachusetts defended the measure upon the grounds of military necessity without reference to any other arguments. Everything else had failed, now conscription must be tried.[640]

---

[637] *Ibid.*, p. 1261.
[638] *Ibid.*, p. 1234.
[639] *Ibid.*, pp. 1253-1255.
[640] *Ibid.*, p. 1289.

Thaddeus Stevens even tried the novel expedient of blaming the necessity for the bill upon the democrats. If the bill to enlist negroes had passed, he declared, this bill would not have been necessary. The timid Senate had been frightened out of passing the negro bill simply because of the clamor of the democrats. As to democratic gains in the recent election he had an easy explanation. Democrats had stayed at home and voted while republicans were fighting the nation's battles on the field. Did the democrats really wish the omission of the "treasonable practices" clause? Well enough, he was willing to grant it, especially since it might be interpreted to include such outspoken persons as his friend Vallandigham.[641] Stevens could well afford to assume this tolerant and condescending tone, considering the surety of the early passing of the bill.

The net results of the discussion in the House were but very small except to add to the oratorical reputations of some of the members. Yet some of the objections were answered by minor amendments during the hour allotted for that purpose. The detention of draft resisters by provost-marshals was given up, and the "treasonable practices" clause was likewise omitted, thus tending to substitute more of civil rather than military law for civilians. But this was the only gain except a few amendments for purposes of clarity. A motion by Vallandigham to substitute civil for military arrests in the case of draft obstructors lost by a vote of 57 to 101. A motion to limit the draft to white men lost by a similar margin. In a like manner one very progressive amendment was rejected. Democrats like Pendleton, Vallandigham, and William S. Holman,

---

[641] *Ibid.*, pp. 1261-1262.

combined with republicans like Schuyler Colfax, Roscoe Conkling, and John Sherman to get section 13 with its concession of substitution and commutation removed bodily, but failed by a vote of 67 to 87, party lines being abandoned. Finally the amended bill passed by the decisive vote of 115 to 48,[642] thus proving decisively the preponderating sentiment of the House.

The belated opposition in the Senate was merely a repetition of what had gone before in the House. Senators James A. Bayard of Delaware, David Turpie of Indiana, Anthony Kennedy of Maryland, Garrett Davis and Lazarus W. Powell of Kentucky, William A. Richardson of Illinois, and Willard Saulsbury of Delaware in turn attacked the bill and sounded the lowest depths of despair over the sad state of the country. A speech by Senator John S. Carlile of Virginia is also referred to but, in violation of promise, it does not even appear in the appendix.[643] Of these eight, six it will be seen were from loyal slave states, and their anomalous position as well as their feeling of betrayal, in the movement toward emancipation, is reflected in their words.

It was by the efforts of Senator Bayard that these and a few others were allowed to register a record of protest against the bill. Under a motion for indefinite postponement made by Bayard, their speeches were in order, and by calling for a division in the vote, their names were definitely recorded against the measure. This motion, the significant one for the Senate, was defeated by a vote of 11 to 35,[644] about the same ratio as in the House.

---

[642] *Ibid.*, pp. 1291-1293.

[643] *Ibid.*, pp. 1363-1367, 1367-1370, 1373-1375, 1377-1380, 1380-1384, 1384-1386, 1387-1389 respectively. Reference to Carlile's speech is on p. 1371.

[644] *Ibid.*, pp. 1363, 1367, 1389.

While this momentous piece of legislation was disturbing congress, the people at large seem to have had little knowledge of what was in store for them. Only the largest metropolitan newspapers maintained efficient Washington correspondents. Smaller papers copied extensively from the larger. Even these Washington correspondents do not seem to have caught the drift of the legislation contemplated. The *New York Tribune* merely reported the progress of the legislation from time to time, and as late as February 28, the date of the final legislative action upon the bill, displayed an utter lack of comprehension by referring to it as the "Militia Enrolling Bill." [645] Yet by the middle of the summer the very life of the nation seemed in peril as the result of the inequities and operation of this act.

[645] *New York Tribune*, February 28, 1863.